STAR TREK MOVIE MEMORIES

Besides starring in seventy-nine television episodes and seven feature films as Captain James Kirk, Montreal-born William Shatner has also written six non-Star Trek science fiction novels. He is a resident of Los Angeles.

Chris Kreski is the editorial director for MTV and co-author of *Growing Up Brady*.

Voyager

WILLIAM SHATNER
With Chris Kreski

Star Trek Movie Memories

HarperCollins*Publishers*

Voyager
An Imprint of HarperCollins*Publishers*
77–85 Fulham Palace Road,
Hammersmith, London W6 8JB

This paperback edition 1996
1 3 5 7 9 8 6 4 2

First published in Great Britain by
HarperCollins*Publishers* 1994

Cover photographs: STAR TREK® and © by Paramount Pictures
Cover design © by Chip Kidd
A catalogue record for this book
is available from the British Library

ISBN 0 00 638792 6

Printed and bound in Great Britain by
Caledonian International Book Manufacturing Ltd, Glasgow

For the one who meant the most—
See you in dreamland.
—W. S.

For Dawn, who's still the grooviest
chick in school.
—C. K.

ACKNOWLEDGMENTS

My recollections of the movies and the shenanigans that went on in making them are far fresher than those of *Star Trek* the series, which constituted the first book. Memory is a strange thing. It's very personal, remembering the best of times in some instances and the worst in others. The desire to tell the truth presents complex issues: Are my recollections valid? Is my memory being selective? Does that selectivity constitute an untruth? Is my version of events really what happened or from my singular point of view only what I think happened? How can I depict circumstances as they were except by having a camera shooting from at least four different angles and then being able to play it back in slow motion?

Failing to have had a camera in position for the drama of my life, and having somewhat aged film stock behind my eyes, I sought to get other people's perspectives on the events contained here. Putting these views together, using other people's internal lenses, and striving to be fair have constituted the real challenges of this book. Helped by the talents of Chris Kreski, I hope I've been equal to the task.

To the people who gave me their time and their energy, I thank you from the bottom of my heart.

The authors would like to thank the people who supported, encouraged and put up with us throughout the writing of this book: Wendy Wolf, whose patience, talent and red pen never slept; Kevin McShane and Carmen LaVia of the Fifi Oscard Agency, whose competence and honesty might actually give agents a good name; Mary Jo Fernandez, whose tolerance has now proven completely unshakeable; Paramount's Larry McCallister and Ann Ling, whose photographic assistance and red-tape cutting were appreciated immeasureably; and Richard Arnold, whose brain is of truly Talosian dimensions.

Special thanks are also extended to Harve Bennett, Rick Berman, Stephany Byrne, Eileen Campion, Joe Davola, Michael Dugan, David Gautreaux, Tracy Grandstaff, Amelia Kreski, Harold Livingston, Nicholas Meyer, Malcolm McDowell, Judy McGrath, Ricardo Montalban, Ron Moore, Patrick Stewart, Abby Terkuhle, Laurie Ulster, Phil Weyland, Ralph Winter, Robert Wise . . . and, of course, Leonard Nimoy, DeForest Kelley, Nichelle Nichols, George Takei, Jimmy Doohan and Walter Koenig.

Your knowledge and generosity were overwhelming.

CONTENTS

DOG
DAYS

N

ASA's calling. They need my help, fast. I spring into action immediately, jumping the first jet east. Six hours, three bags of peanuts and one truly horrendous chicken à la king meal later, I'm in Florida, where immediately upon landing I'm glad-handed by a pair of aviator-sunglassed NASA representatives and shoved into a Jeep. I'm then shuttled off to NASA's Cape Canaveral, where I've been assigned the task of serving as the "surprise guest" at a party honoring one thousand of the agency's staff engineers. It's a difficult mission, one that could very well involve a lot of forced smiling, waving and schmoozing. Still, as any good starship captain can tell you, the needs of the many outweigh the needs of the few or the one, and with that in mind, I rise heroically to the occasion, sacrificing my personal comfort for the good of the United States space program.

Actually, this party's real purpose is to venerate the NASA engineers who've recently reached the milestone of completing their preliminary research and computations in regard to the upcoming *Apollo 11* manned Moon landing. Their countdown to liftoff now stands at exactly one year, and with the majority of their paperwork behind them but the majority of their nuts-and-bolts production still to come, NASA's powers that be have decided that this would be a perfect time to provide their biggest-brained employees with a large ceremonial pat on the back.

With that in mind, they've pulled out all the stops and converted one of their biggest aviation hangars into the setting for what has to rank as the most colossal pep rally in history. Enormous sections of the actual rocket that will one day carry man to the Moon, plus full-scale mock-ups of *Apollo 11*'s capsule and lunar module, are sprinkled about the concrete floor of the hangar like enormous party favors. Nearby, a buffet table roughly the size of Rhode Island is straining under the weight of a potato-salad hemisphere, sculpted to vaguely reproduce the lunar surface. An open bar lurks seductively between a seafood salad and the midsection of the rocket's fuselage. It seems to garner the lion's share of attendee attention.

I'm above it all—hiding behind a maroon velvet stage curtain alongside future *Apollo 11* inhabitants Neil Armstrong, Michael Collins and Buzz Aldrin. Flanking us all around are about a half-dozen of NASA's highest-ranking rocket scientist types. Below us, the honored engineers are now beginning to arrive, with most milling aimlessly about the cavernous confines. Once they've taken their seats, the brainiest-looking of the scientists is presented. He speaks to the attendees, stroking them about what a great job they've done and repetitiously urging them to "keep up the good work."

Meanwhile, the rest of us are killing time, still hovering behind our curtain while we wait to be introduced. I've just completed writing "See You on the

Moon—Best Wishes, William Shatner" on the side of a model-kit version of the U.S.S. *Enterprise*, which was assembled by six high-ranking NASA types and presented to me by the trio of astronauts for my autograph. They tell me it will one day hang fuzzy-dice-style in the "cockpit" of *Apollo 11*. Grinning uncontrollably at that flattering piece of trivia, I hand this thing back to Neil Armstrong, who thanks me, returns my smile, then watches in horror as the entire hull section of this plastic mini-*Enterprise* just falls to pieces, plopping and clattering to the concrete floor. Now, as I try my best not to laugh out loud, I watch some of NASA's very brightest rocket scientists huddling around their damaged dime-store creation, brows furrowed, swearing and sweating over their own embarrassing inability to construct a model kit recommended for "ages 8 and above." Finally, with the aid of some Juicy Fruit and masking tape, the faux *Enterprise* is whole once more, if a bit wobbly.

Meanwhile, I can't help but notice that Armstrong, Aldrin and Collins have understandably gone a bit pasty. I mean, these guys have just bravely signed on for a trip to the Moon, to go *literally* where no man has gone before, only to then stare in horror as the handiwork of NASA's premier engineers self-destructs in their hands. Now, as they gaze upon the hastily "repaired" starship, a pathetically jerry-rigged mess, I find little beads of sweat forming on Armstrong's upper lip.

At any rate, throughout the ensuing proceedings, compliments are tossed all over the hangar. There's verbal backslapping and asskissing all around, one by one the scientists and astronauts-in-waiting have their say, and toward the end of the festivities, I'm introduced. I emerge at last from behind that curtain and I'm absolutely stunned by the thunderous ovation that greets me. These guys are literally standing on their chairs cheering, even chanting from the floor. Trust me—I was excited just to be in attendance, but to receive this sort of overwhelming reception was beyond belief. Somehow it just didn't seem credible that a make-believe space explorer should merit the center of attention amid these real-life heroes.

I spent the rest of my day at NASA like a kid in a candy store, climbing aboard the actual *Apollo 11* lunar module and touring the base, all the while shaking hands, signing autographs and posing next to scientists and engineers as they passed Instamatic cameras back and forth. I believe I said the word "cheese" 900 times that day. By the time it was over, the sides of my face hurt from smiling, and my corneas were reeling from a barrage of those blue, semipermanent flashbulb splotches.

Late in the afternoon, I exchanged thank-you's and good-byes all around, then sped back toward the airport and climbed aboard a plane pointed back toward L.A. Within a week we'd begin shooting *Star Trek*'s third season, and as this 727 shot westward, extending a vivid orange sunset as it traveled, I found myself feeling really good about the show. My spirits had been buoyed tremendously by the events of the day, and for the first time I'd seen tangible and irrefutable proof that despite *Star Trek*'s mediocre Nielsen numbers, the series *was* truly appreciated. And let's not forget that NBC's new fall schedule found us penciled into a high-profile "can't-miss" time slot, and, further stacking the odds in our favor, that Gene Roddenberry would be returning to the show on an everyday basis. *Star Trek*, I mused, was going to be around for a long time.

Things have taken a decided turn for the worse. Almost immediately upon my return to L.A., I'm told that NBC has made some last-minute revisions to its upcoming prime-time lineup: *Laugh-In* has commandeered the early-evening Monday spot that had originally been assigned to *Star Trek*. Making matters worse, *Star Trek* has consequently been bumped to the network television graveyard, Friday nights at ten. The time slot is a perennial loser for the network, and especially inappropriate for *Star Trek* in that the majority of our audience is composed of kids and young adults. This new NBC schedule virtually guarantees that the larger percentage of our potential viewers will now be out on dates or safely tucked into their beds snoring by the time we come on the air. My optimism in regard to the upcoming season is gone.

Shortly thereafter, Gene Roddenberry is gone, too. Angered by NBC's scheduling decisions, and well aware of the highly probable resultant decimation of our already mediocre ratings, Roddenberry offers NBC an ultimatum. "Return *Star Trek* to Monday nights at seven-thirty," he says, "or I walk."

"Been nice working with ya," they reply.

With that in mind, Gene effectively deserts his sinking starship. He moves out of his office at Paramount, takes up similar residence at Universal Studios, and throws all of his energies into writing a feature film entitled *Pretty Maids All in a Row*. Gene's departure vaporizes the last of NBC's dwindling faith in *Star Trek*, and within the week they've decided to hedge their bets and cut some of their probable losses by hacking generously at our budget.

Over the course of the next eight months, *Star Trek*'s

cast and crew went through the motions of producing the series' final twenty-eight episodes, trying our best to keep our upper lips stiff and to fight the good fight, but with weakened creative abilities and a disemboweled budget, the show suffered noticeably. We could no longer afford to shoot on location. We couldn't afford to create many new sets. We couldn't afford many special effects. We couldn't even afford scripts that required any number of guest stars. Additionally, our third-season budgetary restrictions forced us to shorten our shooting schedule from six days per episode to five. That demanded less rehearsal, fewer takes of each scene, less time to perfect the lighting or design of any given set, less complicated camera moves, and less ability to experiment. In short, it straitjacketed our creativity while allowing the tension level on our set to soar.

The crew of the U.S.S. *Enterprise* was effectively grounded, walking through entire shows without ever leaving the bridge. As co-producer Bob Justman says, "We had a budget almost large enough to do a really good radio show."

With the cards stacked against us, we did what we could, but *Star Trek* continued sliding further and further toward cancellation. Finally, just before Christmas, with our ratings, scripts and spirits all sinking to the abysmal level, the show was put out of its misery. The *Enterprise* was mothballed. Having limped through three seasons of sporadic creative greatness and Nielsen ambivalence, the series could now be officially categorized a failure. And then things got decidedly worse.

Throughout this same period, and far more important, my marriage was in deep trouble, ultimately deteriorating to the point where it, too, could be officially categorized a failure. It was a confusing, heartbreaking situation for my wife and me, one that seemed to defy all efforts toward healing. Somehow the love, caring and closeness that had once made up the foundation of what I believed would be a lifelong relationship had gradually and inescapably been replaced by disillusion and distance. Attempts to maintain the charade for the sake of the children were useless, and over the course of the past several months, it had become increasingly clear that the marriage was simply over. Separation and divorce followed.

It was an absolutely horrendous time. I resigned myself to the breakup, but couldn't shake a nagging grief and loneliness in regard to what I'd lost. Worse than that, I could not even *begin* coming to grips with the fact that my three daughters, more beloved to me than anything else on the face of the planet, were suddenly gone, living, sleeping, laughing, singing and playing in a different house. I learned that there's nothing more disheartening than the luxury of forced free time. Without the kids' distractions, I spent a lot of time desperately trying to convince myself that my newfound peace and quiet was actually enjoyable, halfheartedly "relaxing" with the newspaper or distractedly savoring a long dinner with friends, all the while wishing I could exchange the adult leisure activities for a spirited game of Candyland. I actually found myself nostalgic for that nauseating aroma that wafts out of brand-new cans of Play-Doh, even longing for an opportunity to once again assume my usual role as Ken in one of my daughters' free-form after-supper Barbie improvisations.

Five days out of every seven passed without my kids, and it was driving me nuts. By month's end, I'd begun regularly counting down the 132 hours between the time I'd drop the girls back with their mom on Sunday evenings and pick them up the following Saturday. Sometimes I'd even find myself keeping a notepad tally sheet of "hours passed" versus "hours to go."

Further, the words "divorced" and "unemployed" almost immediately conspired to leave me in a tough spot financially. In fact, I was pretty much broke. My wife's divorce settlement, arranged prior to *Star Trek*'s cancellation, was based in large part upon my average "TV star" salary of the past three years. Needless to say, with *Trek* now dumpstered, I was earning a lot less than I had in the past. The financial settlement, alimony and child support decisions were sizable enough that I *had* to find work, *any* work, fast, so that at month's end I could write nonbounceable checks for my ex-wife, my kids and of course the lawyers who allowed me to fall into such a penurious situation.

Job hunting was not easy, and I quickly found that my prospects of getting work on another television series were slim. Somehow the image of a green velour–clad Captain James Tiberius Kirk still lingered indelibly in most producers' minds, effectively preventing them from considering me for other roles. To keep myself busy and financially solvent, I decided to jump back into the theater. A phone call to my agent proved fruitful, and by the time NBC had aired the final first-run episode of *Star Trek*, I was already traveling the Northeast with a small troupe on the straw-hat circuit, directing and starring in standard summer-stock comedies like *The Seven-Year Itch* while touring resort towns from late May through early September. My dog, Morgan, a beautiful, wet-nosed, black Doberman, was with me.

Like gypsies, we'd take a play with a company of actors into a new resort town every few days, giving four or five performances at each stop, then packing up our tents and heading off to the next town. Our first destination that summer was in Connecticut, and I was staying at a truly no-frills-style motel when an unpleasant mixture of travel costs, hotel bills and my checkbook quickly convinced me that these days I couldn't really afford even the most economy-style accommodations.

At that point, I went out and purchased a beat-up secondhand Chevy pickup truck. It wasn't pretty, it wasn't the most luxurious ride in the world, but it ran pretty well; in fact, it was pretty much indestructible. Even by the time the Fourth of July rolled around, it had already more than paid for itself by virtually erasing my expense lines in regard to rental car and hotel.

"And hotel" is not a typo. This dirty, rusted-out, six-cylinder warhorse actually provided me with shelter as well as basic transportation. That's because filling up the pickup bed of my truck, and tossed into the deal at no extra charge, was one of the strangest sheltering devices ever to house a human being. Best described as a sort of collapsible aluminum camper, this thing spent most of its time as a compact metallic rectangle. I'd haul it from town to town as we toured, and upon scouting out a prime location in the theater of the week's parking lot, usually under a tree, I'd slide this kit off the truck, open her up, get out the directions sheet, insert "tab A" into "slot B," prop the whole thing onto four telescoping legs, tighten up a couple of Phillips-head screws, hook up the generator, and within forty-five minutes, voilà, I had my own freestanding hovel.

It certainly wasn't the Ritz, it wasn't even the Motel 6, but this thing really wasn't all that bad. In fact, it actually boasted all the necessities, if not the luxuries, of home. The attached generator was quite powerful, and it allowed me to run a small stove, a fan, a tiny refrigerator, even a minuscule television set. Additionally, once I'd filled the unit's water-storage tanks, I could shower, brush my teeth, go to the bathroom, and I was in business. I could survive adequately, if not entirely comfortably, and it was cheap. Hell, it was free. In those bleak post-*Trek* days, anything else would have been extravagant.

I lived that way all summer, moving into a new neighborhood every Monday, nearly all of them black-topped and half-filled with cars. I'd just park, build my house, unpack, rehearse and spend the bulk of the next seven days depressed, lonely and forlorn. It was terrible. I hadn't even adjusted to my girls living in another house when suddenly they were on another coast. You can't imagine the guilt that comes part and parcel with the irrational feeling that you've abandoned your kids. Even worse is wondering whether they might agree with you. I suddenly began sinking a lot of my hotel bill savings into pay phones, dedicating full rolls of dimes to transcontinental kid/Dad conferences. It helped, a little.

JULY 20, 1969:
EAST HAMPTON, NEW YORK

I'm now in the small, seasonal community of East Hampton, New York, driving in circles around the town square, sweating, swearing and cursing the fact that the tiny local theater has no parking lot. My "front lawn" has ceased to exist, and I'm forced to begin a search for some place, *any place*, to rest my weary poor man's Winnebago. Finally, one of the local stagehands suggests I homestead in a nearby vacant lot, not too far from the ocean. Once there, I set up shop quickly, constructing my prefab camper amid the mosquitoes, oppressive humidity and million-dollar beach homes indigenous to the area. I'm working faster than usual this afternoon, sweating through my home-building routine so that I might finish in time to check out the progress of NASA's *Apollo 11* mission on my tiny TV. Blastoff was four days ago. Today Neil Armstrong walks on the moon.

Twenty minutes later, I'm lying across my camper's sponge-rubber mattress, diagonally, so that my feet won't hang over the end. On my chest, a black-and-white six-inch television set, with an antenna concocted from a wire coat hanger, some Scotch tape, and a hunk of tin foil that I'd salvaged off a takeout cheeseburger, undulates with my every breath.

My head is propped on Morgan's haunches. He actually makes a pretty comfortable pillow, although he could *really* use a bath. One thing I've learned over the course of this long, strange summer is that the combination of big dog and small living space can be quite pungent.

Thus I watch in amazement as Neil Armstrong's "one small step" makes history, his "giant leap for mankind" encompassing about two and a half inches of my blurry, ghost-ridden television screen. As the spectacle continues to unfold, I employ some further bodily contortions to clarify the set's reception, my left hand constantly monitoring the vertical hold knob, my right focusing a magnifying glass between my eyeballs and the screen. It keeps me from squinting and allows me to get a better sense of what's going on 238,900 miles away. Despite the lousy view, I'm awestruck by the magnitude of the day's events.

I am also well aware of the irony. Less than a year ago I was on top of the world, playing the lead in a network television series, making good money, hobnobbing with real astro-celebs, and thoroughly enjoying my good fortune, my work and my family. A year later, they're all gone. I live in a tin box, broke and alone except for a large malodorous Doberman. Somehow I can't help but feel like the victim of some grand cosmic plan whose sole purpose is to kick the shit out of me.

MID-AUGUST 1969: MILLBURN, NEW JERSEY

The dog days of August are burning at full force, creating steam and melanomas all over the Northeast. Still, the August heat foreshadows the onset of autumn and the long-awaited light at the end of the tunnel. I'm now counting the days until I can pack up my sheet-metal motel for the last time and haul it the length of Route 66, speeding cross-country, back to my kids and all the sticky-fingered hugs they can dish out. Today Morgan and I have made it as far as New Jersey.

It's a nice little theater called the Paper Mill Playhouse, made nicer by the fact that one of the theater's volunteer workers has kindly invited me to forgo my standard parking lot location and set up my camper in her driveway. Actually, she'd originally offered me her spare bedroom, but after she met my four-legged, hundred-pound, drooling, trained-to-kill traveling companion, we both agreed that the driveway might be a better solution.

So now my rig is standing on its four thin pipe legs, looking not unlike *Apollo 11*'s four-legged, freestanding lunar module. Four weeks have passed since that first moon landing, but the resultant media hysteria and public fascination have yet to die down. I learn this one morning while brushing my teeth.

As I stand there at the sink, massaging my molars and peering out my small, grubby bathroom window, I notice something streaking toward the trailer. Turns out to be a kid, redheaded and crew-cutted, maybe seven years old, who's pedaling a red, banana-seated Schwinn with all he's got. Suddenly, as he runs parallel with the bathroom window, he stomps on his brakes, skids, stops and stares wide-eyed at my camper. He then proceeds to stay there for ten full minutes. I have no idea what he's doing. Finally, in an effort to understand this bizarre behavior and to make some actual human contact, I open my front door about halfway, poke my head outside and say "Hi!"

The kid sees me, gasps loudly, then remounts his two-wheeled steed and bolts.

The following morning I'm shaving. Foam-covered, I'm going about my business when I see this same kid rolling toward my front door. Once again he skids to a stop, once again he stares, once again he stays there marveling at my truly unimpressive housing. Once again he scurries away at the first sight of me. Now I'm really confused.

Morning comes once more, and I'm jostled from unconsciousness by the cold, slimy alarm clock that is Morgan's nose. I try my best to ignore him, but within minutes my cold clammy alarm clock has been replaced by a warm one, equally unpleasant. It's Morgan's tongue, which he's now applying liberally to my eyelids. The game's over. Morgan's won. I've got to get up.

Fifteen minutes later, the two of us have completed our second lap around the block. One of us is bleary-eyed. We're just approaching my front door when in the distance I can hear the distinct sound of baseball cards flicking through bicycle spokes. I come alive immediately, determined to finally make contact with this prepubescent stalker and find out what in the world draws him so uncontrollably to my weird little home. Morgan and I make a beeline around the side of the camper. The kid moves in, taking his standard approach.

While he's closing in, I shoo Morgan back inside and take up a position slightly in front of the camper, trying my best to look accessible and nonthreatening. The kid pedals closer. I wave to him, smiling broadly and shouting "Hi there! How are *you* today?!" The kid now smiles at me, waves back and rolls, full speed, into a shrub.

He's lying there, mussed, oozing blood, snot and tears, when I arrive. "You okay?" I ask him. He nods at me, embarrassed.

"Is Spock on the Moon?" he asks.

That's when the obvious finally hits me. The kid thinks I'm Captain Kirk, and that my camper, looking not unlike the real thing, is some sort of lunar module. I'm impressed with his imagination, though a bit concerned about his physical well-being. "Yes," I say to him, "I left Spock up there with Bones and Chekov. I'm gonna go pick them up on Monday. You want a Band-Aid or something?"

"Cool," the kid replies, still picking pine needles out of his ears. "That your ship?"

"Uhhhh, yeah."

"Can I see it?"

"Uhhhh, yeah," I repeat, ushering him toward the screen door.

Once inside I squirt the kid with some Bactine, slap a bandage onto his skinned left elbow, and show him around the "*Enterprise* shuttlecraft." I show him my ship's control panel, which I'd cleverly disguised as a tiny electric stove, complete with burner knobs that control the accelerator, brakes and steering wheel. Inside my small square refrigerator, I show off some of the reconstituted food I'd recently whipped up from its freeze-dried powdered beginnings. I even show him my top secret transporter bay, a tiny, tiled area with two high-tech chromium knobs. One is marked "H" and the other "C." "H" stands for "hover in space," I tell him, and "C" stands for "come back." It was the best I could think of on the spur of the moment.

"Wow!" yells the kid, thrilled with the knowledge that I routinely allowed my entire being to be sucked into a pitted shower head. "But why is there a dog on your ship?" he asks, changing topics faster than I can keep up.

"Uhhhhh," I counter feebly, while Morgan chews the local newspaper into confetti.

" . . . uh, . . . no, that's not a dog, it's a, uh, miniature Klingon horse, I've captured him and I'm bringing him back to the zoo on . . . uh . . . Rigel Seven."

"Oh," says the kid. "He really smells."

"Well, of course," I answer, "all Klingons smell like that. You get used to it after a while."

"Gotta go," he tells me, reaching for my hand. "Thanks a lot." He smiles at me, one of those big, broad, no-bullshit, no-pretense smiles that only kids up to about the age of eleven can muster. We shake and part, both of us thoroughly delighted with the unexpected close encounter. He's made contact with a space hero, and I've made a friend, for a while, anyway.

If I don't see my daughters soon, I *am* going to die.

LABOR DAY WEEKEND, 1969: WILLIAMSTOWN, MASSACHUSETTS

Jerry Lewis is three inches tall. He's wearing a tiny tuxedo and mugging like a maniac, live from Las Vegas, as he raises money for his kids. He's flickering amid a pile of dirty laundry as I hastily, even gleefully, pack up my belongings for the long trip home. Pots and pans go in one box, books and papers get shoved in another, and . . . that's about it. I must be the oldest bohemian in Williamstown.

I'm finally going home. Full-color Vistavision fantasy previews of my father-and-daughters reunion take up the bulk of my brain, but other, less pleasant thoughts creep in as well. I worry about how I'll adjust to the transition between "TV star" and "unemployed actor." I wonder what I can do to help rebuild the friendships and business relationships that have undoubtedly been damaged by my abrupt disappearance from the face of the earth. After this long, lonely summer, I even wonder if I can still converse face-to-face with another human being.

I have now survived a one-hundred-day sentence in purgatory, with no exit from a shallow, transitory, empty place, wherein your entire life is kept at arm's length, where you work all the time because you simply have nothing else, where business acquaintances have to pass for friends. It's not an unpleasant world, it's merely devoid of any real human contact, devoid of passion. It's a place where everybody likes you, but nobody loves you. However, against all odds, I'm still smiling, reasoning that if I can survive just one more matinee, I'll have beaten this abominable summer, free to head home and get reacquainted with my grubby little angels.

Curtain time arrives, and over the course of the next 120 minutes, we finish what's normally a two-hour-and-thirty-minute play. It seems I'm not the only one champing at the bit to get home. Afterward, cast and crew pass quick congratulations all around, and make insincere promises to keep in touch. Two sips of champagne later, I'm back in the truck. After a preliminary scan of my road atlas, I aim my rusted road warrior due west. I've got my tinny AM radio cranked, I'm singing along with the Beatles, and I find myself feeling happier and more energetic than I have in a long time, perhaps since that last time I was heading west into a summer sunset.

Twelve hours later I'm still at the wheel, groggy, baggy-eyed, and semiconsciously grunting the words to the Archies' "Sugar Sugar," which now blares, for the fifth time today, out of my sound-distorting dashboard speaker. When the farm reports begin, I decide to crash at the first roadside motel, allowing myself four hours sleep before resuming my westward trek. In the morning, I wander dull-eyed into a local diner, where I order a couple of scrambled-egg sandwiches and a veritable bucket of coffee to go. No sense wasting twenty minutes over my food. While the eggs are sputtering on the grill, I make two phone calls. The first is to my kids. I tell them that I've made it as far as western Pennsylvania and that I should be home soon. When my change runs out, I change gears, calling my agent collect. He's requested, actually demanded, that I check in with him at least once a day while I drive. He accepts the charges.

"Bill, ya bastard, where the hell are you?"

"Uh, Pennsylvania, I think, why?"

"Listen, turn that rusty hay wagon of yours around and get back to New York right now," he juicily decrees.

"Huh?" I reply.

"Whassa matter, you got potatoes in yer ears, babe? Pay attention this time, okay? Get in your car. Turn the key. Then turn the car around so that it's pointed toward New York and get your ass back there. Rose Kennedy, THE Rose Kennedy, was apparently a big fan of *Star Trek* . . . go figure. Anyway, she wants you to sit at *her* table at a charity event this Thursday night."

"Can't do it."

"Wha? . . . who? . . . wha?" sputters my apoplectic rep. "What are you, nuts?! You don't say 'no' when the

Kennedys want you. Jesus, why don't you just piss on the Queen of England while you're at it?"

"Look, as much as I admire the Kennedys, I *have* to see my kids. I promised them, I promised myself, and there's nothing you can say that can change my mind about this. I'm going home."

There's now a silence on the other end of the phone that's so long and awkward I actually begin wondering if maybe I've given my agent a coronary. " . . . Okay. All right . . . go kiss the girls," he tells me. "But call me again tomorrow, because, well, you know, you never know."

"No problem," I reply, surprised that he'd given up that easily.

I pay for my now greasy paper sack of egg sandwiches, pound back a couple slugs from my coffee tureen, and I'm off, spending the ensuing day and most of the night staring zombielike at the white line painted down the middle of Route 66. I stop only for gas, restrooms and takeout food. Morgan hangs his head out the passenger-side window for a full three hundred miles. The wind blows his ears back and molds his face into what appears to be a big smile. In my punchy state I find myself laughing hysterically at that all through the Midwest. When I'm doubled over to the point where the truck begins swerving, I pull into the first motel I find and try my best to sleep, while the large, pink neon sign outside my window blinks "HEATED POOL" at me all night long.

By the time the sun nullifies the neon, I'm back on the road, rolling through the Midwestern plains. By nine, I've racked up another hundred miles, and Morgan's stomach is rumbling loudly. Mine, too. We pull into a truck stop, where we both scarf down takeout orders of blueberry pancakes. I then check in with my agent while still sucking syrup off my fingers. Thirty seconds later, he has me grimacing.

"Look," he begins, "I know you don't want to hear this, I know you want to get home to the kids, but the Kennedy people called me four times yesterday. They won't take no for an answer. They really want you to come to this charity thing, and they're offering to do whatever it takes to get you there. You *have* to do this."

"I . . . uh . . . don't have a tuxedo with me," I reply, feebly scrounging around for any additional excuse that might help keep me pointed west.

"C'mon already."

"Sorry, but as much as I admire the Kennedys, and as much as I'd like to go to this thing, I can't. I've *gotta* go home, I've *gotta* see these kids, I *can't* wait any longer."

The phone goes silent now, save for the sound of my agent chewing a Tums. "Call me tomorrow," he sighs, and hangs up.

The next twenty-four hours come and go in a haze of sleep-deprived, adrenaline-driven speeding. By morning, I'm in Arizona. Barring disaster, I should be home by suppertime. I'm fixated now on those first three hugs at the door. I can't stop smiling. I check in once more with my agent, just as a formality.

"Where are you today?" he expostulates in lieu of "Hello."

"Phoenix," I reply, preparing myself for his next volley.

"What if I told you the Kennedys just called me again, and now they're willing to send their private jet to Phoenix, pick you up, fly you to New York, and then back to Phoenix after the event? You can continue home from there. Start to finish you'll just lose one day. You can live with *that*, can't ya?"

My eyeballs are now rolling up into my skull. "Aw, c'mon, don't do this to me."

"Don't do this to *you*, don't do this to ME!"

"Listen, I know this sounds crazy, and I know it makes me look like an asshole, but I'm drawing a line in the sand here. I'm going home."

So now, having spent the better part of a week parked upon a nearly springless vinyl truck bench, having slept only two or three hours per night, having consumed mass quantities of grease and cholesterol, and having pissed off my agent and insulted the most powerful family in America, it's time to go home. It's time to collect my reward. I drive like an escapee from Alcatraz. Then it hits me.

About an hour outside of L.A., I'm struck with a stunning blow. My eyes widen from their weeklong tunnel vision, and I realize that I could have had the Kennedy plane come to Phoenix, pick me up, then hop across the rest of Arizona to L.A. There I could have collected my kids and all of us could have flown to New York. We could have had a wonderful all-expenses-paid adventure. I was astonished by my own lack of creative thinking, but somehow in my tunnel-visioned drive to get home, I'd simply blocked any variation on that theme from my head.

Later, about five miles away from the kids' house, Morgan's stomach is growling again, big time. Big, rolling, gurgling rumbles that he accompanies with the saddest puppy-dog face he can muster. It's a powerful weapon, and it quickly brings me to my knees. I decide to pull over and grab a pizza to bring home for the girls, as well as a meatball sandwich for the dog. Before I order, I call the kids to see what they want on top of the pie.

"Hi, Lisabeth," I say to the daughter whose phoneward lunge has vanquished her sisters and won her possession of the receiver. "Daddy's almost home, honey, I'm just down the road at the pizza place."

"Oh . . . uh . . . "

"I'm on my way, sweetheart!" I add with a melodramatic flourish.

"Well, uh, that's great, Dad, I guess we'll see you tomorrow then."

All the air in my body comes heaving out. "Tomorrow?"

"Yeah, we're all going to a slumber party tonight. We're on our way out the door right now."

"Oh . . . uh . . . that's great . . . great," I squeak out defeatedly. "I'll see you guys tomorrow. Kiss your sisters for me, okay?"

"Okay, see ya!" she chirps.

I spend that evening alone with Morgan, the two of us drowning our sorrows in meatballs and an entire Sicilian pizza. Afterward, we just lie there, bloated, like two beached whales, cursing the fates. The adrenaline and excitement that had kept me moving for the past ninety-six hours have now been yanked from my body by a simple little girls' slumber party. Exhaustion sets in quickly, and I collapse into a nearly comatose sleep.

I awake before sunrise, so early that even Morgan is still belly-up. I'm instantly energized, and I quickly shower, shave, dress and proceed to pace around my living room until I get the call that tells me my kids are home. At that point I practically sprint out the front door and break several local speed laws careening toward my kids. When I get there, they're waiting at the door, faces pressed unwisely against the bug screen. I screech to a halt outside, beep the horn, and they tumble forward, racing toward me, arms open wide, the word "Daddy" squealing in triplicate as they approach. The moment of impact arrives about halfway between sidewalk and front door. They clobber me with a barrage of bear hugs, kisses, happy tears and "I love yous," and we collapse into the sod. For a few moments nothing else in the world exists. Nothing else matters. I can worry about the future tomorrow.

Over the course of the next several years I accepted all offers, and was lucky enough to keep busy as an actor. Some of the roles, a guest villain shot on *Columbo* and featured spots on shows such as *The Name of the Game* and *Mission Impossible*, were quite good. Others, like hawking Promise margarine all over television, or battling *The Six Million Dollar Man*, were equally bad. A few, in films such as *Big Bad Mama* and *The Devil's Rain*, can best be described as just plain ugly.

Still, with a lot of hustling, I was able to keep my head above water. The bills got paid, my kids stayed fed, Morgan got fat, and my post-*Trek* life moved forward without regrets.

Meanwhile, all across America, an unexpected, convoluted and nearly unbelievable series of events were conspiring to change my life forever.

MEANWHILE....

NBC actually did *Star Trek* a favor by canceling it. With declining ratings and free-falling creative content, the show was mercifully yanked from the airwaves before it had the chance to alienate its legions of fans. Rather than stumbling anemically through a fourth or fifth season, we left our audience wanting more. Kirk, Spock and company had beaten it out of town before they could leave a bad taste in anyone's mouth. Subsequently, *Star Trek* would be remembered fondly, as a great show that got screwed by the network, rather than as a good show that got worse and worse over time.

By the autumn of 1969, however, *Star Trek* still hadn't quite dropped dead. A few of its vital signs were still faintly noticeable, and they grew a bit stronger as the show began playing in syndication. Playing five nights a week, in a few small and medium-sized markets, the show was initially offered up by Paramount in an attempt to recapture some of the money the studio had lost in producing this ratings disappointment. Had *Star*

Trek fared better in its original prime-time incarnation—and not hemorrhaged money out of the Paramount lot—we might never have gotten to syndication at all. Once again, *Star Trek*'s abrupt cancellation was actually working in its favor.

And then the unthinkable happened. *Star Trek* became a hit.

Apollo 11's exhaust trail had apparently stretched the length of America, drawing the imagination of an entire country into outer space. Somehow, despite the cheesy special effects and melodramatic storylines, *Star Trek* had become a bit less unbelievable, a bit more exciting, and its audience quickly began growing almost exponentially. A brand-*new* audience, one that had never bothered with the show in prime time, was now suddenly enamored of the series. Add into the mix the existing band of hard-core *Trek* devotees, and *Star Trek*'s reruns quickly became a big success, boasting a sizable, enthusiastic and steadily increasing viewership.

Program managers at local TV stations all across the country were suddenly turning cartwheels at their water coolers. They'd sucked up a cheap hour's worth of programming for a song, only to find it becoming the most popular program on the channel. News of this minor miracle spread rapidly among industry types, and before long there wasn't a television market in America, big, small, or minuscule, that wasn't airing *Star Trek* reruns at least once a day. Paramount was finally cashing in, their ugly duckling slowly growing into a beautiful swan.

Over the course of the next eighteen months, ratings for the original seventy-nine *Trek*s continued to grow even after they'd been aired three or four times over. Instead of getting bored, fans of *Star Trek* actually seemed to enjoy watching repeats of our repeats, studying every episode to the point where they not only knew each storyline, but most of the dialogue as well. Star Trek parties began springing up on college campuses, where whole groups of Trek-nuts got together to watch the show and celebrate their fascination with the series. Trek fans, it seemed, weren't just enthusiastic, they were fanatical. This would be proven beyond a shadow of a doubt when a strange and heretofore unheard of entity began springing up around the country—the Star Trek convention.

Partly the result and partly the cause of Star Trek's continued vitality, these mass celebrations began sprouting like dandelions, attracting thousands of fans into musty convention halls and economy hotel meeting rooms all over the country. There they'd mingle amid their fellow addicts, screening old episodes en masse, buying up whatever Star Trek merchandise they could lay their hands on, and sometimes, when they were really lucky, mingling with members of Star Trek's original cast and crew.

By early 1972, Gene Roddenberry himself was addressing the pointy-plastic-eared crowd, holding court among the admirers and widening their eyes by doling out the anecdotes and inside information that were his alone for the telling. The conventioneers were generally awestruck at first, intimidated in the presence of the man they themselves had deemed the "Great Bird of the Galaxy," but in time, Gene's big laugh and willingness to chat always melted away their fears. Soon they'd be quizzing him about specific episodes, about his legendary fights with the network and about his future plans.

Inevitably, the conversation would begin to center on whether or not Gene thought it might be possible to breathe some new life into his recently deceased television show, and just as inevitably, Gene would light up, smile broadly and conjure up some cryptic statement along the lines of, "Well, I would love to bring *Star Trek* back. I'd love to see it return to television, or maybe even on the big screen, but the networks and film studios just won't get behind it. Perhaps with your continued enthusiasm and support, they'll see the light and give us a chance. Would you folks like that?"

At that point the attendees would invariably rise, their decibel levels rattling the rafters at Gene's prompting. What they couldn't know was that despite all his cheerleading, Gene had absolutely no intention of resuscitating the object of their desire, at least not yet.

As early as 1972, Paramount came to Roddenberry, asking him to return to the lot and start thinking about bringing *Star Trek* back, either as a TV movie or perhaps a very-low-budget big-screener. Gene turned them down immediately. He knew that his original contract prohibited the studio from moving forward with any new *Star Trek* project without his participation, and he quite correctly theorized that the growing cries for new *Trek* material would only get louder with the passage of time. He could tuck *Star Trek* neatly into his back pocket, forget about it and concentrate solely upon creating new programming.

Actually, later that year there *was* one exception to that rule. When Filmation Associates came to Gene pitching an animated Saturday-morning version of the original series, offering Gene total creative control, he jumped at the chance. He quickly installed *Trek* staple Dorothy Fontana as story editor/associate producer, and she in turn was able to persuade some of the original series' finest writers to pen scripts for the animated go-round. Dorothy, who'd written some of the very best

*Star Trek*s ("Charlie X," "Tomorrow Is Yesterday," "Journey to Babel," "Friday's Child"), succeeded in luring *Trek* colleagues Paul Schneider ("Balance of Terror," "The Squire of Gothos"), Sam Peeples ("Where No Man Has Gone Before"), Stephen Kandel ("Mudd's Women," "I, Mudd"), Margaret Armen ("The Gamesters of Triskelion," "The Paradise Syndrome") and David Gerrold ("The Trouble with Tribbles") to the series. With these highly competent key personnel in place, the animated series, which premiered in September 1973, practically ran on autopilot. It required very little of Gene's time, paid him rather handsomely, and allowed him to remain focused on several non-*Trek* projects he'd been banging around.

As story editor, Dorothy would assign scripts, shepherd them through a rewrite or two, and pass the completed manuscripts along to Gene, who had assumed the title of "executive consultant." Gene would then read each script, perhaps make a suggestion or two, and sign off. It was that simple. Roddenberry had found the perfect vehicle. The animated *Star Trek* required almost none of his time, it kept his most durable brand name alive, and it served as a lightning rod, rallying the forces behind the cry to "Bring back *Star Trek*!" In their minds, and this was carefully groomed by Gene at countless conventions, they'd won their first battle. The animated *Star Trek* should be seen not as a reward in and of itself, but as the first step back toward new and improved live-action *Trek*s, be they on television or the silver screen. Over and over again, fans were urged to keep fighting.

Meanwhile, having been burned by the feature film industry, Gene's efforts were now almost entirely directed toward the creation of new television series. *Pretty Maids All in a Row*, the film he'd written for

Universal during *Star Trek*'s last season, had become a major critical and box office embarrassment. Additionally, his subsequent silver-screen plans to re-create Tarzan as a sexually hyperactive superhero never got beyond the preliminaries. A bit shell-shocked by his lack of cinematic success, Gene now refocused his sights toward television, and set about rebuilding some of the bridges he'd burned at the networks throughout the prime time run of *Star Trek*. It seemed to be working.

By early 1973, with several irons in the fire, Gene was most enthusiastic about a pilot entitled *Questor*. The proposed series, which had been in the works at Universal for some time, would have followed an android named Questor through a series of adventures in which he'd search for his creator while striving to elude a mysterious group of government scientists hell-bent upon dissecting him. As a final kicker, set to play the cool, dispassionate, highly intelligent, unfailingly logical Questor was the obvious choice, Leonard Nimoy. Despite their rocky relationship throughout the original run of *Star Trek*, Nimoy and Roddenberry had agreed to reunite for the project. Leonard explains:

Questor came from the word quest, in this case a search. The basic storyline was one in which a diverse group of scientists come together from a number of nations to create a humanoid being, a sort of futuristic Frankenstein story.

Now, as this character is being developed, evolving on the operating table, it reaches a conscious state. And in this conscious state, he overhears this contingent of scientists arguing with each other about things like international ownership, rights, licensing and so forth. He has become the subject of a global tug of war, a battleground. He quickly realizes that he's in great danger. That evening, after the scientists have left the lab, he rises from the table and completes his own construction.

At that point, in theory, he'd go off on a series of adventures, sort of like *The Fugitive*, only instead of searching for the one-armed man, Questor is looking for the one individual he trusts of all these scientists who've conceived him. He's looking for his creator, trying to understand his own reason for existing. He simply wants an answer to the question "Why am I here?" It sounded rather intriguing.

So now I sign my contract at Universal, and I'm set to play the Questor character. I had some meetings with Gene about it, and we talked about the various aspects of the character that we could explore. We'd done the same thing with Spock years earlier. I was actually a little nervous, because in the draft I read there were some pretty obvious Spockian references. I wanted to be really careful. Questor shouldn't be able to tap into men's minds, or have the neck pinch ability, or play off the equivalent of a Bones McCoy, who'd needle him about his lack of humanity. It just wouldn't have worked.

Gene and I had some very helpful discussions about all of that, and things were progressing nicely, until one day the director of the *Questor* pilot, a man named Richard Colla, came into my office and told me that Robert Foxworth had just been hired by Gene to play Questor. To this day I have no idea why it happened, although you'd have to assume someone at the studio must have shared my concerns about Questor looking like Spock revisited, especially with me in the title role. At any rate, I called Gene's office immediately and demanded an explanation.

Gene and I had a tough time about this. We didn't yell, we didn't argue, but we did have a final conversation in which he came up with a whole song and dance about how the studio had hired Foxworth behind his back. According to him, he had no inkling that this had happened until my phone call. It was patently and transparently untrue, but I just couldn't bring myself to get into any sort of cross-examination.

Instead, I said, "You know the press is going to jump on this. What will your answer be when someone says to you, 'You came to Universal specifically to develop this series for Leonard Nimoy. What happened?'" At that point, there was a long pause, after which Gene said, "I'll just say that you were unavailable."

I said, "But Gene, that's not the truth. I *am* available. I'm right here. I was specifically hired for a year to develop this project, and you were brought here to develop this project for me." I said, "If they ask me what happened, I can't say, 'I'm unavailable.'"

Gene answered, "You tell your story, I'll tell mine."

I mean, how do you deal with that? How do you deal with a producer who says to you, "I will lie, not *for* you, but *about* you"? You know what I did? I just quickly shifted gears and said to myself, "You know something? You're well out of this." I was devastated, but I thought to myself, *Why should I have expected anything else*? By this time I had become totally disillusioned in regard to my relationship with Gene.

With NBC showing interest in the project, *The Questor Tapes* (now retitled) got as far as the pilot stage, and at that point, one of two things happened. Either, as Roddenberry always stated, he got disgusted when the network demanded that he amputate Questor's basic search for his creator and replace it with more action and less philosophizing, or as the network states, they simply looked at the pilot, didn't like it, and thought it was far too similar to ABC's then-current hit, *The Six Million Dollar Man*.

Either way, Gene had at least one more ace up his sleeve. *Genesis II*, a pilot he'd been working on for some time, was now being produced in conjunction with Warner Brothers, and was generating some serious interest from CBS. The premise, much darker than *Star Trek*'s, depicted a future nowhere near as utopian or altruistic as Roddenberry generally espoused. Civilization had in fact disintegrated, torn apart by a societal inability to look beyond selfish needs. In *Genesis II*'s near-future, things like water supply, food, medicine and shelter, once taken for granted, have become scarce, the victims of overpopulation, waste and greed. In the face of these grave crises, mankind's nobler instincts get squashed beneath a wave of riots, looting and gang warfare. The carnage soon escalates to the point where most of mankind and all of civilization are destroyed. The year is 1983.

Flash forward 150 years, and Gene's pilot begins. Dylan Hunt, a twentieth-century NASA scientist, is awakened from a state of suspended animation by a group of futuristic scientists called PAX. They tell him that the Earth he recalls now lies in ruins. They explain the horrifying events of 1983 and describe how the small number of survivors of that devastation immediately banded together in small tribal communities scattered across what was once the United States of America. Those communities, now populated by the survivors' descendants, have since evolved into widely varying civilizations. Some are highly advanced, others simply barbaric. It is PAX's goal to preserve and protect the nobler aspects of mankind, their books, their knowledge and their spirituality, while slowly guiding these tribal civilizations toward rebuilding an all-inclusive society and recapturing the glories that their species had once attained.

Thus Gene hoped to rekindle his own creative glories and surpass his own *Star Trek* achievements. The pilot aired on CBS on March 10, 1973, and despite a critical shellacking, it racked up rather impressive Nielsen numbers. Intrigued with the product, CBS ordered up six scripts, and Gene immediately went to work. However, within a month's time, Fred Silverman, then the head of CBS, did an about-face and dumped *Genesis II* entirely, deciding that the network budget could handle only one expensive science fiction series, and that *Genesis II* simply wasn't the most attractive project on the table. He opted instead to adapt the *Planet of the Apes* films into an episodic small-screen format. The result was an expensive disaster, both creatively and in the ratings.

Drop-kicked by CBS, Gene took his pilot to ABC. They expressed some interest in the project, and after several rounds of creative changes, a *new* pilot was filmed. Now entitled *Planet Earth*, this offering came off rather poorly, and ABC quickly passed. At about the same time, another project, this one a ghost-and-goblin chaser entitled *SPECTRE*, co-written with *Star Trek* veteran Sam Peeples, was unceremoniously canned by Twentieth Century-Fox. Gene was beginning to sweat. It was time to fall back on his sure thing. By mid-1974, Roddenberry and Paramount were once again negotiating and pondering the future voyages of the Starship *Enterprise*.

At the same time, partly to help fuel the demand for new *Star Trek* product and partly because after five years of failed projects he really needed the money, Gene began hitting the *Star Trek* conventions big-time, working the crowds hard and turning almost every question-and-answer session into a boisterous rallying cry for *Star Trek*'s return. He'd love to bring *Star Trek* to the big screen, he told the rabid devotees, if only Paramount would let him. It was "Up to you folks," Gene rallied them, "to make sure the studio knows how badly you all want this."

Meanwhile, even as Roddenberry was whipping his hardest-core supporters into a frenzy, *Star Trek*'s fan base was booming. By now the classic seventy-nine episodes had become a syndicated fixture, seeping into every nook and cranny of the country five nights a week. Unfounded rumors began flying constantly that we were on the very brink of returning to the small screen, or graduating to the silver. For a while, there was even a volley of gossip declaring that it was absolutely certain . . . *Star Trek* was going to return as a full-blown Broadway musical. Those of you who've had the chance to become familiar with my now classic renditions of "Mr. Tambourine Man" or "Lucy in the Sky with Diamonds" can attest to the improbable nature of that particular idea.

Can you imagine? Kirk beams down to an unknown

planet and grapples with a hostile alien. They fall to the ground, locked in a hostile clinch. And then something wonderful happens. They exchange their first truly meaningful glance, their eyes meet, their hearts leap, and suddenly they're not angry anymore. Kirk scoops his ex-nemesis into his arms . . . and sings, "Isn't it rich . . . aren't we a pair, me here at last on the ground, you with . . . green hair."

Anyway, though the rumors were always unfounded, *Star Trek*'s renaissance was apparently very real. I, however, had absolutely no idea that any of this was going on. I had remarried, my kids were beginning to spend more and more time with me, I was working fairly steadily in TV or theater, not getting rich, but paying the bills and for the first time in a long time clutching a couple of bucks in my pocket. It was a truly wonderful period of time. *Star Trek* was the last thing on my mind.

I had even managed to scrape up the down payment on a nice little shoebox of a house: living room, two small bedrooms, kitchen, bathroom, what else do you really need? Loud, chaotic and most often filled with some combination of my kids, their friends, our dogs and my wife, Marcy, the house was generally overflowing with happiness. We even had a tiny aboveground pool, complete with a slide, that I, my kids, the neighbor kids and even Morgan the Doberman would whoosh down maniacally, screaming and plummeting into three and a half feet of ice-cold water at every opportunity. I couldn't have been any happier.

I was also almost entirely unaware that anything was brewing in regard to *Star Trek*. My residuals had run out long ago, and though I knew the show was once again airing in reruns, I had no idea it was becoming something of a phenomenon. I simply didn't pay it much attention. In fact, my first realization that *Trek* was indeed rising from the dead came on a ski slope.

It happened like this. I'm away on a ski vacation, sliding wobbily around California's Mammoth Mountain, minding my own business, when all of a sudden, this sort of mildly drunken guy comes schussing up next to me. So now we're skiing along side by side, and half a ski run goes by during which this guy just keeps staring at me. And then he speaks.

"Hey man . . . you're Spock!" he yells.

"Uh, no. Kirk," I grumble as I try to ignore him and involuntarily begin gritting my teeth.

"Oh, Kirk . . . yeah, right. Hey, have you seen the *Star Trek* thing down at the lodge bar?"

Now the jerk's got me. I'm intrigued, and with my forehead wrinkled I yell back, "What do you mean? The reruns?"

"No way, Kirk [again with the "Kirk"], not the series, this *other* stuff. Dude, I never knew you were so funny!!"

So now I snowplow to a stop, and he does the same. I say, "What are you talking about?"

And he says to me, I swear, "Mr. Kirk . . . uh, I mean Stratner . . . dude . . . William . . . you just have to check it out for yourself."

So of course I make a straight run down the hill, and I get to the bar just in time to watch images of me and Leonard being projected onto a bedsheet that's acting as a makeshift screen. And as this thing progresses, I watch the entire cast of *Star Trek* flubbing lines, falling down, kidding one another and generally running around this bedsheet looking like inmates of a mental institution. Meanwhile, all around the bar, inebriated après-skiers are falling all over each other, doubled up laughing. Immediately I recognize the images as a compilation of *Star Trek*'s funniest bloopers, which in the days before Dick Clark and Ed McMahon beat the concept to death on network television, provided a truly unique viewing experience. This stuff was genuinely funny to watch, but at the same time it was also totally illegal and unapproved.

You see, throughout the prime-time run of *Star Trek*, the weeks before Christmas would invariably find the show's editors digging through mounds of discarded film clips searching for all of the season's more humorous outtakes. Once they'd completed the search, they'd begin assembling the funniest, silliest and stupidest moments into a collection that would ultimately find every cast member playing the fool. It was private footage, most often focusing on Leonard and me being undone by some of the idiocy that was part and parcel of our jobs. Anyway, the editors would then put music to all of this stuff and premiere the thing at our staff Christmas party.

There, the whole cast and crew, which was already quite well bonded, would laugh as we made idiots of ourselves. It was great fun, goofy, unpretentious "family" stuff, the equivalent of dropping your pants or wearing a lampshade on your head in some dumb eight-millimeter home movie. They were to be unreeled, enjoyed, destroyed and forgotten. Obviously that wasn't the case. Somehow, somebody, somewhere, had allowed them to leak out of the Paramount vaults. "Somebody" was Gene Roddenberry.

Gene, struggling through some tough post-*Trek* years and desperately committed to feeding and maintaining the public's inexplicably ravenous appetite for all things *Star Trek*, had pushed his actors' foolishness to the surface in public. I shrugged the whole thing off as a misguided but well-intentioned publicity stunt, but in truth, Gene would continue to cash in on the blooper reels for years to come, both by licensing them for "midnight movie" showings, and by making them the centerpiece of his traveling lecture, "Gene Roddenberry's World of Star Trek." Over time, thousands of Star Trek fans, each paying an admission fee, were made to feel like privileged insiders with the unveiling of this "backstage reel." It was a tool that would help see Roddenberry through some of his leaner years, and one that would also continue to damage his relationship with Leonard Nimoy. Leonard explains:

The whole thing really bothered me, and I actually filed an injunction with SAG against Roddenberry on the issue of this stupid blooper reel. I was so angry that at one point, I even wrote Gene a very impassioned letter in which I said privately and personally, "Gene, what this is really about is creating an atmosphere on the set wherein an actor cannot take a chance on making a mistake lest that piece of footage someday be used in some way that he had not authorized. You just can't do that. You are destroying the creative atmosphere and the privacy of the set. That's why spectators aren't allowed to watch shooting. Actors need to be able to make a mistake. That's what this is all about. If an actor makes a mistake on the set and then feels as though that footage is fair game, you will kill his creativity. In effect, you're saying, 'Anything that you're doing while the camera is rolling, I may use.'"

I wrote, "Gene, how would you like it if I came into your office late at night after you'd been struggling at the typewriter all day, and I pulled all of your crumpled rejected ideas out of the wastebasket and published them as *Gene Roddenberry's Bloopers?*"

The upshot was he offered me my own copy of the blooper reel. He just didn't get it, because for Gene, it always came down to money. He was somehow convinced that what I was *really* angry about was that he was making money with our bloopers, and I wasn't. He thought I was only after my own fair share, so he said, "Okay, you can have a print too." He thought that I would go out with the print on my own and show up at conventions and charge five bucks a head to show the blooper reel. He didn't get it at all.

Despite Leonard's best efforts, once that gorilla had gotten out of its cage, there was no recapturing it. For years our foul-ups continued to thrive in multiplexes and drive-ins everywhere. Today, with the advent of the VCR, nearly all Trekkers have not only seen the blooper reels, but most own their own personal fuzzily pirated VHS copy. Don't tell anybody this, but I have one myself.

By the mid-seventies, there was simply no denying the durability of *Star Trek*. Six years after breaking into syndication, the ratings on our reruns were extremely strong and still rising. *Trek* conventions had grown from yearly to twice-yearly to commonplace events. Not a weekend would pass without some group some-where throwing its own convention and attracting liter-ally thousands of fans. Still, at this point I had absolutely no idea what went on at them, and I'd avoided them like the black plague. *The attendees must be nuts*, I thought to myself, *sci-fi kooks obsessed with some old TV show*. I assumed they were unbalanced. I assumed they were nerds. And at the risk of repeating my own tired catchphrase, I truly assumed that they needed to "Get a life!"

And then I accidentally got smart. Early in 1975, I was appearing in a little one-man show that I used to do, full of Shakespearean sonnets, monologues, poetry, all kinds of stuff, all of it highbrow, none of it bearing the slightest relation to *Star Trek*. Still, every night the theater would be mostly full of people curious about seeing Captain Kirk live and in person. I was not naive enough to believe otherwise. *Star Trek* had gotten them in the door, I mused, but perhaps my performance might open them up to the Bard.

Each night as I went through my paces, the audiences seemed to genuinely enjoy my performance, and their applause as I took my bows was always more than polite. Still, it seemed to me that something was missing. The audience wanted more, some stronger connection. A stagehand figured it out for me.

"They probably just want to talk to you," he told me. "These people aren't here to see you act, they're here because they admire you, and because they feel like they know you. You're in their living rooms every night, and while the conscious part of their brains knows you're just an actor, on some gut level, I think they see you as a friend. Somehow, watching your friend reading the greatest sonnets ever written isn't nearly as interesting as having a simple, face-to-face chat."

The following evening, after the final curtain fell, I tried something new. I said to the crowd, "Tonight, if it's all right with you folks, I'd like for us to spend some time together. I'd like to throw the floor open for questions."

Over the next sixty minutes, I fielded whatever questions the audience wanted to throw at me, and as I expected, nearly all of them were *Star Trek*–related.

However, what I didn't expect was that the questions were smart, thoughtful and extremely insightful. I was amazed at the depth of feeling these people held in their hearts for the show, and touched by their appreciative insights. What had previously been missing each night was suddenly everywhere. By the time the night was over I had decided to take this experience a step further—attending my first *Star Trek* convention.

Several weeks later, I was in New York City, standing backstage awaiting my introduction to the crowd. Unprepared and unrehearsed, I'd just sneaked in through a back door at the last minute, assuming that I'd take a few questions, schmooze a little bit with the couple of hundred fans in attendance, see what this whole convention thing was all about, then hop back to the hotel for a late dinner. "Ladies and gentlemen, William Shatner!" boomed a loud, squeaky voice over a musclebound PA system. That was my cue. With a hammy flourish, I threw open the stage curtain, stepped out onto the hardwood and stopped dead in my tracks. My jaw dropped. My face went white, my eyes rolled up into my head and I was genuinely stunned. Five thousand people were now staring back at me, all of them cheering, all of them standing atop their chairs, all of them expecting me to be charming, full of absolutely fascinating *Trek* lore, and unceasingly entertaining. I was horrified.

And then they sat, all of them plopping into their wooden folding chairs nearly as one. The clattering wood roar slowly faded away, replaced by my own deafening silence. I had gone blank, the circuit breakers in my head overloading with astonishment and panic as to what I might do next.

"Uhhhhhhhhhhhhhhhhhhhhh . . . " I said lamely, following my brilliant opening statement with another.

"Uhhhhhhhhhhhhhhhhhhhh . . . does . . . uh, does anybody have a question or something?"

Five thousand hands shot into the air. My stomach shot into my throat. "How 'bout you?" I stammered to a young man down front.

He smiled and asked his question, which I answered to the best of my ability, throwing in a joke at Leonard Nimoy's expense for good measure. The joke got laughs, I got some applause, and I finally began feeling more comfortable among this crowd. I continued chatting, joking and bonding with these people for the next two hours, at the end of which time I was ushered away, having barely made a dent in the crowd's inventory of potential questions. Still, despite the rocky start, I really had a wonderful time, and came away feeling great. I had now seen for myself some of the faces behind *Star Trek*'s continuing popularity. We'd exchanged ideas, and when it was all over I felt as if I had begun to understand what it was that attracted them to the series. Their enthusiasm was actually quite contagious, and that afternoon, for the first time in my life, I actually found myself beginning to wax nostalgic for the old show. In the weeks to come I began looking at our old reruns every once in a while, and on one occasion I even went so far as to revisit the stages where we actually shot the old show. It was a visit I will never forget.

I had just begun shooting a new series for Paramount and ABC entitled *Barbary Coast*. It was a fairly standard western, primarily set in and around a fairly wild San Francisco casino. I was thrilled with the chance to once again be playing the lead in a network television series, and I have to admit I thought this show was absolutely great. In no time, I mused, people would stop typecasting me as a Starship captain and start pigeonholing me as a cowboy.

We shot this series almost entirely on the Paramount lot, lensing the bulk of our scenes outdoors, on a phony Western street made up to look like the San Francisco of the late 1870s. This street could be found running parallel to Paramount Studios' main entrance, way up toward the Melrose Avenue side of the lot. Star Trek, which we'd also shot at Paramount, was always shot on soundstages located way off in the studio's opposite corner.

Still reveling in my postconvention glow, I decided to blow off my Monday morning lunch hour, opting instead to grab a baloney sandwich and walk over toward the old Star Trek stages. That way I could eat and wander down memory lane at the same time. It took me a good ten minutes to walk the length of the lot, and when I finally reached my destination, I have to admit I was disappointed that I'd even bothered.

The stages were now empty and run-down. The doors were wide open, the floors filthy, garbage strewn all about, and to be honest, I felt no pangs of nostalgia at all—just disappointment. Still, since I wasn't due back on the set for another forty-five minutes, I decided, just for old times' sake, to wander over toward the building that had always housed Star Trek's dressing rooms and office space. I'd take a quick look around, then stroll back to work.

The building looked absolutely deserted. A layer of dust was the only thing preventing our old makeup room from looking exactly as it had in the past. Co-producer Bob Justman's nameplate was still on his office door, and it quickly became apparent that no one had used these offices in more than five years. I looked around for a while, but after about ten minutes of nostalgic archaeology, I was just about ready to leave. And then I heard something.

Way off down the hall toward where Roddenberry's office used to be, I could hear someone typing. It seemed out of place in such a decrepit working environment, but I figured some low-level writer or producer must now be squatting in our abandoned old space, having logically commandeered for himself the lot's best available office. At least that would explain why the side door was open. I continued forward.

Along the way I could now hear the sound of paper being angrily yanked from a typewriter carriage, crumpled mercilessly and slammed into a metal trash can. I smiled at that, remembering Gene's similar old habits. As the typing began once more, I got even closer, and noticed that the name GENE RODDENBERRY still presided over the office door in large brass letters. I then poked my nose inside the office and saw a ghost.

There, sitting at Gene's old desk, puffing on a Camel unfiltered, eyebrows furrowed, meathooks pounding mercilessly upon a battered set of manual typewriter keys, was . . . Gene Roddenberry. I hadn't seen him in five years.

"Hey Gene!!!" I yelled at him through the doorframe, "didn't anybody tell you? We got canceled!"

"Whaddya mean?" he said, not looking up but continuing to type. "I'm almost finished revising our 1968 scripts!"

We laughed, and I quickly followed it up with the obvious reply. "No, really," I asked him, "what the hell are you doing up here?"

Gene smiled, leaned back in his chair, folded his arms behind his head and said, "Don't tell anybody this, but I'm writing *Star Trek*, the movie."

With that I came to the conclusion that Gene had finally lost his mind. He'd snapped. Somehow, this guy had now lost his grasp of reality and refused to acknowledge that *Star Trek* was gone. Here he sat, returning to the dilapidated surroundings of past achievements, typing the script for a movie that no executive in his right mind could possibly care about. I mean, didn't he know that *Star Trek* was dead as far as Paramount was concerned? Didn't he know that the next big thing was going to be *Barbary Coast*?

Turns out *I* was the delusional one. *Barbary Coast* got yanked after thirteen episodes. Gene, on the other hand, was just beginning a long, strange voyage that, after monumental delays and setbacks, would ultimately prove him the soothsayer.

In the spring of 1975, Roddenberry and Paramount had negotiated a preliminary agreement in which Gene was given back his old office and hired to write a low-budget, feature-length *Star Trek* movie script that would cost the studio, start to finish, somewhere between two and three million dollars.

Paramount would then read Gene's work and decide upon one of three options. They could produce it for theatrical release, as a TV movie, or trash it altogether.

Which brings us back to Gene's office, where he's now elbow-deep in a script entitled *The God Thing*, first-drafting at a fever pitch, at least until I come along and break his concentration. "What's it about?" I inquire, still not quite sure about Gene's sanity. With that, Gene rises and gives me the specifics.

"Somewhere out there," he starts off, his eyes widening as he continues, "there's this massive . . . entity, this abstract, unknown life force that seems mechanical in nature, although it actually possesses its own highly advanced consciousness. It's a force thousands of times greater than anything intergalactic civilization has ever witnessed. It could be God, it could be Satan, and it's heading toward earth. It demands worship and assistance, and it's also in a highly volatile state of disrepair."

He goes on to tell me that the original crew of the *Enterprise* are now being embraced as heroes all over the galaxy. Spock has gone back to Vulcan to become head of their Science Academy. McCoy's married and living on a farm in the Midwest (although his wife, following in the time-honored tradition of women dumb enough to fall for an *Enterprise* crewman, is promptly killed off). Everyone else has been given hefty promotions, and continues to serve on active duty. Additionally, Starfleet has offered Kirk a prestigious but deskbound admiralcy, but he's passed, preferring to retain his rank as captain while acting as a sort of consultant/troubleshooter aboard Federation spacecraft. As we find him, he's visiting the recently overhauled *Enterprise*, supervising her new captain, Pavel Chekov.

Throughout the bulk of the next two hours Kirk rounds up the old crew, while studying and ultimately battling this "God thing." As the drama builds and we finally approach the craft, the alien presence manifests itself on board the *Enterprise* in the form of a humanoid probe, which quickly begins shape-shifting while preaching about having traveled to earth many times, always in a noble effort to lay down the law of the cosmos. Its final image is that of Jesus Christ.

"You *must* help me!" the probe repeats, now bleeding from hands, feet and forehead. Kirk refuses, at which point the probe begins exhausting the last of its energy in a last-ditch violent rampage, commanding the *Enterprise* crew to provide the assistance it needs in order to survive.

Without warning, the force summons up the last of its remaining strength to blast Sulu, severing the crewman's legs in the process. When Spock attempts to comfort the mortally wounded Sulu, he, too, is blasted and left for dead. With that expenditure of energy, the vessel is weakened to the point of vulnerability, and the *Enterprise* unleashes a barrage of firepower that destroys the craft.

"With that," says Gene, "we begin pondering the notion that perhaps mankind has finally evolved to the point where it's outgrown its need for gods, competent to account for its own behavior without the religiously imposed concepts of fear, guilt or divine intervention."

I was dumbfounded. Gene's rough storyline was tremendously powerful, truly impressive, and I immediately became enthused about the project. Still, I couldn't imagine Paramount or any other studio agreeing to make such a controversial, perhaps even blasphemous film. I mean, here was a terrific story that basically pondered whether God could actually be an alien life form, a mechanical intergalactic bully! Kirk might be the conquering hero, but for the first time in history, God was gonna be the bad guy.

Gene completed his script in August 1975. As expected, Paramount president Barry Diller quickly and flatly passed, then asked him to take another crack. At the same time, unbeknownst to Gene, the studio began interviewing other respected science fiction writers, asking that they, too, submit outlines for the proposed *Star Trek* feature. Harlan Ellison was one of their first targets.

Ellison, as every decent Trekker knows, is the author of many of the finest pieces of science fiction ever written, as well as the man behind what's generally considered *Star Trek*'s finest episode, "The City on the Edge of Forever." He's also a bit . . . eccentric. In fact, as legend has it, when he was asked by Paramount to write up his story outline in regard to a possible *Star Trek* movie, he balked, opting instead to commit his idea to memory. Once that was accomplished, he set up a meeting with a Paramount development executive, wherein he ran through a forty-five-minute monologue and verbally unveiled a *Star Trek* adventure of truly epic proportions.

Pacing about the office, speaking loudly and gesturing broadly for dramatic emphasis, Ellison conjured up a tale involving time travel back to prehistoric times, complete with battles against an evil race of reptiles and Captain Kirk's kidnapping of the entire *Enterprise* crew. Exhausted after his performance, Ellison supposedly turned to the executive and asked, "Well, whaddya think?" at which point he was told, "Hmmm, it's okay, I guess, but I was just reading this book right here called *Chariots of the Gods* and in this thing, it says that the ancient Mayans were visited by creatures from outer space. Think you could squeeze some of those Mayans in there?"

Ellison, being Ellison, quickly, loudly, bluntly and politically suicidally pointed out the inherent stupidity of the man's idea, making clear the obvious fact that there were no Mayans in prehistory.

"Aw, so what," the executive supposedly replied, "nobody'll know the difference."

Ellison chimed, "I'll know the difference, you idiot." He then punctuated his remarks with a stream of profanity, a hasty exit and a strident door slam. Needless to say, his idea was quickly rejected, as were the offerings of *Trek* veterans John D. F. Black and Robert Silberberg shortly thereafter.

By January 1976, Gene was once again pounding a keyboard, this time collaborating with a very talented, very young writer named Jon Povill. Povill had previously worked for Roddenberry as a researcher and, when times were especially hard, as Gene's handyman, patching and doing repair work on Gene's two homes. Together, although Povill states that *he* did most of the actual writing, the pair concocted a tale that begins as we find the *Enterprise* and her entire crew dead, the victims of an imploding black hole. Suddenly, however, they're mysteriously reanimated, repaired by some sort of glowing intergalactic goo. What follows is a wildly complicated tale involving repeated time travel, heated arguments with Albert Einstein, Adolf Hitler, Winston Churchill and Mao Tse-tung, clandestine meetings with John F. Kennedy, and culminating with the *Enterprise* ultimately becoming responsible for the start of World War II.

Gene, this time with Povill, had again concocted an intelligent and powerful tale. However, although Gene loved this particular idea and would continue pushing for its production through nearly every *Trek* sequel, it was also confusing, convoluted, gigantic in scale and nearly unshootable. As they had done once before, Paramount rejected Gene's script. However, the idea of making a *Star Trek* movie stayed hot, continuing to bubble on the studio's front burner, thanks largely to NASA and their brand-new space shuttle.

The space agency, having conquered the moon, was now beginning a brand-new, very-high-profile adventure, and an entire nation was being taken along for the ride. Not since the *Apollo* launches had the American public become so caught up in space exploration, and with that in mind, the agency's public relations department hatched a plan asking the American public to come up with a name for its prototype shuttle. Almost immediately, they were deluged under postcards and letters from thousands of *Trek* fans, demanding it be christened *Enterprise*. Although he publicly played it cool, even going so far as to feign annoyance with the idea, it should come as no surprise that Roddenberry was absolutely thrilled by the turn of events. He'd soon like it even more.

Any other film project having met with this much failure would have been shelved by the studio long ago. *Star Trek*, however, was an entirely different animal. Despite a stack of rejected scripts, Paramount *knew* there was a growing audience out there that was primed and ready to spend their money in exchange for the privilege of watching the further adventures of the Starship *Enterprise*. With that in mind, they not only continued searching for an appropriate big-screen vehicle, they upped the pace. At the same time, they virtually quintupled the film's proposed budget, to about eleven million dollars. *Star Trek: The Movie* was now failing upward at warp ten.

On September 17, 1976, the space shuttle *Enterprise* was officially christened amid pomp, circumstance, military drill teams, and a multimedia press circus that immediately allowed the events to explode all over the world via radio waves, cathode tubes and of course the Sunday paper. Unless you were living in a cave, Trekker or non, you saw for yourself just how big this thing was getting.

At Paramount, our two-to-three-million-dollar quickie feature with no script had now been greenlighted at ten million plus, and key personnel were beginning to get hired. After being rejected by directors such as Steven Spielberg, Francis Ford Coppola, William (*The Exorcist*) Friedkin, George Roy Hill (*Butch Cassidy and the Sundance Kid*) and George Lucas (who was busy over at Fox at the time), veteran filmmaker Phil Kaufman took over the big chair. At about the same time, Jerry Eisenberg was hired to produce. Next up in the writers' on-deck circle were a Roddenberry-approved pair of British writers named Chris Bryant and Allan Scott, whose recent credits included the critically acclaimed period drama *Joseph Andrews* and the genuinely scary thriller *Don't Look Now*. They got to work immediately, banging out a story entitled *Planet of the Titans*, which opened with the *Enterprise* hurtling through space in an effort to answer the distress call of a fellow Federation starship.

However, upon arrival at the distressed starship's supposed coordinates, there is nothing to be found. The *Enterprise* has been duped. Just then, strange energy waves blast across the bridge, searing Kirk's brain in the process. Although the captain initially appears to have escaped injury (only Kirk could have his brain seared and escape injury), he slowly goes mad, eventually hijacking a shuttlecraft and blasting toward what seems to be an invisible planet. When rescue efforts fail, Mr. Spock, logically presuming the captain to be dead, although intuition tells him that his friend has indeed survived the disappearance, moves on.

Slow-lapse dissolve, and it's three years later. Spock, still firmly believing that Kirk is alive, journeys back to the area of his former captain's disappearance. There he finds the previously invisible planet of the Titans, home to an ancient, once-believed-mythical race of supremely intelligent and advanced humanoid creatures. Beaming down to the surface, Spock truly feels he's also closing in on Kirk. At the same time, his preliminary studies of the planet are horrifying, revealing that it will soon become engulfed by an enormous black hole.

Meanwhile, a Klingon bird of prey has intercepted communications detailing the findings and is now speeding toward the planet of the Titans, intent upon pillaging the vast intelligence and resources of the inhabiting superrace. However, Spock ultimately finds his captain alive and well, upon the surface of the planet. Kirk explains that this planet is not inhabited by the Titans at all, but by the vicious and brutish Cygnians. They mindlessly destroyed the Titans long ago, but were far too primitive to reap the rewards of their teachings. Very soon, the Cygnians decide that the crew of the *Enterprise* must meet the same fate.

What follows is a three-way battle against time, with the crew of the *Enterprise* trying to salvage the surviving riches of the Titans while simultaneously surviving attacks from both Cygnians and Klingons. In the end, with no way out, Kirk orders the *Enterprise* through the very black hole that will soon destroy the entire planet. Of course, this being science fiction, the *Enterprise* makes it out the other side just in time to watch the hole swallow up the Klingon ship, the Cygnians, and the entire planet of the Titans and implode.

That basic storyline would be tugged at, rewritten and obsessed over by Bryant and Scott, Eisenberg, Kaufman and Roddenberry to the point where none of them were entirely happy with it. Finally, as deadlines loomed ever more ominously, Bryant and Scott hid from the rest of the cooks in this kitchen, retiring to a hotel room, locking the door, and pounding out their tale. After allowing both Roddenberry and Kaufman to recommend changes, they turned it in.

Just as before, Paramount rejected the idea. The only difference was that this time they also pulled the plug. After spending the better part of three years vainly trying to nurse *Star Trek* back from the dead and onto the silver screen, Paramount had finally gotten disgusted. No acceptable script had yet been written, large sums of money had now been wasted, and as the final nail in

Star Trek's coffin, Twentieth Century-Fox had just released a similar science fiction film and watched it explode into a huge and unexpected blockbuster. There was no way, Paramount reasoned, *that* sort of lightning could *ever* strike twice. The astounding success of *Star Wars* effectively killed *Star Trek* . . . at least for the moment.

DÉJÀ VU ALL
OVER AGAIN

So there we were, slapped right back to square one. And then, on June 10, 1977, while nobody was looking, it hit. Suddenly, from out of the blue, there came a surprise announcement from Paramount, one that would allow *Star Trek* to wriggle out of the hangman's noose yet again. This time around, salvation came in the form of Paramount's chairman, Barry Diller, president, Michael Eisner, and a very young, rather green executive named Jeffrey Katzenberg. Together, they called a press conference and announced that a plan they'd been working on for some time now was about to become a reality. Paramount was going to launch a fourth network. *Star Trek: Phase II*, as it was entitled, would become that network's first original series. Mouths dropped open all over Hollywood. In these pre-cable-ready days, when even syndication was a fairly new idea, Diller and Eisner had basically come up with a risky and highly imaginative nuts-and-bolts plan for Paramount to create its own programming and then peddle the homegrown productions to a series of local independent television stations all across the country. They then brought in Katzenberg to supervise the day-to-day machinations of the new network, and fleshed out their plan.

In the beginning, they'd fill just one night a week, Saturday, with *Star Trek* manning the 8:00 to 9:00 P.M. slot, and made-for-TV "Movies of the Week" (another Diller invention) carrying viewers from nine to eleven. Later, should the great Saturday evening experiment prove successful, Paramount would begin adding programming to their independent "network" one night at a time. Indeed, a small-screen episodic version of *The War of the Worlds* was already waiting in the wings for a chance to kick off the potential Sunday night block.

Suddenly, Paramount's cancellation of the feature film version of *Star Trek* made perfect sense.

Throughout Roddenberry's last creative go-round on the feature, Paramount had remained quietly supportive. Should they have been overwhelmed by the Bryant/Scott/Roddenberry/Kaufman collaboration, the likely scenario would have found the studio releasing a new *Star Trek* feature film, hyping it to death, then parlaying the probable success of that film into the creation of the new TV series. Ideally, they'd have simply coasted into their independent network on the coattails of *Star Trek*'s big-screen success.

However, with the launch of a *Star Trek* feature continually bogged down at the creative level, the studio simply changed direction and went straight (back) to the small screen. They immediately ordered thirteen episodes of the new show, plus a two-hour pilot that would serve to relaunch the *Enterprise*. However, having continually battled Roddenberry (and the production delays that seemed to follow him everywhere) throughout *Star Trek*'s first incarnation, Paramount was taking no chances this time around. This time they hired TWO producers to work alongside Gene at all times. The first, Robert Goodwin, was a solid line producer with a well-established reputation for bringing his projects in *on* time and *under* budget. The other, Harold Livingston, performed in an almost entirely creative capacity, developing the new series' storylines and scripts in conjunction with Roddenberry, story editor Jon Povill and, most significantly, many of the same talented writers who'd penned the best of our original *Star Trek* adventures.

Meanwhile, Roddenberry became "executive producer" and during the early stages of preproduction began working on the series' "bible," a sort of instruction manual for writers outlining the basic structure of the new series and briefly detailing the characters, their relationships, their duties and their personalities.

As in *The God Thing*, Captain Kirk has once again refused a promotion to admiral, only this time it's so that he can reclaim his position as captain for the second five-year mission of the newly refitted Starship *Enterprise*. As in the original series, the parameters of this particular mission were rather nebulous, involving no specific duties, instead simply entailing an exploration into the farthest reaches of space. Kirk and nearly all of his original crew had once again signed on to "boldly go where no man has gone before."

This time around, however, Kirk would be ably assisted by a brilliant and sexually supercharged female navigator, a Deltan named Ilia. Bald but stunningly beautiful, she would also boast "an intellect as impressive as her more obvious attributes." Her actual duties aboard the ship, aside from tossing off rapid-fire sexual innuendos, were less succinctly defined.

Will Decker, a brilliant, handsome and extremely competent young crewman, was to begin assisting Kirk even more closely. As penned by Gene, he'd been placed aboard the starship as Kirk's heir apparent, studying alongside the captain while gaining the knowledge and experience that would one day prove invaluable when he takes over the biggest chair on the *Enterprise* bridge. That day may have been close at hand.

Even as *Star Trek: Phase II* was in its infancy, Captain Kirk was fighting for his life. The reasoning behind this turn of events found that the actor who played Kirk was getting older, more expensive and more opinionated with every passing year. Knowing the man quite well, I can attest to the fact that all three of those things were true. The character of Decker was clearly an insurance policy. He'd become a featured player throughout *Star Trek: Phase II*'s first thirteen episodes, and should the character have become accepted and embraced by *Star Trek*'s legion of fans, one of two things would have happened. Kirk could have quickly become relegated to minor character status, really just wandering into and out of episodes as a glorified cameo, or killed off entirely. The "cameo" scenario would have gone into effect if I'd accepted a huge pay cut, and the "killed off" scenario would have heralded my refusal. Either way, Kirk's days at the helm of the bridge were nearing an end.

At the same time, Spock's tenure on the *Enterprise* was already over. Leonard, whose relationship with Roddenberry had never been very good, was now carrying the additional baggage of the pair's several recent skirmishes. The *Questor* situation, and the ongoing dispute over *Star Trek*'s blooper reels had combined to all but sever ties between the two men. Furthering the separation was Gene's refusal to assist Leonard in an ongoing lawsuit he'd been fighting against Paramount, which, under the inevitable mounds of legalese, boiled down to this:

With *Star Trek*'s continued renaissance came the inevitable avalanche of related merchandise, and millions of dollars soon began changing hands all over the globe in the marketing of *Star Trek* T-shirts, trading cards, action figures, toothbrushes, comic books, coloring books, pencils, pajamas, gum, posters, fine china and hundreds of other items, virtually all of them bearing likenesses of the *Enterprise* crew. For this, manufacturers received hefty profits, Paramount earned sizable licensing fees, Gene Roddenberry earned a small percentage, and the rest generally got sucked up by lawyers, accountants and the infamous "miscellaneous" line. Like The Monkees and David Cassidy before us, we who merely *owned* the faces that were being plastered all over the globe got almost nothing. It was a truly unfair though commonplace business arrangement of the time.

Leonard, however, wouldn't stand for it, at least not without a fight. Spurred into action by a chance encounter with a London billboard bearing three beer-swilling, beer-shilling Spocks, Leonard had now instigated a lawsuit against Paramount in trying to ascertain whether or not they had any legal claim on his likeness. The action would drag on for years, but at this point, the most noteworthy aspect of the case is that while Leonard felt that Gene should have come to his aid in this battle, Gene was caught between a rock and a hard place. Once again hired by Paramount, Roddenberry was still desperately trying to bring *Star Trek* back from the dead, and with that in mind, instead of standing up for his actor in court, Gene opted to avoid biting the hand that fed him.

Never one to create unnecessary waves, Roddenberry stayed true to form and simply avoided the confrontation entirely, fading into the woodwork and remaining nearly invisible throughout the litigation. Leonard never forgave him.

All of those things, combined with the fact that like me, Leonard, too, was now getting older and more expensive, resulted in the character of Spock being virtually eliminated from the planned series. Leonard explains:

My battle with Paramount over merchandising rights had dragged on for years. At the same time I had been banged around by Roddenberry over the blooper reels and the problems on *Questor*, so my relationships with nearly everyone involved with *Star Trek* were pretty bad.

But then my agent called me and said they were planning to make a new *Star Trek* movie. I met with Phil Kaufman, who was going to direct it, and before I'd had time to really mull over the pros and cons of the situation, the whole idea of doing a feature film fell apart, and Paramount decided instead to go with the idea of turning this thing into a special two-hour TV movie, which would be followed up by a new *Star Trek* TV series.

When that came to pass, I rejected the offer completely, because I was asked to appear in only two of every eleven episodes. In effect, it would have been a part-time job. I couldn't believe it.

Later, my agent called them and said, "Guys, I think you're making a big mistake with this offer.

Why would you offer my client such a limited opportunity? Why aren't you instead saying to him, 'How many episodes would you like to do? Would you like to be in all of them? Just a few? An occasional guest-starring role? What would you like?'" They replied, "Oh no, we're standing firm on our offer and this is how it has to be." I was told that this offer and this rejection of the Spock character were coming from Gene Roddenberry himself. He and I never actually discussed the issue, so I really don't know what his thinking was. Perhaps he thought that offering me a limited role, one that wouldn't tie me down for months at a time, might be more appealing to me. Still, no matter how you look at it, my participation in this series was being restricted, limited to a small number of appearances. That bothered me a great deal. That's why I passed.

With Leonard now officially out of the picture, Roddenberry and Livingston quickly replaced the Spock character with a very young, very brilliant full-blooded Vulcan science officer named Xon. Rumored to be even more intelligent than Spock, Xon is nonetheless apprehensive in regard to adequately filling the slippers of the legendary Vulcan hero. Unavoidably compared to Spock, Xon seeks to better understand his predecessor's genetically programmed, genetically conflicted psyche. With that in mind, he fights a constant battle to begin understanding such uniquely human attributes as humor, love, anger, joy and sorrow. He would even go so far as to try and comfort a melancholy Bones by consciously, though clumsily, attempting to rile the cranky doctor into a typical Spock versus Bones argument session. McCoy, touched by the Vulcan's kindness, would have quickly become the new science officer's closest friend.

At that point, with the character roughed out, it was time to find the actor who would play him. An extensive search was begun, and when the dust had finally settled, an unknown actor named David Gautreaux was being fitted for a brand-new set of pointed polyvinyl ears. He tells the story:

Every actor I knew was being called into Paramount to screen-test in regard to the role of Xon in *Star Trek: Phase II*. Of course, I immediately wanted a shot at it myself, but no matter how I tried, I couldn't get in for it.

At the same time, I'd been dating a girl who was a secretary at a very prestigious theatrical agency. She said to me, "The problem with you is that without an agent, you can't be submitted for this part." I said, "Maybe you can help me?" and she did. *She* submitted me, and I got an interview with Pat Harris, who was Paramount's casting director at the time. She interviewed me, liked me and said, "You'll have to come back tomorrow and speak with the producer and director." I was told that should I get the role, I'd be signing a six-year deal. I practically fainted.

So I came back the next day and met Bob Goodwin, and a director who'd just been hired named Robert Collins. I read for them, they gave me two thumbs up, and the next step was the screen test.

September 26, 1977. I remember that day

vividly. I showed up on the set and immediately began laughing, because all around me were these seven other Xon hopefuls, and all of us were standing around looking very serious, while wearing ridiculous synthetic eyebrows and pointed vinyl ears. I'd say there were at least eight of us testing for the role: dark-haired, tall, short, slender, fat, all shapes and sizes, all of us vaguely alien-looking. At the same time, there were probably an equal number of men trying out for the role of Commander Decker. At any rate, I won. I was told, "You got the part."

At the same time, the Paramount lot was buzzing with Trek-related activity. Construction crews hammered furiously upon a reincarnated and tremendously upgraded Enterprise bridge, and where the cheapest possible materials had once combined in clamping and gaffer-taping our original sets into existence, only the finest materials were now deemed acceptable. Sparing no expense, heavy three-quarter-inch plywood now formed the framework of a vast array of prefab Enterprise interiors. Genuine NASA surplus was integrated into our ship's controls, replacing the hastily glued, cheap plastic doodads of the past. Costumes, in a total departure from the inexpensive, not to mention itchy, velour of days gone by, were now being tailored in the finest available fabric. Star Trek, in short, was no longer a bargain-basement special.

Meanwhile, back at the office, the creative aspects of Star Trek: Phase II were also continuing forward, steadily if not entirely smoothly. First-draft scripts were beginning to arrive, and for the most part, they were very good. However, the working relationships between Roddenberry and the producers around him were deteriorating rapidly. In particular, Roddenberry and "creative producer" Harold Livingston were locked in a no-holds-barred power struggle.

Livingston had been hired to supervise the creative processes behind scripting the initial thirteen episodes of Star Trek: Phase II. Normally, that would be a fairly cut-and-dried job description, but in this case, with Roddenberry still on the job as well, things were bound to get sticky. As expected, after a brief period of professional courtesy, the two men developed an intense dislike for one another. Livingston makes no secret of the fact that he thought Gene was a fairly lousy writer, and with that in mind, his resentment over having to make sure every draft of every script received the official Roddenberry stamp of approval becomes quite understandable.

Roddenberry, it would seem, had equally little regard for Livingston's talents, constantly criticizing Livingston's creative input and churning out unsolicited rewrites of his scripted offerings. Tensions between the two men were nearing the breaking point. When it came time to script Star Trek: Phase II's two-hour pilot film, they would get even nastier.

Roddenberry got the ball rolling by unearthing some of the old story outlines that he'd created for the failed series Genesis II. One of them, "Robots Return," piqued his interest to the point where he contacted science fiction novelist Alan Dean Foster (who'd recently written a series of quickie Star Trek novelizations), asking that he try to rework the tale, customizing it to fit the episodic parameters of Star Trek: Phase II. Foster was happy to oblige. Two days later he returned, bearing a thirty-page outline that he'd retitled "In Thy Image." This was apparently carried out without consulting Livingston.

Foster's outline starred a high-powered intelligence-seeking space probe that has been traveling the universe for hundreds of years, soaking up an absolutely immense amount of knowledge along the way. The probe, having evolved to the point where it is now capable of original thought, has begun pondering such philosophical questions as "Who am I?" and "Why do I exist?" With that in mind, it begins a search for its creator, heading toward Earth and destroying anything and everything that gets in its way, including the "parasitic, carbon-based life forms currently infesting the creator's planet." Kirk and company are of course called upon to save the Earth.

In a rare moment of total agreement, Livingston and Roddenberry were both impressed by Foster's story, and together they decided to flesh it out as the series' two-hour pilot. It was perhaps the last time the two men would ever agree—about anything. Although the story was almost immediately greenlighted by Paramount's genuinely enthusiastic Michael Eisner, Livingston and Roddenberry soon found themselves at loggerheads over who should turn Foster's story into a full-blown screenplay.

Roddenberry had assumed that his friend Foster, although relatively inexperienced, would carry his story through the entire scripting process, guided no doubt by the Great Bird of the Galaxy himself. Livingston, perhaps sensing a double-teaming in the making, openly questioned the wisdom behind gambling with a fairly green screenwriter on such an important project. He asked to see samples of Foster-penned scripts, and upon reading them, made the politically incorrect decision that the screenwriter behind "In Thy Image" would *not* be Foster. Instead, after a talented young writer named Steven Bochco proved unavailable and another, Michael Cimino (future auteur behind *Heaven's Gate*), proved uninterested, the project was awarded to a very talented, very experienced writer by the name of William Norton. Norton, it was believed, was a sure thing; he was very familiar with *Star Trek*, extremely competent, and certain to finish the job with a degree of polish and professionalism that simply could not be expected from a less seasoned veteran.

Norton spent the better part of the next ten days locked up in his office trying desperately to get started writing "In Thy Image." Early one morning, he called Livingston's office and quit. He had come to the conclusion that he simply wasn't the man for this task.

With the first day of principal photography now just ten weeks away, Norton's abrupt departure was a devastating blow. Panic was beginning to set in.

Meanwhile, across town, young David Gautreaux had landed an agent and a contract for the series pilot: "They [his agents] did a very good job for me, and I ended up getting $15,000 for the pilot, which was really just four weeks' work. Once they'd done that, I let them negotiate my six-year deal for the series."

David's agents secured a solidly constructed, financially rewarding, ironclad "pay-or-play" contract. It was fairly standard operating procedure, simply stating that David would get paid whether or not *Star Trek*: *Phase II* ever made it to the small screen. Still, since the series was inked into the cornerstone position for an entire new network, no one paid that particular clause much notice. David had agreed in principle to the contract, and all he had left to do was sign on the dotted line. That, however, almost never happened:

Boom! I had gotten the job, but before my hand had a chance to even touch the new contract, I got an "emergency phone call" from Paramount saying, "We need to do a second screen test, right away."

I said, "I don't understand, I thought we'd already eliminated all of the competition."

"Uh, yes, there's some . . . technical problems." They then asked me if I'd come down to the studio and talk to the producer and director about my role. I said, "Sure, I'd love to. I'm very excited and committed to this project."

Now I go down to the studio, and I meet with Bob Goodwin, Harold Livingston, and the director, Bob Collins. They said to me, "There are some problems that we have to deal with. Majel Barrett, who played Nurse Chapel in the original series, always had a bit of an unrequited love for the character of Spock, and she feels that casting a younger Vulcan would be 'unsettling to the arc of her character.' Therefore, she is bringing in another actor, a bit older than you, to test for the role. He's British, and to be honest with you, she's really pushing for him to get the part."

All of a sudden I've got competition again.

I should take a moment to explain that although David's tale sounds incredible, you've got to remember that Majel Barrett had by now graduated from Gene Roddenberry's girlfriend to Gene Roddenberry's wife. With that in mind, Nurse Chapel was once again shoehorned into the continuing adventures of the Starship *Enterprise*, although she'd now been given full-fledged "doctor" status. She also decided that with her character's longtime love interest now conveniently ensconced back on Vulcan, her minor role might simply slip away no matter how well connected she may have been. For those reasons, Mrs. Roddenberry pulled out all the stops and used her considerable clout to demand a screen test for her own hand-picked version of Xon. David continues:

When they finally told the whole story behind the new screen test, it bothered me to the point where I told my agent, "I won't do the second screen test for free." I was very hungry. I then suggested he tell the *Star Trek* people that in the ten days since they told me about the second screen test, I'd gotten another offer. My agent then called them and made up a story, saying, "David's just been offered a job as a guest star on *Fantasy Island*. It pays $2,500. You guys will have to make a choice."

They made a choice—they paid me the $2,500.

When I arrived for my second screen test, Bob Goodwin told me that they still hadn't found their Decker. He told me that today they'd be testing "ten of the hottest young actors in Hollywood" for the role, and he asked if I'd play against them and help out. I said, "Sure."

Anecdotally, those "ten hottest actors in Hollywood" were idiots. I've never seen men less prepared for anything in my life. These guys were jackalopes. I was astonished that most of them needed to have their script pages Scotch-taped onto the bridge console. I was also astonished to find that some of them had done cocaine just prior to their screen tests. I know that because it

DAVID GAUTREAUX, VULCAN WANNABE

was obvious as they tested, and also because I've since confronted them, literally confronted them. I have since seen these "ten hottest actors in Hollywood" here, there and everywhere, and I do not misunderstand, even for a second, why their careers never came anywhere near "hottest actor in Hollywood" status. It was a funny day, to say the least.

I should break into David's story at this point to add that less than a week after this round of screen tests, a debate suddenly began over the character of Decker and whether or not he'd actually be necessary beyond *Star Trek: Phase II*'s pilot episode. At the same time, my own contract negotiations suddenly and inexplicably became a lot more pleasant, and I began repeatedly having my ass kissed about how important it was to "keep James T. Kirk standing tall on the bridge of the *Enterprise*." No longer was the good captain a terminal case. In the past, I've always been told that this abrupt change of heart came about because in writing the series' first thirteen stories, it began to emerge that Decker really served no dramatic purpose, that while he was created to be a captain-in-training, on paper he always just sort of came off as Kirk's personal assistant. All of that may be true, but I think, in talking with David Gautreaux, that I've finally gotten the rest of the story. David continues:

I was already in the makeup chair when this gentleman from London came onto the set, surrounded by a formidable entourage. The producers were with him, the director, and of course Majel was fawning all over him. It was as if Sean Connery had just flown in to test for the role of James Bond. I was alone, and I understood that.

It would have been political suicide for the producers and director to do anything different.

Were they seen fawning all over *ME*, they'd have accomplished nothing, and at the same time they'd have made a very powerful enemy. Their job was to make a television show, and they desperately wanted to get it done. If that required taking care of someone's ego, so be it. They'd simply take care of that problem as quickly and efficiently as possible. My feelings were secondary. I understood that. I was alone.

I then said to Freddie Phillips, who was still working on my ears, "Do your damnedest. Do your best job and make me look great. I'm gonna kick his butt." And he looked at me and very quietly said, "Go for it!"

And as it turned out, this gentleman from London was absolutely abominable. It was embarrassing. I hung around the set to watch him test, and I left that day feeling very good about my chances.

Across the lot, under the ugly greenish haze of a half-dozen fluorescent tubes, the *Star Trek* creatives still had a script to write. "In Thy Image," having now been abandoned by William Norton and due to be finished in less than three months, was stuck in a no-win situation. A round of inquiries found that the best writers in town were all simply too busy to jump into the task at this late date, and those who *were* available were ultimately deemed unsuitable by Livingston and/or Roddenberry. Still, *somebody* had to write this thing . . . and fast.

With that in mind, Livingston, under enormous time pressure and lacking confidence in Roddenberry's abilities, took the task upon himself. He turned the bulk of the series' story editing duties over to Jon Povill, locked himself into his office, and spent the next month pounding "In Thy Image" into a complete first-draft screenplay. Down the hall, Roddenberry was not happy.

Livingston's first draft took Alan Dean Foster's basic storyline and added into it a lot of material that would have acquainted audiences with the new characters of Xon, Ilia and Decker, while reacquainting them with all of their old friends aboard the *Enterprise*. Kirk and Xon would stumble into a new friendship, a past relationship and lingering sexual tension would be established between Decker and Ilia, and our renegade space probe now had a name. It was "V'ger," which would of course be proven short for "Voyager 6" during the last ten minutes of the film. In the end, even without Spock, Livingston's first-draft script was really quite close to the one that would ultimately become *Star Trek: The Motion Picture*. The only real difference was the ending.

In this draft, there is no confrontation with V'ger, no glimpse into the specifics of its vast and wondrous knowledge, and no ultimate communion with the human element ultimately provided by Decker. Instead, Kirk simply talks to V'ger, chewing scenery through a long-winded speech about the inherent goodness of man, which ultimately dissuades the omnipotent entity from zapping all the inhabitants of the Earth into charcoal briquettes.

Still, except for the last few pages (which even Livingston found unsatisfying), the initial reviews were good. Povill gave it a thumbs-up, as did Collins, Goodwin, even Roddenberry, who went so far as to offer to do the second-draft "cleanup" himself. Harold Livingston continues:

brought in. my script on a Friday afternoon. I gave it to Gene and he said, "Okay, now you've done your job. Let me do mine." He then goes home, and rewrites the whole goddamn thing over the weekend. Monday morning, he hands out copies of his revised version to Goodwin, Bob Collins, Jon Povill and me, and at first glance, I immediately notice that the cover page now reads "*In Thy Image*, by Gene Roddenberry and Harold Livingston." He'd put his name on top of mine.

So now we all go into our offices, we all start reading this thing and maybe an hour or so later, we'd all finished. At that point, everybody congregated in my office, saying, "What are we gonna tell him? WHO'S gonna tell him?"

So I picked up his script, walked into his office, and while he was sitting there with this expectant grin on his face, I said, "Gene, this is SHIT!" just like that. And the grin remained frozen on his face, so I got myself excited, and I asked him, "Why'd you do this? When something works, you don't piss in it to make it better!" He was furious. He ultimately sent both scripts up to Michael Eisner, and insisted that HE make a final decision as to which one was better.

So about two days later, we go up to Eisner's office, and as we're all sitting around this enormous conference table, Eisner's juggling these two scripts, one in each hand. He says, "Gene, your script is a television script, Harold's script is a movie! It's a lot better." Shit, you coulda heard a pin drop. The gasp that came out of Gene was like a shot of thunder, and he never forgave me.

Eisner's decision ultimately widened the chasm between Roddenberry and Livingston to the point where it became virtually impossible for the two to continue working together. Creative discussions in regard to the script now inevitably degenerated into a deadlocked, voluminous clash of wills, until finally, with the clock continuing to tick, the pair accepted director Bob Collins's offer to objectively fuse the best parts of both scripts into a mutually acceptable hybrid.

Throughout the ensuing three weeks, Collins struggled at the typewriter, desperately trying to come up with a script that would defy logic *and* the old cliché by being able to please everyone. When he was finished, he presented his work to Roddenberry, Livingston, Povill and Goodwin. The opinions were unanimous: It was horrible.

Now, less than six weeks away from the start of principal photography, they were undeniably up shit creek without a paddle. There was simply no way they could get the *Enterprise* launched on schedule. However, through a strange twist of fate, they wouldn't have to. Once again, Vulcan-in-waiting David Gautreaux had the best view:

We were now closing in on the third week of October. I'm sitting in my little garage apartment in Hollywood on Sierra Bonita, which cost me $105 per month, and at about six o'clock, my phone rings. It's Bob Goodwin, and he says, "David, c'mon down to the studio. I've got an ice-cold drink waiting for you, the job is yours, and we've got some great news." My eyebrows went up.

When I got to the Paramount lot, I swear to God it felt like the gates flung open for me. I don't think I even had to tell the guard my name. I pulled into the Roddenberry offices and was greeted by Jeff Katzenberg, Gene Roddenberry, who had a smile from ear to ear, Bob Collins, Harold Livingston and Bob Goodwin. Every single one of them had a drink in their hand and they went, "Surprise! It's gonna be a motion picture!" I said, "What?" They said, "As of today, *Star Trek: Phase II* has become *Star Trek: The Motion Picture*."

I said "Uh, great!" That's all I could think of.

Suddenly, and without warning, Paramount and parent company Gulf + Western had gotten cold feet about the economic feasibility of starting a fourth network, and in a matter of weeks, the whole concept managed to travel from the studio's front burner to the trash heap. At the same time, *Close Encounters of the Third Kind* had opened to rave reviews and enormous box office success. Rumor has it that upon viewing the film, Michael Eisner, at that point knee-deep in *Star Trek's* political muckraking, raised his hands toward the screen and shouted, "Jesus Christ, this could have been us!!!" *Star Wars*, whose success had previously been seen as a mere fluke, now seemed more like the pioneer offering in a whole new genre of filmmaking. Knees jerked all over Hollywood, and as Paramount's fourth network came tumbling down, Diller, Eisner, Katzenberg and company almost immediately hatched a plan. They could salvage "In Thy Image," rework it, spend about eight million dollars in shooting it, and still usher it onto the silver screen in time to cash in on this latest round of sci-fi chic. Even in a worst-case scenario, even if the film ultimately took in only half the box office of *Star Wars* or *Close Encounters*, they'd still be able to make a decent return on the money they'd already lost in trying to give birth to the ultimately miscarried fourth network. In a best-case scenario, they stood a really good chance of making one of the greatest science fiction epics ever made.

But of course, that didn't happen.

STAR TREK:
THE EMOTIONAL PICTURE

n our last episode, the Starship *Enterprise* had sustained heavy damage, and her universe had grown rather volatile. She had suffered a failed low-budget attempt at launching her onto the big screen, only to muddle through a confused, chaotic and ultimately aborted return to television. Animosity and distrust among our producers and writers had gradually become standard working procedure, and making matters worse, one of our most important and irreplaceable cast members had virtually disowned the franchise. Remarkably, however, despite all of these negatives, *Star Trek* not only survived, but prospered as well.

With an abrupt left turn, the *Enterprise* now began plotting a course toward cinematic resurrection, greenlighted and front-burnered by Paramount with a tentative original budget of about eight million dollars, fairly modest even by 1978 standards. However, that budget got tossed out the window even before the week was out. By production's end, it had grown absolutely obese.

Back at square one, Gene Roddenberry rolled up his sleeves, got down to business .... and went to the movies. Wolfing down a steady supply of chocolate bars in the darkness, Gene screened both *Star Wars* and *Close Encounters* several times over, ultimately coming away a bit queasy, and absolutely convinced that *Star Trek* could no longer rely on the fishing-line, spit-and-tin-foil effects that got us through the original series. With that in mind, he gathered up a recent draft of "In Thy Image," hooked up with director Robert Collins, and immediately began visiting Hollywood's top effects houses, comparison-shopping for opticals worthy of the Jedi stamp of approval.

Having left the Paramount lot with a total budget of eight million dollars, they ultimately returned with their jaws hanging, their eyeballs wide, their faces flushed and their bellies fizzing with Alka-Seltzer. What Roddenberry and Collins had learned in their travels was that amid the cutting-edge technology and slim competition in the rapidly emerging world of computer-generated special effects, there was no such thing as a bargain. Special effects alone were going to set this eight-million-dollar production back somewhere between nine and ten million bucks!

Reeling with sticker shock and seeking to loosen the Paramount purse strings, the pair immediately met with Jeffrey Katzenberg, who'd been reassigned after overseeing the birth of Paramount's canned fourth network and now found himself toiling as the *Star Trek* feature's "Executive in Charge of Production." Katzenberg, in turn, met with Michael Eisner, who undoubtedly met with Barry Diller, and when the smoke had cleared and the budget meetings had finally subsided, we came away ten million dollars richer. Our budget now stood at *fifteen* million, with the studio's unwritten guarantee that they'd be willing to go as high as eighteen million in a pinch. Little did they know that the pinch would soon arrive, clamping lobster-style onto the backside of this production and ultimately intensifying to viselike proportions.

Back at the bungalow, in an effort to hitch a ride on the coattails of Star Wars and Close Encounters, Paramount was determined to get their Star Trek feature into the movie theaters as quickly as possible. For that reason, the script for "In Thy Image," which had already caused more than its share of heartburn around the production office, was now getting a total makeover, being hurriedly pounded and fluffed into suitably "big-screen" proportions as quickly as possible.

Basking in the afterglow of a virtually quintupled effects budget, and fearing that their gargantuan TV-movie script would ultimately just seem puny on the silver screen, Roddenberry and company began revising that script, puffing and packing it with long, loving exteriors of the Enterprise, dramatic space walks, and decidedly Star Warsian visuals. However, their basic story, still lacking a satisfactory ending, remained largely unchanged. At the same time, several major changes were being made around the office. In fact, personnel began dropping like flies.

Harold Livingston had been the first to go, dumping the project in disgust shortly before it got punted back toward America's multiplexes. Shortly thereafter, he explained his hasty exit like this:

R oddenberry and I really began to get at each other's throats. December came along and my contract was coming up. Before they could fire me, I quit. We had too many problems there. I

just didn't think that Gene was a good writer. He
for his part, I'm sure, considered me a total inter-
loper. Who the hell am I to come in? He had his
own formula, which worked, and he had a great
following. Here I was getting on his nerves.

Director Bob Collins and producer Bob Goodwin were
unceremoniously shown the door shortly thereafter, the
indirect victims of our rapidly ballooning budget.

It worked like this. Collins and Goodwin had both
spent their respective careers directing and producing
almost entirely for television. With that in mind, they'd
been perceived as solidly qualified and far more than
competent to shepherd *Star Trek* onto Paramount's proposed fourth network. When the project was ultimately
transformed into a low-budget feature, Paramount
remained willing to take a chance that their talents and
familiarity with the project would allow them to more
than adequately step up to the task of churning out a
cheap theatrical release. However, throughout the waning days of 1977, as our film's budget began growing
and the studio's gamble simultaneously became more
potentially calamitous, the suits suddenly started to
sweat. For those reasons, shortly after ringing in the
New Year, Goodwin and Collins were ultimately shown
the door, both of them replaced by a man of such
unquestionable talent, flawless cinematic vision and
unparalleled acclaim that even *they* couldn't really
argue with the decision. That man was Robert Wise.

Arguably one of the most revered directors in the
history of the cinema, Wise began his illustrious career
as an editor, cutting his teeth on a little project entitled
Citizen Kane. As the years passed, he ultimately made
the leap into the big chair, directing and sometimes
serving double duty as producer of a remarkable and

eclectic string of films including *West Side Story* and *The Sound of Music* as well as science fiction classics like *The Day the Earth Stood Still* and *The Andromeda Strain*. For all of those reasons, Robert Wise ultimately took the helm of our *Star Trek* feature, and simultaneously allowed Paramount's studio executives to begin sleeping much better at night . . . at least for a while. Wise begins his story below:

I got a call from Mike Eisner about making this *Star Trek* movie, and I said, "Well, I'm not really a Trekkie, and I never got hooked on the series at all, but I will come down and talk about it." So then I went in and talked with Eisner and with Jeffrey Katzenberg, and I finally said, "Yes, I'm interested, but before I make a final decision, and before we get started, I think I'd better see some of the episodes." I really wasn't up on this stuff at all.

They said, "Sure," set me up in a screening room, and over the next couple of weeks, I watched about ten episodes. I liked them, thought they were all pretty good, and a couple of them were really exceptional. So I then went back and talked with Michael and Jeffrey one more time, and at that point, things really started falling into place. I'd made *The Andromeda Strain*, I'd made *The Day the Earth Stood Still*, what better way was there to continue forward than with the crew of the *Enterprise*?

And when I first came into the film, I was told by Michael and Jeffrey that they were out to make a "top-notch picture," and that our budget stood at somewhere between fifteen and eighteen million dollars. They didn't expect we'd be able to actually spend that much, but before they locked down a number, they wanted to leave us some freedom in terms of creative ideas. The look of the film, the feel, the costumes, the sets, they wanted us to start thinking about all of those things.

At the same time, while I didn't know much about *Star Trek*, my wife, Millicent, and her father were absolutely devoted to the show, so when I brought the script home, and they saw that Spock wasn't in it at all, they both practically yelled, "Hey, what's this? You can't POSSIBLY do *Star Trek* without Spock! It just won't work, because he and Captain Kirk have such a thing going."

The next time I went into the studio, I said to Michael and Jeffrey, "I'm ready to commit to this

ROBERT WISE TAKES OVER THE BIG CHAIR

picture, BUT you just can't do it without Spock. He's so identified with the series that I think there would be a real hole in the film without him." They agreed with me almost immediately, and they told me they'd been thinking the same way. So we sort of all decided to take a shot at bringing Leonard on board.

And that, my friends, brings us to the next installment of our continuing drama. As we begin, we find that Leonard Nimoy has been rather busy these past nine years, co-starring on the television series *Mission Impossible*, touring the country on stage as Sherlock Holmes and as Tevye in *Fiddler on the Roof*, creating books of his own poetry and original photographs, even going so far as to exorcise his own lingering demons with the publication of a literary self-portrait entitled *I Am Not Spock*. With all that in mind, and sprinkling into the mix that Leonard had also spent these years sporadically battling with Paramount over merchandising matters and with Gene Roddenberry over *Questor* and the *Star Trek* blooper reels, it should come as no surprise that my friend Leonard approached this film in a manner not unlike the way a mongoose generally approaches a cobra. Leonard explains:

I was in New York, doing a play, when my agent, Sandy Bresler, called me, and by this time so much water had passed under the bridge that I was angry with the studio, angry with Gene and angry with the whole *Star Trek* process. For those reasons, I literally said to him, "If you EVER call me again about *Star Trek*, you're fired!" I really meant it. So then a few more days went by, and one night just after I'd gotten home from the theater, my phone rang. I picked it up, and it was my business manager, Bernie.

"Hi, Leonard," he says, "how are you? How are you doing?" And after five minutes of back-and-forth schmoozing, he reveals to me that Sandy, the agent whom I've warned not to call me lest he be fired, has instead called *him*, asking that *he* try to talk me into doing this film. This is the work of a great agent.

Sandy had apparently told Bernie that Paramount was being very persistent, and that they really were eager to make a deal and lock me into the picture. Still, I wanted no part of this. These people had done nothing but leave me unsatisfied and unhappy.

But this thing just refused to go away, and I was told that there was a new young guy at Paramount who was anxious to talk to me. That was Jeff Katzenberg. Later that afternoon he called and introduced himself over the phone. He said, "I'd like to come to New York. I'd like to see you in your play." With that he immediately scored two points by stroking the actor's ego. Y'know, this guy was willing to fly all the way to New York, and sit in a theater for two hours watching me do *Equus*, for no good reason except to establish a relationship with me. He also stated that he'd like some time to talk with me, and to find out about my concerns. He knew that there was a lot of bad blood involved here, and he really wanted to find out exactly what had transpired. He genuinely wanted to be helpful.

"Fine," I said, "if you want to come to New York, that's fine with me."

Two days later, he sees the show, comes backstage and asks, "Do you have time for a cup of coffee?" So we went to the Backstage Deli on 45th Street and started talking. Over the course of the next two days, we spent three more sessions together, each lasting three or four hours. Jeffrey came to my apartment during the day, and we sat and talked about the whole history of the TV series, and about the fallout afterward. We talked about the blooper reel, we talked about the *Questor* incident, we talked about my merchandising battle with the studio, all of this stuff came up. I told him about this whole history that led me to the point where I really didn't want to speak with Roddenberry or Paramount about *any* future *Star Trek* project.

Katzenberg then asked me if I'd seen the script, and I said, "No, I'd prefer not knowing anything about this particular project." He brought up the fact that it's not at all unheard of, even considered acceptable in this industry, to be fighting a lawsuit against a company while simultaneously going to work for them. I said, "I just can't do that, I'm sorry." He said, "Well, then, let me go back to the office and see if I can straighten things out."

A few more days passed, and my lawyer called. He told me that Paramount had suddenly approached him about settling the lawsuit. They also expressed a desire to have me read the script for *Star Trek: The Motion Picture*.

"I'll be happy to read the script," I told them, "and I will do so immediately after our lawsuit is settled, not a minute earlier."

The play now closes, I go back to L.A. and the

lawsuit is settled that Friday. A check is delivered to me at five o'clock that afternoon, and a copy of the screenplay arrives at six. By seven P.M. I've gotten a phone call, asking if I'd make myself available for a meeting the next morning. I read the script that night and early the following morning Roddenberry, Bob Wise and Katzenberg came to my house.

Bouncing back across town, I asked Bob Wise to tell me about that meeting, and to describe what he and Roddenberry might have been expecting to hear from Leonard.

We thought that getting Leonard to come back and play the role of Spock would probably present a rather large hurdle. And I can recall that Gene, Jeffrey Katzenberg and I went to Leonard's house one Saturday afternoon to meet with him. He'd read the script by now, and of course Spock wasn't in it yet, so Gene and I basically spent the better part of an hour talking about how we saw the character of Spock fitting into this script.

Y'know, Gene was sitting there, trying hard to sell all of his ideas, trying to put a real writer's spin on everything, but our main goal was to do whatever it took to try and get Leonard in the mood to say, "Okay, I want to go with this film." But he didn't bite, not right away.

Actually, Leonard nearly avoided biting altogether. He explains:

They arrived the following afternoon, and it was a very delicate meeting, because, in a way, Gene's talent was on the line. His presentation was this script, and his obvious first question was, "Well, what do you think?" My response to that was another question. "Well," I said, "is this the screenplay you plan on shooting?" That way I felt I could at least *suggest* that I had some trepidation about it. I mean, I wasn't about to say, "I think this thing sucks." I couldn't do that, but I *could* make certain demands on the issue of where the Spock character would fit into the scheme of things.

So I asked, "Is this the script you're going to shoot?" and Jeff said, "Yes, we're making *this* movie." He was there as the studio spokesperson, standing up for the project. He had to do that, and I understood. So now I say, "Well, what did you have in mind for the Spock character?"

Gene pauses thoughtfully, then says, "I had in mind that we'd discover Spock has gone back to Vulcan to try and expunge from himself any remnants of humanity or the emotional side of his character, and he's had the Vulcan equivalent of a nervous breakdown."

I couldn't believe it. I couldn't figure out why I'd want to go to a movie and see that, let alone play it. Who cares? What's it got to do with the story? There was nothing writable there, nothing playable. There was no indication of where Spock would fit into the bigger picture. I took it as Gene really being lost on that issue. He was just farting around, trying to shoehorn the character into the basic framework of his existing screenplay.

Still, by now every other cast member had

signed on to appear in the film, I'd settled my fight against the studio, and I realized at that point I really had nothing to gain, and a lot to lose, by refusing to do this picture. I was sure that if I didn't participate, I would be answering the same questions about it for the next two to five years. You know, "Why did you refuse to be in the Star Trek movie?" "Why were you the only holdout?" It'd all be very negative. How could I answer those questions? "I didn't like the script"? "I hated Gene"? "I was angry at the studio"? I would be carrying that negative shit around with me for the next five years, at least. So I thought, *Okay, if I'm in this film, I can at least make some investment in the character, and try to create some semblance of usefulness for Spock in the picture.*

Ultimately, I trusted Bob Wise, but I was also scared of making this film, mainly because I felt that we had accomplished something amazing with our seventy-nine television episodes. I really did. I was very proud of that series, and I felt like the driving force behind the film project might not be creativity, but profit potential. It scared me to think that the *real* impetus behind finally putting the Enterprise on the big screen might have been provided solely by the box office receipts of Star Wars. People would say to me, "It's gonna happen. We're gonna get the budget." And I would always be thinking, *Well, what's it ABOUT? What are we going to DO?* I didn't want to be embarrassed, and I didn't want to embarrass the franchise. I thought we had left behind a legendary accomplishment. I really mean that. *Legendary.* Certainly we had made our share of turkeys, but there was always a very real sense of conviction in what we were doing. There was a core to it, an idea behind it, a continuity. I took real pride in that.

While Leonard was busy soul-searching, I, having already agreed to appear in the film, was busy starving myself to death. As the *Enterprise*'s countdown to relaunch began drawing near, my bathroom mirror and I had simultaneously come to the unpleasant and unmistakable conclusion that with the passage of nearly a decade since my last intergalactic adventure, both middle age and my own middle section were rapidly creeping up on me. With that in mind I immediately began running a *lot* and eating very little, determined that by the time Captain Kirk finally reassumed his command, he'd be in absolutely terrific shape, more physically fit than even his occasionally beefy TV form. As the weeks passed, I came to hate that decision.

Throughout late 1977 and early 1978, my consumption of anything that might actually be defined as "food" basically ceased. Instead, sprouts quickly became my mortal enemy. Plain white yogurt began coursing through my tired veins. Sugarless gum got recategorized as dessert. Still, my torture continued, ultimately escalating to the point where I began jogging six or seven miles at a clip, sweat-soaked and zombie-eyed, through the hills near my home, getting progressively more lightheaded and hungry with every mile. I was never so miserable.

My sleep became tortured, haunted by highly sensual dreams: pouty-lipped grilled cheese sandwiches beckoning me to dive into their rich, creamy goodness, voluptuous mounds of angel-hair pasta steaming for me and me alone, seaweed rolls busting out of their seams and driving me mad with their exotic Oriental beauty. It's an ugly, hellish lifestyle that no middle-aged father of three grown daughters should ever be forced to withstand.

Meanwhile, back on the Paramount lot, Gene Roddenberry had finally filled in the hole left by the sudden departure of Harold Livingston. Dennis Clark, a young writer/avid Trekker (whose most notable screen credit found him writing the critically acclaimed *Comes a Horseman*), arrived smiling and promptly moved into Livingston's old digs, full of enthusiasm, full of energy, and genuinely looking forward to the formidable task at hand. Roddenberry, too, seemed pleased by this infusion of fresh blood, and within days it was clear that whereas the relationship between Roddenberry and Livingston had never been very good, he and Clark actually . . . couldn't *stand* one another.

Things between the two men just sort of started off on the wrong foot and got progressively worse. In fact, as legend has it, Clark had barely been in the office long enough to unpack when he became the victim of one of Gene's least successful practical jokes. Apparently, Clark arrived in the office one morning to find that his assistant, a woman Clark truly admired (and later married), had been fired. In her place sat a wisecracking, minidressed, nose-blowing, gum-chewing, love-beaded, black-wigged, spit-curled and heavily toilet-watered monster—our own Yeoman Rand, Grace Lee Whitney, in disguise.

"Who the hell are YOU?" she asked, snapping her gum and staring down her new boss upon their introduction.

"Excuse ME?!!!" replied Clark, rapidly turning a half-dozen shades of purple.

Just down the hallway, Roddenberry was watching, laughing, waiting for Clark's ultimate realization that he'd been had, and the accompanying hilarity that was surely bound to ensue. However, none of that happened. Instead, Clark's nose widened and flattened, his forehead wrinkled, the veins in his neck bulged ominously, and he immediately let out a high volume tirade so bloodcurdlingly loud, so heartfelt, and so genuinely enraged that Whitney actually feared for her own personal safety. Quickly she and Roddenberry scrambled to explain their gag, but they'd already dug themselves into an inescapable hole. Clark would ultimately go on to spend the better part of the next three months miserably battling Roddenberry, losing arguments and his patience on a regular basis. Finally, after one particularly volatile exchange, less than ninety days into his new job, Clark's employment was terminated on Gene's behalf by Robert Wise.

Sluggishly deteriorating throughout this creative clash of wills was our script, which after a slow start had now begun completely unraveling, much to the chagrin of the studio suits. Shortly thereafter, springtime and Harold Livingston both returned to the Paramount lot.

With the sudden departure of Dennis Clark, and attempts to satisfactorily complete our feature script continually bogged down at the creative level, Katzenberg and Eisner swooped in to stop the bleeding. Scheduling a meeting in Gene's office, and ultimately playing a bit of good-cop/bad-cop, the pair convinced Roddenberry that the only way his film might still be able to stay anywhere near "on schedule" (they were now hoping to start shooting by June 1, 1978) would be for him to swallow his pride and drop the script back into the lap of the man who'd carried it through its earliest incarnations, Harold Livingston. Later that night, Gene made a very difficult phone call, officially reinstating his strangest of bedfellows. Livingston continues:

By the time I left, Gene and I were ready to kill one another. I couldn't stand the son of a bitch, so I left, went to work for Aaron Spelling, and then one day about three months later I got a call in the middle of the night from Gene. I had heard that the movie had grown, Nimoy was aboard, and they had gone through another writer who also didn't get along with Gene, so I knew he was in trouble.

I met with him the following morning, and afterward he messengered me a script, which I read. One day later, I went back in to meet with him and Robert Wise and I told him that they might as well go jump off the bridge, because there was no way they could've shot this fucking thing.

Still, in the end, I came back because they offered me a huge raise and I'm really greedy . . . I wanted the money.

Livingston agreed to return, on the condition that Gene's hands stay off the typewriter, and together, for the good of the film, the two men even went so far as to pronounce an interoffice cease-fire. Shaking hands through tentative smiles, the two men espoused a new spirit of cooperation, promising to work together without any of the bickering or artistic clashes of their first go-round. The hatchet had been buried. The Road Runner and Wile E. Coyote had kissed and made up. All was calm, all was bright . . . for about ten days.

Less than two weeks into their trial reconciliation, Roddenberry and Livingston were once again making like Ali and Frazier. Livingston explains his return to the fire like this:

When I came back, it was with the understanding that I would be writing this thing, and rewriting it alone. Roddenberry basically agreed to leave the typewriter alone. And then, two days later, I rewrote a chunk of the script, with Robert Wise practically looking over my shoulder, and we gave it to Gene's office, to be transmitted to Michael Eisner and Jeffrey Katzenberg, who were in Paris at the time. Next thing I know, I get a call from Eisner in Paris, and he's yelling at me, saying "C'mon, Harold . . . What is this shit?!" I said, "What are you talking about?" and he starts to read me things from the script that I simply hadn't written. They were totally foreign to me, and I finally had to stop Eisner in his tracks by saying, "Wait a minute, we didn't write that!"

What had happened was Roddenberry had gotten hold of it, decided he wanted to do his own rewrite, and then sent his draft off to Paris. Robert Wise once said to me, with a strange look on his face, "In forty years I've never had an experience like this."

Afterward, Gene was very apologetic, but that didn't stop him from doing the same kinda thing over and over again. It drove me nuts, and I ultimately quit this picture three times. I just walked away from ten thousand dollars a week!

Roddenberry and Livingston would continue to do battle almost nonstop throughout the production of this picture. And while the specifics of their quarrels never much mattered (they generally blew up over plot points or unsolicited dialogue changes), the manner in which they were played out always seemed to maintain a fairly standard pattern. Basically, Roddenberry would have an idea for the script. Livingston would hate it, and leave it out of his next rewrite. Roddenberry would then read Livingston's work and rewrite the rewrite, putting in whatever idea he'd originally espoused. Livingston would read this re-revision and blow a gasket. In fact, even as we began shooting the film, alternating script revisions began arriving on the set every couple of hours, with each one dutifully initialed by the author. Y'know, REVISED 12:30 P.M. G. R. might be followed by RE-REVISED 2:45 P.M. H. L. and so on. Yelling and threats to quit would then generally ensue, and only lengthy standoffs and looming deadlines could ever bring the two men back together. Theirs was a relationship without room for even the slightest compromise, their actions not entirely unlike those of the mountain rams you often see butting heads to the point of exhaustion on those public television nature shows.

Meanwhile, despite the fact that our script was nowhere near final, the entire cast was called together around one of Paramount's most enormous black lacquer conference tables for our first readthrough. Smiling, catching up, and generally doing a lot of hugging, we were all genuinely pleased to be reunited, genuinely excited about the work ahead of us. Nichelle told me I looked "skinny," and I was thrilled. I kissed her on the spot, while secretly hoping that her lipstick might not contain too many grams of fat. Additionally, it was at this preliminary readthrough that we Starfleet veterans got to meet our newest cast members, Persis Khambatta and Stephen Collins.

Khambatta, a stunningly beautiful model, was also

a stunningly bad actress, once proving that assertion by requiring a whopping nineteen takes of a single line, "No." Originally hired almost a year prior to our meeting, she was to have become a permanent cast member on the *Star Trek: Phase II* TV series.

With her shoulder-length brunette tresses gleaming beneath even the standard-issue fluorescent tubes of the Paramount conference rooms, she was already openly dreading the day when she'd have her head shaved in preparation for her role as our chrome-domed Deltan navigator, Ilia. "Don't worry," we assured her. "You'll look great. After the first minute or two, no one will even notice that you're bald." When she pressed us for further specifics as to the probable results of her upcoming scalping, we all stammered out variations of the same cliché. "You'll look really . . . uh . . . unusual," we told her, "exotic and sexy." What can I tell you, she was nervous, we lied.

Stephen Collins, hired to play Captain Decker, was most certainly NOT one of the ten "jackalopes" described earlier by David Gautreaux, but instead a solid young actor, cast by Robert Wise, who immediately impressed us all with his enthusiasm and good-will toward our project.

In the end, we all came away from our unfinished

script-reading with an unshaken belief that we were getting involved in something terrific. Sure there was some story work to do, but there was no doubting the gut-level appeal of the basic tale of a machine returning from hundreds of years in deep space having grown its own organic consciousness, and now searching for its maker. With Gene back in the producer's office, Robert Wise manning the director's chair, and full-blown *Star Wars*–style opticals on their way, we all felt assured that once this picture was complete, there was just no way it could be anything short of great. We left that meeting with our spirits soaring. And then we heard nothing.

Weeks passed, and ultimately months, during which the entire cast of *Star Trek: The Motion Picture*, hired and put on hold by Paramount, simply sat back, collected checks and waited for an official green light. Robert Wise filled me in on what was going on throughout this period of enforced leisure:

One of the first things I did was to really give the sets a makeover. Most of them had already been built by the time I came onto the picture, and when I took a good look at them, I really didn't like them very much. So we took apart the *Enterprise* engine room and basically started over from scratch. We threw the ship's corridors into the trash, and we tried to make everything look a bit more functional, a bit more realistic. At the same time, we also tossed out the costumes that had originally been designed for the film, because to me, they just looked like men's pajamas.

We were also spending a great deal of our time working on the script. At the time, I think we had a rough idea about how the first act might play, but the final two-thirds weren't anywhere near shootable. But at the same time, the cast was all under contract, and they had all been getting paid since their original TV deals. This just went on and on, and Paramount just kept extending everyone's contracts, until finally they just said "Enough of these extensions, we've got to start shooting right away!" So that's what we did. The script *still* wasn't in any kind of shape, so we had to start rewriting and shooting all at the same time. It was a hell of a way to make a picture.

For those reasons, on Wednesday morning, August 9, 1978, the Starship *Enterprise* was officially hauled out of dry dock for the first time in nine long years—ten weeks behind schedule. With Robert Wise sitting quietly, staring intently upon his canvas folding throne, we then spent the entire day shooting a grand total of two camera setups, both of them housed smack in the middle of the previously familiar confines of the *Enterprise* bridge. Throughout this rather sluggish first day on the job, I found myself consistently musing about two things.

First, I hated our new uniforms. Ugly, form-fitting, pastel-colored, one-piece jumpsuits, these things itched even worse than our old TV series togs. Far worse was the fact that due to the design of these outfits, it was virtually impossible for any male member of our

ABOVE: Kirk arrives at Starfleet HQ
BELOW: A lot of the extras in this shot were fans

cast to sit down without seriously endangering his ability to procreate. All day long, our set was peppered with the pitiful high-pitched yelps and wailings of castmates discovering this particular design flaw for the very first time. Nichelle tells me that the outfits were equally uncomfortable for our female cast members, but I find that hard to believe.

By lunchtime, four-by-eight sheets of pressure-treated three-quarter-inch-thick plywood have been arranged, flanking our set on all sides. Between camera setups, it becomes commonplace to find some combination of myself, Walter Koenig, George Takei, De Kelley, Jimmy Doohan and Leonard propped up against them. Leaning, I learn rather quickly, makes a truly unsuitable alternative to sitting. This could be a lo-o-ong shoot.

My second thought of the day has nothing to do with my groin, and it is markedly more pleasant, centering around my genuine amazement that the camaraderie and chemistry that always made our *Star Trek* series so much fun to shoot seem to have survived our rather lengthy hiatus without the slightest deterioration. I find myself genuinely happy to see these people, and they, in turn, seem pleased to be working with me. Nichelle has once again commented on my hard-won sveltitude, and I find myself musing about how she's always been my favorite co-worker.

As our first weeks of production wore on, it became rather obvious that Gene and Harold still hadn't quite gotten a handle on how we might actually finish this story. Script revisions, sometimes arriving as late as thirty minutes prior to the start of the day's shooting, began coming in on a regular basis, and whether signed off with an H.L. or a G.R., it was obvious that the continual interoffice creative clashes were really beginning to hurt the film. Finally, Livingston quit the project, for the third time. With his departure, Leonard and I began trying to help out wherever we could, often meeting with Robert Wise and Roddenberry attempting to smooth over some of the script's potholes and rewriting much of Kirk and Spock's dialogue so that it better suited the characters. Leonard recalls:

ou and I were constantly getting together. I remember sitting around in your dressing room and saying, "We've really got to come up with some shit here." I mean, Kirk and Spock were just basically standing around that fucking bridge, staring at a bluescreen [literally a large blue screen, ultimately eliminated in the final print and replaced with special effects] at the mercy of this . . . thing, for pages and pages. Y'know, the best episodes of the old series always seemed to focus upon the crew of the *Enterprise* encountering a dilemma, formulating a solution and then implementing that solution, most often overcoming a lot of obstacles and resistance along the way. We had none of that here, and so we were always seeking to make these characters a bit more active.

And at times we *were* able to come up with some good ideas. I remember that at one point I thought I had got a handle on things and was able to articulate it through an isolated moment wherein Kirk discovers Spock at his station crying. Kirk says, "What is it, Spock?" And Spock says, "I am weeping for V'ger as I would for a brother." Suddenly there's a bond between Spock and V'ger. V'ger's lost, alone, wondering, "Who am I?" "Who am I supposed to be?" and Spock has certainly known all of those feelings.

ILIA AND KIRK, CIRCA TAKE SEVENTEEN

And as things came to pass, Bob Wise kept saying, "We'll shoot that, we'll shoot that" . . . and then it was all cut. It was left out of the theatrical release. Sometime later, when they did the re-edited home video version of the film, they added back almost twelve minutes of cut footage. And I think it helps.

But you and I shared a real camaraderie and we were in mutual agreement about what the script's problems were. So we began working out a lot of those problems together. The biggest change we came up with actually made it into the final film. It was rather major movement toward the middle of the picture in which Kirk says to Ilia, who's become overtaken by V'ger, "We're going to do so and so," and she says, "No, you can't do that," and Kirk says, "Fine, then you stay here and do it yourself," and we start to leave her on the bridge. Remember, the idea was that she was acting like a child, so we close her in her own room to have her tantrum. It tightened that particular scene, made it less talky, more interesting, and it actually served to strengthen the film's basic story structure.

Leonard and I roughed that scene through, and I then acted it out for him playing all the roles myself. When I'd finished, Leonard skewered my impression of Spock, then said, ". . . but the rest of it's great. Let's go show it to Bob Wise." At that point, the two of us wandered over to Bob's office and cornered the director, who'd been foolish enough to leave his door unlocked. "Bob," said Leonard, "Bill's got something terrific to show you . . . Go ahead."

Bob's facial expression was now screaming the words "Oh NO!!!" but I remained undaunted, playing the scene once more, acting out all the parts, and although I have to admit my performance had really dropped a notch since its first presentation, Bob was terribly enthused. He really liked the idea, and Leonard was actually kind enough to inform him that "the on-screen performances will most likely be a lot better than Bill's."

The three of us began a discussion about how we might best sell Roddenberry on the idea. Leonard and I suggested triple-teaming Gene right away, but Bob Wise ultimately talked us out of that idea, and instead phoned Gene's office himself, scheduling a meeting between all four of us later that evening, shortly after we'd completed the day's shooting.

The hours pass. We all reassemble in Bob's office, and Bob opens the meeting by saying, "Gene, the boys have some terrific ideas they want to suggest." Gene's face, already screaming "OH NO!" even louder than Bob's had, nearly explodes from his skull when Bob says, "Bill's gonna perform them for you, okay?" With that, exhausted from a full day's shooting and performing for a very intimidating audience that I'm sure would rather I just crawled under the nearest rock and let him get back to work, I perform the entire scene one more time. I have to admit, my performance was pretty bad. "Jesus," cried Leonard, "today's matinee was WAY better than the evening show."

In large part due to the fact that Bob Wise was obviously in support of these ideas, Gene actually grumbled, sighed and said, "Okay, I'll start writing it tomorrow morning." At that point, the reasoning behind Bob Wise's delaying tactics finally became clear.

At the precise moment that Gene said, "I'll go to work on this in the morning," Bob Wise practically jumped out of his seat, saying, "Excuse me for just a minute, gentlemen, would you?" and he left the room. So now Gene, Leonard and I are trapped together in this office, muddling through a very embarrassed silence.

Gene's quite obviously boiling over the fact that we've come up with a fairly tight, workable solution for the film's third act. In the weeks since Livingston's departure, Gene had been struggling with this problem and had come up dry, adding a lot of the talky exposition and lengthy transitional scenes that Leonard and I had just effectively eliminated. So while Gene's forehead throbs, I'm basically staring at the office doorknob and praying for Bob Wise to reenter and smile and sort of smooth things over. None of us had any idea why he'd disappeared, what he was doing, or when he might return. The easiest way out, it seemed, was to simply continue sitting silently, awkwardly awaiting Bob's return.

Finally, after what seemed like a month, Bob came bounding back into the room saying, "Gene, there's a phone call for you. Would you take it in the other room?"

Gene exits. Bob Wise sits down, and Leonard asks, "Uh, Bob, is Gene going to write this?" He was suggesting, and I believe rightly so, that by this point in time Gene might have been burnt out, dry, creatively drained from having written literally thirty different versions of this third act, each of which became progressively more expository. Leonard now pressed Bob once more as to who might write the scene in question.

"We'll see," says Wise, "that's what's being dealt with right now."

Turns out that shortly after our previous meeting, Bob Wise began maneuvering on the phone with Jeffrey Katzenberg, and by the time we all assembled in Bob's office, Jeffrey was already standing by his office telephone, awaiting Bob's cue.

Quite obviously, when Bob mysteriously bolted from our meeting, he simply rang Katzenberg's office, prepared him to speak with Gene, then reentered our meeting, shepherding Gene toward Jeffrey's line. At that point, Katzenberg told Gene three things: that the suggested changes would be made, that Harold Livingston had once again been rehired, and that he was standing by to do the rewrite.

Needless to say, when Gene came back into the room he was in a full blown rage, red-faced and yelling, "I'm not going to be rewritten by Livingston." He ultimately stormed out of the room, slamming the door behind him. The silence he left behind was deafening. I stared at Leonard, he stared at me, Bob Wise paid inordinate attention to the acoustic tiles of his office ceiling, and we all came away feeling a bit uneasy about what had just transpired. We'd won our battle, but in the process, we watched Gene Roddenberry get steamrollered, flattened by studio politics. There was no victory celebration. Harold Livingston has also gone on the record, further illuminating his on-again, off-again relationship with this project and the maneuverings of Wise and Katzenberg. His side of the story:

After my third resignation, they really went behind Gene's back. I got a call at home saying, "Mr. Katzenberg would like to see you at seven o'clock this evening. He says it's very important." So of course, I went into the studio, up to his office, and when I walked in, his secretary asked me, "Can I get you a drink?" and I said, "Well, I don't really . . ." and she said, "You drink Beefeater Gin, don't you?" I said, "Uh . . . yeah," and at that point, she ran outside and almost immediately came running back in with this huge glass of gin with ice. She must've had it waiting outside. So I'm now sitting there in the office thinking *This is really strange*, and as the secretary leaves, I can hear the door click locked. I'm locked into the fucking office.

At that point I said to myself, "Aw, what the hell," and I proceeded to spend the next half-hour waiting for Katzenberg and polishing off this drink. By the time he arrives, I'm half whacked out of my head, and he says, "You are not getting out of this office until you agree to come back and work on this picture." So I knew I was in a strong negotiating position, and I used the opportunity to soak him for a big raise, and an additional script commitment.

So I came back one more time, but things still weren't very good. Gene annoyed me so much that I refused to speak to him. I couldn't stand him, and I told him one time, "Gene, you wouldn't know a good story if it was tattooed on the end of your prick." He would take this from me, and I was always walking on razor blades because he was twice as big as me, and I kept waiting for him to haul off and pop me, but thankfully that never happened.

At the same time, back across town, David Gautreaux had some script questions of his own. He was *still* under contract to play Xon, although there had been absolutely no sign of Gene's new improved Vulcan in our script as yet. David was working in the theater, and had now begun wondering whether or not his ears would ever be pointy again.

By June, I still hadn't heard anything official, so I called Gene. I said, "Gene, I'm getting the impression with Spock back on board that Xon, character, will be sort of unnecessary." I said to him, "I just don't want to see Xon carrying Mr. Spock's luggage on board the ship. I mean, realistically, do you *need* two science officers?" And Gene said, "David, you are part of this family. You are a member of this family. You are in this motion picture." I then said, "But Gene, I'm in preparation of the character of Xon, a full Vulcan, and I am putting all of my energy into being that person for you. Is that character going to appear on-screen or not?"

"We're in rewrites," he told me. "We're working on it."

I waited through July and August. However, by September, it had been almost a year since I'd gotten the job, principal photography was at least halfway finished on what would ultimately become *Star Trek: The Motion Picture*, and I really just wanted to get on with my life. I wanted to force their hand, literally saying, "Play me or trade me." So my agent made the call, and by the end of the week, a UPS guy had already delivered my check, payment in full for the feature film. I think it was for $35,000.

Obviously, at that moment in time, September of 1979, they decided once and for all that Xon was out, but strangely enough, the news made me feel good. I could finally go on with my life.

By the time Halloween had come and gone, we'd been shooting for almost three months and we *still* hadn't finalized the last act of our film. As a result, the rewrites got even more frantic, and we often began shooting scenes less than twenty-four hours after they'd been yanked from Harold Livingston's typewriter. With that in mind, every morning at seven, Leonard and I began meeting with Bob Wise, Livingston and sometimes Gene Roddenberry (who had by now begun withdrawing from the project). Together, dull-eyed and bushy-tailed, we'd go over the upcoming day's script pages, all of us making creative suggestions on the fly. When we were through, the scenes without need of revision would get shot first, and those that needed some more pounding were rewritten and returned to the set later in the day. Our production schedule became a work of fiction, and our already turtle-esque pace became downright snailian.

As you can imagine, as the weeks began piling up, the workload, the confusion, the stress and the length of our shoot all began taking their toll. All of us were exhausted, rather punchy, and before long, that really

CONSTRUCTING V'GER'S INNARDS

began showing up on the set. However, instead of getting tense or angry with one another, we of the Starship *Enterprise* somehow just got transformed into uncontrollable, giggling idiots. For example, when Leonard managed to flub a line about "the heart of the nebulae" into "the *liver* of the nebulae," I lost all sense of self-control, giggling all over the bridge and spouting back, "The 'liver'? You must be kidneying. You've got the guts to say that to me?" Honest to God, the two of us absolutely howled over those awful puns for a full ten minutes. Things got even more out of hand that afternoon, when I accidentally referred to my Vulcan pal as "Mr. Sponk." It was not pretty. Things got even worse late in the day when Persis Khambatta innocently mala-propped her scripted "intersect course" into . . . well, you get the picture. Needless to say, we gleefully rolled ourselves into an early wrap.

Things, however, never truly reached bottom until the following morning, while we filmed a scene in which the crew of the *Enterprise* watches V'ger releasing a series of unknown cylindrical objects in our direction. Coffee in hand, we all gathered sleepily together on the bridge for the first time that day, reading through our scripts in an effort to block and rehearse the upcoming scene. However, we would accomplish neither.

You see, with our brains beaten into mush by months of mind-numbingly tedious film production, we simply no longer had the inner strength or maturity we'd need to avoid laughing like demented schoolboys at Uhura's first line of dialogue: "Captain, the alien has expelled a large object and it's headed in our direction." Almost immediately an entire bridgeful of middle-aged actors began giggling, spitting out juvenile remarks like, "Look out!!! Flying turd!!!"

While we were all flailing about in the toilet, the line

was hastily changed to read, "Captain, the alien has ejected a large object." Bob wisely sent us to the commissary for an early lunch.

An hour later, trying our best to keep our faces straight, we all reassemble to resume shooting. Amid a few scattered and lingering giggles, we once again take our places upon the bridge, fried, exchanging glances and smirks about the scene to come. Bob Wise now retakes his position behind the lens and calls out, "Okay, guys, let's try and get through this one time on film, shall we?" Thrust into an actual camera take much more quickly than we'd expected, all of us now began biting the insides of our mouths, doing math problems in our heads, thinking about the Rams, anything to avoid being the first to break up on set. "Speed," yells our soundman, and I know we're in big trouble.

Seconds later, Nichelle hasn't even finished saying, "Captain, the alien has ejected a large object," when ALL of us, as if having been unsuccessfully shushed by our third-grade teacher, virtually explode with laughter. Even Leonard, normally unflappable, is beside himself. As we all fall about the bridge, Robert Wise, himself normally a bit of a stoneface, cracks up as well, refusing to shut off the cameras. Our cinematographer, thoroughly delighted with the twisted turn of events, just can't hold it in any longer, and he, too, begins to blow.

"Keep . . . haaaaaaaa . . . heeeeeeee . . . keep going," Bob Wise laughs. At which point George Takei delivers his next scripted line, which read (I swear), "Oh my God, it's released another one . . . now two . . . and three!!!"

Now, as you might expect, we're all sprawled about our posts, crying, roaring, rolling and thoroughly punch-drunk amid our uncontrollable base-level glee.

Teamsters are now howling phlegmily. The script girl is literally lying on the floor, having fallen from her chair, and above us the lighting crew is rattling their catwalks underneath their uncontrolled foot stomping.

De Kelley speaks next, saying, "Let's just hope those things don't hit this ship!!" It marked perhaps the only time in my life when I can recall laughing so hysterically that I couldn't breathe.

And now it's Leonard's turn. Standing tall at his post, still trying to retain some semblance of decorum, some shred of dignity, he's got his eyes squeezed tight, his hands visibly trembling, and he's shaking his head from side to side, silently refusing to speak.

"C'mon, Leonard, don't get all blocked up now," I ad-lib as we all just keep on rolling.

"I would . . . hmmmmmmmmm prefer to remain, ohhh-hhhh, silent," says our rapidly cracking Vulcan.

"Leonard, line, PLEASE?!" cracks Robert Wise, knowing full well what's in store.

"Oh, Jesus," says Leonard, having given in to his human side once more. Sighing, then speaking, he pronounces his line flawlessly. "Captain," he says, "I must tell you that the objects released are at least a hundred times more powerful than *anything* any of *us* has ever encountered."

We had to break for twenty minutes. During that time, we all splashed cold water on our teary-eyed faces and thought about things like world hunger, sickness and death in the hope that we might be able to regain our composure at some point in the near future. A half-hour later, we'd made it back to the set, but throughout the rest of the day, we just kept blowing takes, with each one of us at fault at least one time, laughing out of context at the mere memory of our unhinged loss of restraint.

Believe it or not, as the weeks kept piling up and our shooting finally moved off the bridge and into the enormous "bowels of V'ger" set, Harold Livingston finally nailed down our ending. Employing an idea originally concocted by Gene Roddenberry (much to Livingston's chagrin), Livingston's scripted brainstorm allowed V'ger to ultimately succeed in its quest of becoming one with its creator, by unloading its vast and wondrous stockpile of knowledge into a willing human being, conveniently provided by the rather expendable character of Decker. The resultant union would allow man and machine to combine, achieving an entirely new state of consciousness. Finally, after months of fiddling, our script had found its "big finish." Shooting it, however, nearly killed me.

Our newest and most impressive set would take Kirk, Spock, McCoy, Ilia and Decker deep within the bowels of V'ger. Looking not unlike the stylized inner workings of a personal computer, the set was absolutely stunning, deep gray metallic interiors spreading spiderweb-style over a gleaming black underlayer with all walls and angles leading the eye toward the heart of V'ger, the banged-up twentieth-century information-seeking deep space probe, *Voyager 6*.

The set, however, proved to be almost as deadly as it was beautiful. Constructed about five feet above the studio floor so that electricians and lighting crews could wire the set to appear luminescent, the floor of V'ger was created almost entirely from thin black plastic. On top of that, we found a checkerboard pattern of thin plastic and heavy wooden octagonal steps. Color-coded, the dark gray octagons were made of plastic, and the light gray had been constructed of solid wood. That's where you walked. Step on the dark gray octagons or the black plastic flooring, and you'd

simply plummet straight through the set and down into the maze of wires and lights below. I learned that firsthand.

On our first day of shooting on this set, I was standing around, casually chatting with my stand-in, when we heard a stomach-turning crunch followed by an electrical zapping noise and the unmistakable smell of burning human hair. I looked over to find that two of our lighting guys had fallen through the set as they worked; one of them, holding onto a metal light stand, received a terrible shock. It put the fear of God into all of us, and we immediately knew why these particular scenes had been saved for the END of production.

Later that day, as De, Leonard and I began rehearsing a scene in which we all hurriedly descend toward the center of V'ger, it was nearly impossible to shake the lingering image of our injured crewman from our minds. As a result, we were all extremely tentative, downright scared, during our practice descent. As the cameras rolled, however, I became determined that Captain Kirk would not be seen hopscotching like a nine-year-old girl through this thing and so, as the cameras clicked, I began rapidly and confidently striding toward my destination in a manner more befitting an intergalactic space hero. Three steps later, I stepped onto a booby octagon and went crunching down through the set.

Horrified, my mind immediately flashed upon sudden electrocution, but thankfully, having fallen only armpit deep into the set, my worst affliction became the embarrassment I suffered by just sort of dangling helplessly in front of castmates who were ready and willing to tease me about this for the rest of my life. I still haven't entirely lived it down, and it was most definitely NOT one of Captain Kirk's finer moments. However, despite the chaos on the set, this film's biggest disaster was yet to come. Robert Wise explains:

We had a huge crush on our special effects. We had almost finished shooting when I realized that we hadn't yet received any footage from our effects house, Abel and Associates, so I said I

NEITHER HERE NOR THERE IN THE TRANSPORTER

have to see at LEAST some test footage. When it came in, I knew immediately that we had a big problem. The stuff was not good. They'd had months to play with this stuff, and the results were of really poor quality. They just weren't good enough for all the money we'd poured in . . . close to five million dollars.

So now we were all panicking that we wouldn't be able to make our Christmas release date, but we lucked out. We got Doug Trumbull, and we also got John Dykstra and his outfit, two of the best effects houses in the business. Still, even with both houses helping out, these effects guys had to work around the clock seven days a week to get this stuff done. They really pulled us out of a hole.

The production of what had now been officially entitled *Star Trek: The Motion Picture* continued like the tortoise, slow, but . . . well, slow anyway. Principal photography wrapped on the day after Thanksgiving, 1978, and almost immediately, Robert Wise and Paramount began sorting through their special effects mess. Due to the horrendous time crunch in trying to get all of this feature's effects done in time to be added into the film and the film into theaters for its tentative pre-Christmas release date of December 7, 1979, Trumbull, Dykstra and Wise were forced to split up almost entirely. Trumbull's crew, manning the lion's share of the effects work at hand, worked almost independently of Wise, as did Dykstra's. While they began frantically churning out the film's special effects, Wise began locking himself away in darkened edit suites and rough-cutting, desperately trying to piece together whatever scattered bits of this film might not require special effects.

As the unusually hot summer of 1979 slipped unaltered into the autumn, Robert Wise was going through the final torturous turns of this film. With our gala world premiere already penned in for December 4 in Washington, D.C., Bob knew that his film would have to be essentially completed, with music and special effects both locked into place, by mid-November so that 2,000 prints of the film could be produced, color-tested and distributed to theaters by our official opening date of December 7. Now receiving completed effects from both Dykstra and Trumbull on an almost daily basis, Wise found himself absolutely thrilled by their technological brilliance, but at the same time, he was also a bit concerned that many of the effects, the long, sensual pans over the body of the *Enterprise*, the lovingly detailed images of V'ger, seemed perhaps a bit top-heavy, a bit lengthy, perhaps even a bit too detailed. It was as if the effects houses had been a bit too brilliant for the film's own good, providing repeated feasts of inter-galactic photography where maybe a simple snack might have satisfied the audience just as well.

At any rate, with a deadline breathing down his neck and no time to experiment, Bob Wise trimmed a bit of the fat, but by and large inserted the incoming effects unedited (editing them would, in Bob's defense, proba-bly have proven nearly impossible, especially at this late date) into the waiting holes of his film. The result, as you all know, was a movie that, while visually stun-ning, was also deathly slow.

None of us cast members saw that coming. Certainly, we had been less than thrilled by parts of the script and we knew that shooting had been slow, but somehow we all came away from production with the feeling that by the time this film was edited, scored and imbued with all of its special effects, it was gonna be nothing short of ter-rific. With that in mind, we all began getting really excited about our December 4 world premiere. Bob Wise, on the other hand, was basically just getting nervous.

We never sat down and consciously decided to shift our emphasis from the *Star Trek* characters to all of these cutting-edge effects. That came about because of our story and the script. We had a lot of action taking place somewhere out in space, and we had an equal amount of scenes focusing upon our characters' reactions to what they were viewing on the screens of the *Enterprise*. All of that added to our effects load. Honestly, I think the fans who protest that the film relies too heavily upon its effects are correct, but at the same time, there was no way to tell this particular story without them.

And as time passed, we got to the point where I basically had to start putting our effects into the body of the film, one at a time, as they came in from the effects houses. We were on such a tight schedule that I never even had a chance to look at the film as a whole until very shortly before we had to freeze it to make our 2,000 prints.

It's the only picture in all of my thirty-nine which didn't get a sneak preview. We just didn't have the time. Literally, less than a week before our world premiere, I was still getting up every morning at 3:00 A.M., going to the MGM lab and checking their work. We came right down to the deadline, and I saw the completed film for the first time on December 1, just three days before our premiere. Between that Monday and Thursday our editor and I cut about ten minutes out of the film and had a new master printed.

Then, while all of the cast and studio executives were beginning to arrive in Washington, talking to the press about how wonderful tomorrow's world premiere was going to be, we still hadn't finished working. I actually ended up having to carry the first completed print of that film with me, on the plane, on the last flight out of L.A. bound for Washington, the night before the premiere. I slept with it under my bed that night.

The film that was ultimately shown the following evening was essentially a rough cut, the kind of thing you'd show at your first sneak preview. Normally, while the film would be playing, I'd be sitting in the back, aware of the audience, and trying to gauge whether they might be getting restless at times, and getting an overall feel for how the film is playing. Afterward, the audience will generally fill out what they call "preview cards," and that will give you a really good idea about what's working or not working in the film.

You really never know what you have until you get your film in front of a live audience. As an editor, and later as a director, I've seen that dozens upon dozens of times. I've been in so many damn sneak previews that I can tell you with a great deal of assurance that they'll ALWAYS tell you something about your movie that you had never guessed previously. You might get a laugh where it's not warranted, or a scene might just play too slowly, or a plot point get lost instead of highlighted. Ninety-nine times out of a hundred, the audience will tell you that, and when they do, you almost always just smack your forehead and say, "Why didn't I see that? I should have caught that a long time ago."

I have to admit that I attended our huge glitz-enshrouded world premiere event thrilled with the pomp and circumstance and delighting in the paparazzi and news media attention. As the lights dimmed and the film finally unreeled before me, I remained caught up in the excitement and never really noticed the film's sluggishness. Later, however, safely out of my tuxedo and watching the film with a perspective that was a bit more honest, a bit less distracted, I thought to myself, "Well, that's it. We gave it our best shot, it wasn't good, and that'll never happen again."

Shows you what *I* know.

STAR TREK II:

THE WRATH OF BENNETT . . .
AND MEYER, AND MONTALBAN,
AND DILLER, AND EISNER,
AND KATZENBERG, AND . . .

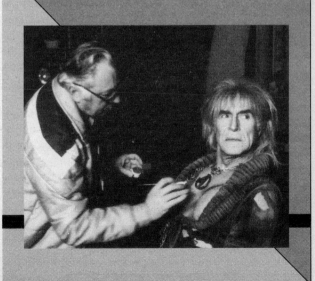

Having spent the entire decade of the seventies battling for a relaunch of the Starship *Enterprise*, Trek fans immediately, enthusiastically and unanimously greeted the release of *Star Trek: The Motion Picture* by stampeding into jam-packed multiplexes all over the country. Starving for ANY new *Star Trek* adventure, they simply ignored the word of mouth and the bad reviews and lined up, most more than once, for a chance to feast upon the seventy-millimeter spoils of their victory. You can see how *Star Trek: The Motion Picture* went on to rack up an amazing one-hundred-million-dollar gross at the box office. Even when you figured in the picture's absolutely ridiculous production costs of forty-five million (which included about twenty million in carried-over expenses from the failed development of *Star Trek: Phase II*), this film fetched home more than fifty million bucks. At the same time, young, green marketing executive Dawn Steel and her enthusiastic merchandising of the film made it the most widespread and lucrative in the history of moviemaking. Combined, they made this molasses-slow, yawn-inducing extravaganza a hit. *Star Trek* it seemed, had once again yanked an upset victory from the gnarled jaws of defeat.

Over time, when the positive returns garnered by the film began to outweigh the debacle of its production, Gulf + Western's chairman, longtime Trekker Charles Bluhdorn, met with his highest-ranking executives and suggested they produce a sequel. Eyebrows shot up all around the heavy oak conference table, but Bluhdorn would not be deterred, and after a lengthy discussion of what went wrong the first time around and how to prevent it from ever happening again, he eventually got his way. By meeting's end, he'd even strong-armed Paramount president Michael Eisner, still smarting from his first big-budgeted creative disaster, into tentative agreement.

Eisner, however, was taking no chances this time around. Robert Wise, as talented as he is, wasn't offered the director's chair. Gene Roddenberry, whose contract forbade such banishment, was eventually kicked upstairs and given the largely ceremonial title of "executive consultant." Paid handsomely and allowed to comment on every story idea and scripted draft of the sequel, Gene was nonetheless stripped of his formerly ironclad "top dog" status. Indeed, as the film progressed and the inevitable battles began to occur, Gene would abruptly come to realize that for all intents and purposes, he'd actually been removed from the driver's seat. In his place was a man named Harve Bennett.

Orderly, systematic and extremely businesslike, Harve's production techniques could sometimes be misconstrued as more methodical than "artistic." However, that was never true. Leonard perhaps best sums up the man's style:

Harve is accustomed to the politics of television production. He sees things in very military terms. When he is producing, HE is the commanding general, and all around him are his field marshals. They get their orders directly from the top, and they're expected to execute them without fail. That's the way he operates. He presses buttons from behind his desk, and his field commanders then execute his orders down on the soundstage. They then deliver to him the end footage, the results of their mission, and Harve goes off and gleefully plays with their work in the editing room. He is very inventive, wildly imaginative, but unshakably used to control. One way or another, he gets his way. He simply tells the executives what he's going to do, and then he goes out and hires people to execute his vision. When it's completed, he hands it in. Simple.

Bennett, almost 180 degrees removed from Roddenberry, came to *Star Trek*'s big-screen sequel by way of Paramount's television division. Normally that just doesn't happen, as producers tend to get pigeonholed into a certain medium or genre and stay there. However, when the powers-that-were at Paramount began mulling over potential executive producers who might competently and cost-effectively deliver a new-and-improved *Star Trek* feature, Harve's name rose to the top of the list. His penny-pinching reputation, combined with his extremely efficient production techniques and past history of producing solid science fiction television like *The Six Million Dollar Man* and *The Bionic Woman*, made him a perfect candidate, and he was almost immediately offered the job. Harve tells the tale:

How I Acquired the *Star Trek* Curse," by Harve Bennett. It is an interesting story. I'd been hired by Paramount in 1980 to do what I had been doing successfully for twenty-odd years, which was simply to make television. I had absolutely no expectation of doing features, but one day only about a week into my new television deal I was suddenly summoned into the office of Barry Diller, who was at that time the driving force and kingpin of Paramount, ably assisted by his right hand, Michael Eisner. So now these two giants of the industry have called me into a last-minute meeting without giving me any sort of hint as to what it might be about.

Lo and behold, I go to Barry Diller's office: "Hi, Barry." "Hi, Harve." "Hi, Michael." "Hi, Harve." And then Diller gets up and says, "Harve, I'd like you to meet Charles Bluhdorn." So now I'm face-to-face with the head of Gulf + Western, a big, energetic man who jumps up, pumps my hand and before I can breathe says, "Did you see *Star Trek: The Motion Picture*?" I said, "Yes, I did." Now, at this moment my mind is going, *Oh, shit, that's the movie where my kids, who usually sit still through a whole movie, kept saying, "Can I have a Coke? Can I go to the bathroom," and stuff like that.*

Anyway, I said, "Yes, I did."

"What did you think of it?"

What do I do in a situation like this? I do one thing, I only have one rule, which is rigorous honesty, so I said, "Well, I think it was really boring."

At this moment Charlie Bluhdorn turns to Michael Eisner and says, "You see, by *you*, a bald woman is sexy." So I'm standing there, nauseous,

HARVE BENNETT, ONE OF THE PEOPLE WHO GOT *STAR TREK* BACK ON TRACK

having no idea what I've just stepped into, what kind of internecine warfare. Now Bluhdorn spins on me—what energy this guy had—and he says, "Can you make a better picture?" I said, "Well, you know, yeah, I could make it less boring—yes I could."

He said, "Could you make it for less than forty-five fucking million dollars?" That was the first question he asked me that I could answer with absolute certainty. I said, "Oh boy, where I come from, I could make five movies for that."

He then said—and I'll never forget this, ever—"Do it." Later that day, at some luncheon in his honor, he crossed the Paramount commissary to find me standing in the corner—you know, the new kid in town, with a tray in my hand. He embraced me in this big Austrian bear hug, crushing my tray of food, and said, "I know you're gonna do a great job. I'll talk to you when it's finished." That's how they got me.

Given a preliminary budget of just eleven million dollars, Harve immediately knew that manning the purse strings on this film wasn't going to be easy. In short order, he also became aware of several additional and equally troubling dilemmas. Gene Roddenberry wasn't at all happy about his assigned position on the bench. Leonard Nimoy wanted nothing to do with *Star Trek* ever again. Directors all over Hollywood, having been scared off by the disastrous first film, wanted nothing to do with the franchise, and writers seemed similarly gun-shy. However, looming larger than all of those problems combined was that Harve knew almost nothing about *Star Trek*. He explains:

I had only seen a few episodes of *Star Trek*, very sporadically, during its great syndication run in the seventies. So, a bit clueless as to how I might make this thing work, I sat alone in projection rooms for three months and watched every episode of *Star Trek* at least once. When I'd finally finished, I felt that en masse, the episodes were about one-third brilliant, about one-third okay and about one-third "ugh," "ugh" being very bad. That's not a bad ratio for a long-running series. I also realized that as a whole, I liked *Star Trek* a lot, because it was optimistic and because it made an inordinate contribution to science fiction by daring to state that human beings would not change a great deal over time. Certainly, we would be out there in space doing a lot of wonderful things, but there would *still* be heavies, we'd *still* fall victim to basic human nature, and mankind would ultimately remain as we are today, well intended, but fallible. That was great, and it made for great television.

Another thing that made a lasting impression on me was the character relationships, especially the triangle of Kirk, Bones and Spock. I saw it as a very classic struggle between decision, passion and wisdom. You know, these three elements battling and ultimately culminating almost presidentially in Kirk having to make a decision, as urged passionately by Bones and dispassionately by Spock. That pattern clearly interested me.

But to me, *Star Trek* seemed at its most basic level a classic Homeric story about heroes, one that could really take place anywhere, about anything. Hence, I was stuck with the following problem: "Why was I so bored by *Star Trek: The Motion Picture*, which was skillfully manufactured and a beautiful tale?" I began to analyze it and I realized that the film wasn't really *Star Trek* at all. It was more of a tone poem, a think piece about God, a very religious essay about the ironies of V'ger returning to search for its creator. The action and the characters that had always been the foundation of the very best *Star Trek* episodes were really just along for the ride, shoehorned into the story in an attempt to make this rich philosophical disputation seem more like a large-scale adventure story.

I was also bothered by the fact that the crew of the *Enterprise* hadn't aged, or at the very least, were trying hard to *appear* as if they hadn't aged. For that reason, the film ended up looking as if it had been shot through gauze, and it took on a very sterile look. For me, that flew in the face of the vivid oversaturated color and unrestrained exuberance of the original series. The best *Star Trek* adventures, as conceived, written and photographed, couldn't help but come across as very alive, colorful, vibrant experiences.

Star Trek: The Motion Picture was none of those things. It was muted, bland, shot in pastels, with crewmen in pale gray uniforms, and actors photographed through a lot of Vaseline and youth-aiding camera tricks—the kind originally invented for aging movie queens like Greta Garbo. All of that combined to make the film seem almost totally unrelated to the larger-than-life, flesh-and-blood stories that Harve had seen in the projection room. For that reason, Harve's first creative decision was that the sequel should honestly and aggressively deal with the obvious, unavoidable aging of the *Enterprise* crew. He decided almost immediately that *his* film would celebrate these characters, wrinkles and all, while allowing them to grow and to move forward in their lives as people. Kirk, for example, would experience a bit of a midlife crisis, made more difficult by the fact that throughout most of the film, he'd be surrounded by a horde of gung-ho young Starfleet cadets. Additionally, it is no accident that this film begins with Kirk's fiftieth birthday and the contemplation of what this milestone might mean to the man. Harve continues:

Kirk is certainly going to live a longer life, but I felt there would be a real danger in trying to have the captain run around the film like a twenty-year-old. When you and I first spoke about this, I was actually kind of surprised that you accepted the notion with such a minimum of anxiety. You know, fear of aging is the absolutely eternal concern for every leading man, and I would have respected that, but in my vision, you settled into the notion quite easily.

Harve's lying. I had to be dragged in, kicking and screaming. However, in a rather lengthy lunch, as Harve and I picked over some of the more edible commissary fare, we talked about the concept of aging, the fact that the captain was now almost fifteen years older than he was in the series, and by the time we both went back to work, I actually found myself accepting, even becoming enthused about Kirk's official graduation into middle age: the eyeglasses, the aching bones, the fully grown son, all of that terrific character stuff served to get me excited about the idea. At the same time, it also seemed like a good way to address and diminish the critics who'd been so quick to point out the fact that we of the *Enterprise* crew now looked a bit long in the tooth to be running around the universe chasing bad guys. It struck me that in openly and purposefully dealing with the advancing age of these characters, we'd avoid looking like we were trying to hide the issue, while simultaneously using it to the film's advantage. Essentially, we'd be turning a potential weakness into a strength. With that, I quickly did an about-face, and began reveling in my wrinkles. Harve's story continues:

The next thing I did was to decide that this film should be a sequel to the television episode entitled "Space Seed." In all the seventy-nine episodes I saw, "Space Seed" popped out as a kind of bas-relief. It was the one I loved the most, and it solved a lot of problems for me.

First of all, it made me feel very safe to do a sequel to an existing episode. As the new boy in town, I didn't want to write something that wasn't within the parameters of the original series. I felt that loyalty and that insecurity. You know, you come into the league, you play by the rules of the league. "Space Seed" had been beautifully done. It was a marvelous combination of menace, action and resolution.

Second, "Space Seed" had a clear, ballsy, theatrical antagonist, which I felt was almost always present in the best episodes of *Star Trek*, and missing from *The Motion Picture*. There, V'ger ultimately shaped up to be more of a misguided spiritual force than a clear-cut antagonist. So I knew we needed a black-hat villain whose reasons for being a villain were clearly defined and clearly motivated. I wanted a classic tale of vengeance, a real "revenge is the best revenge" kind of story. "Space Seed" played into that beautifully and it even had a bit of an open ending. Kirk's last words on the bridge are something to the effect of, "I wonder where Khan will be twenty years from now." It was like a song cue.

I saw that and said, "Thanks, Bill, you just told me what I have to do." And the whole thing was predicated on that emotional feeling. Whew, I thought, *this is going to work*. I never lost that faith, because the path became self-evident.

Harve settled into his new office, began scribbling on a yellow legal pad, and came up with a very basic, very rough storyline. About two paragraphs long, Harve's story proposed that Khan might rally the youth of an entire galaxy into a full-blown revolution against the

United Federation of Planets. In a no-holds-barred quest for revenge, Khan would also frame Captain Kirk as an intergalactic equivalent of Public Enemy Number One, putting a price on his head and marking him for certain death.

Once that germ of an idea had been tied up, Harve called in a writer named Jack Sowards and together they discussed the possibilities and pitfalls of the proposed story, and tried to come up with some idea, ANY idea, that might help bring the thoroughly re-disenchanted Leonard Nimoy back into the fold. Leonard recalls Harve's methods:

I had worked for Harve one time a while back, on a TV movie that he'd produced for Universal, so when he started working on *Star Trek* II, he called me, sort of reintroduced himself, and asked, "Can we have lunch?" I thought to myself, *Oh, shit, here we go again.*

Anyway, when we finally got together, we sat down and I kind of rehashed what had gone wrong in the making of the first picture, about how the characters had been mishandled, handcuffed and buried underneath a lot of unnecessary special effects. Harve agreed, and he went on to speak with a real sense of vision about what was so great about the original TV series. He seemed to understand the ways in which that first film had gone off the tracks.

We talked about what the new movie could be about, and *should* be about, and then he brought up the budgetary issue. Eight million, ten million, twelve million, and that really scared me, because I couldn't help but think to myself,

"Geez, they're really just trying to squeeze a little bit more blood out of *Star Trek*." You know, it seemed the thinking behind the film wasn't "Let's make a *Star Trek* film and do it right this time," but more like "Maybe there's still something left in this franchise that we can exploit. Let's do it on the cheap. We might do less box office, but it won't matter, we'll make this thing so inexpensively that we'll still make some money." I ultimately said to Harve, "Can't you guys just leave this thing alone?" To me, the whole thing seemed motivated solely by profit. They had no creative idea.

So I said, "Look, this just isn't my cup of tea. I go for ideas. If somebody comes back to me with an idea about something that might be interesting to play on screen, I might get excited, but if you're just out to wring some more profit out of this thing . . . I'm out. I'm not interested in playing that game." We were friendly, I wished him luck, and that was that.

A short while later, I was having a social gathering at my house, maybe thirty or forty people, and Harve was there. I asked him, "How's it going?" and he said, "It's coming along really well . . ." Then he sort of leaned toward me and asked, "How'd you like to have a great death scene?" I laughed. "You son of a bitch, let's talk." Harve was clever, he had come up with the idea I'd been searching for.

And then I asked, "Where does Spock's death fit into the film?" and after a thoughtful pause, Harve countered with, "Let me ask you a question. Do you remember a little film entitled *Psycho*?" We laughed, but what came to me was,

"Since I really feel tortured each time I get a call about this thing, maybe Spock's dying is a good idea. If this *Star Trek* movie is really what I think it is, a low-budget attempt to wring out every last drop of blood, maybe the thing to do is die with some glory and say good-bye. Then they can't possibly call me again." It looked to me like a graceful exit. That's what got me involved.

Leonard smiles, the pair shakes hands, and by the end of the party, one more significant aspect of Harve's new storyline has fallen neatly into place. Sowards and Bennett then fleshed out a first-draft screenplay, which pleased the Paramount executives while incurring the first of what would become countless battles with Roddenberry. Harve recalls their relationship:

I first met Gene when I was a network executive at ABC and we always had a cordial professional relationship. When I went over to Universal, Gene was there, too, making his *Questor Tapes* pilot, and during that time, our relationship got a little closer. You know, we'd eat an occasional lunch together and chat. Small talk, really, we never spoke of work. So while I *knew* Gene, it wasn't until I came to Paramount to produce *Star Trek II* that I encountered him on a professional level. The first phase—and I'm not so sure we ever graduated beyond that first phase—involved Gene's attempts at establishing his territorial imperative.

He resisted everything, every suggestion, every idea. I would see Gene every once in a while in the commissary or in the parking lot, and we'd wave to one another and be polite, but that was it. All of our actual business, at Gene's request, was conducted by memo.

Now, I'm a hands-on person, I like to sit in a room, belt it out, get it done, then see where people are having problems and find solutions. You simply can't do that by memo. For example, every story pass, every scripted draft, every thought that sprang from a writer's head and made it onto a sheet of paper, our thoughts, our stories and ultimately our scripts would go simultaneously to Gene and to Paramount management. And management would generally respond with notes of enthusiasm, "Keep going, it's lookin' great," stuff like that. However, Gene's notes would be . . . it's hard to characterize. Defensive, I think, would be a very good word. "This will ruin *Star Trek*" kind of stuff. I saved a lot of them, but I don't ever want to make them public because they're very painful.

No matter what we'd come up with, Gene wouldn't like it, and he'd counter by pitching a story about the crew of the *Enterprise* coming back to stop Jack Kennedy's assassination. The year is 1963 and the *Star Trek* crew comes back, as they had in "The City on the Edge of Forever" and as they would later in *Star Trek IV*, but their purpose here was to muck about and try to stop Kennedy's assassination, which of course they can't stop because that would screw up history. So the end of the story is a lead balloon because we all know that they're not gonna stop anything. Throughout my tenure on *Star Trek*, that story came up four times as a substitute for whatever we were planning. *Star Trek II*, *III*, *IV*, *V*, it didn't matter.

At the same time, there was another piece of the puzzle, and that was Majel. She'd come for lunch and so forth, early on, and she would whisper how wonderful the ideas were, and that things seemed to be coming along well. Basically, she made it clear that she was reading everything. I mean, she would come by and say, "Oh, I just love what you're going to do, making 'Space Seed' is a terrific idea." It was awkward, and I didn't understand it at first, but I subsequently rationalized that Majel most likely just wanted Nurse Chapel to be in the movie.

And from the beginning, Paramount put me in a very difficult, very interesting situation, really the ultimate crunch. Diller and Eisner had said, right from the start, "We'll handle Gene, you just do the picture, and forget about his memos, they have no effect." So if my ethics were different than they are, for better or worse, I would have said, "I have no problem with that, I'll just nod at the memos and I do what I have to do." But it was tough for me. You know, here I was, the new guy, and I'm getting these negative memos from Roddenberry, a man I respect and whose child I am currently taking on a trip. And at the time, I was insecure enough to say, "Well, Gene must know something I'm not getting." I was in a real box.

So the studio just asked that I communicate with Gene, and keep him informed of our creative situation, which I happily did. Basically, I was being asked to serve as the intermediary between the studio and Star Trek's founder, whose presence was no longer requested. We ultimately had a very schizophrenic relationship, cordiality in person, and stiff-necked resistance by memo.

But I was stuck between a rock and a hard place. Gene had been asked to leave center stage and let someone else take over. It wasn't easy for him, and he quickly became very possessive with his child, *Star Trek*. I understood that, and I must confess to similar parental feelings when I produced *The Mod Squad* and when I did *The Six Million Dollar Man* and all those things. As a producer, you just don't want to step aside, to give it up to anybody else.

What I *couldn't* understand was Gene's concept of *Star Trek*. I was fresh from seeing seventy-nine episodes, and I thought I knew what *Star Trek* was in its original form, but when Gene's memos started arriving, they criticized everything we were doing on a basis that was from outer space to me. "*Star Trek*," he said, "is not a paramilitary show." That's not true. "*Star Trek*," in his words from the sixties, "is Horatio Hornblower." That's a paramilitary show to me. The analogy between the United States Navy or any navy and *Star Trek* is so preeminent that you can't possibly miss it. I mean, why then are we dealing with "admirals" and "captains," "commanders," "lieutenants" and so forth? The *Enterprise* is simply a naval vessel at sea, in space.

"There was never," he said, "violence and conflict in the twenty-third century." Well, how do you deal with that when you are fresh from seeing the episodes where there was a *great deal* of violence? There were traditional roustabout fights; there were barroom brawls; there was nerve-pinching; there was exotic weaponry. There were always people doing bad things to people, very bad things to people.

And suddenly I saw the seeds of what had bored me in *Star Trek: The Motion Picture*. It seemed as though Gene, in his statesmanlike personal growth, had now begun confusing his own idealism—which was wonderful—about a peaceful future and man's ability to grow in the years ahead—with *Star Trek*. In my mind, *Star Trek's* vision was very different and very specific. Things will change, parameters will change, technology will change, but human nature will most definitely remain the same. Why do I say that? Because recorded history tells us so.

Go back two hundred years to the seventeen hundreds, what has changed? What has changed since "let my people go" in Egypt and before that, from the recorded history of humankind? Will four hundred years of technology elevate that into bliss and karma? I think not, but somehow Gene had made that assumption in his later years. Or at least that was the basis of all his objections to the things we were trying to do.

Now I could assume one of two things, that Gene had become devoutly sincere about all this and it had altered his vision of what he himself had done on *Star Trek*, or the other possibility was that perhaps unconsciously he resented *anyone*, not just Harve Bennett, coming in, taking over and trying to replicate something that he'd created. If that were the case, and he simply couldn't accept the situation, perhaps he was reaching for any ammunition he could find in resisting my efforts. Perhaps that's what prompted his philosophical stance against everything we were trying to do in re-creating the feeling of his *Star Trek*.

This basic and irreconcilable difference of opinion laid the groundwork for an endless series of battles that would effectively keep Roddenberry and Bennett at odds throughout Harve's four-film *Star Trek* tenure. For the moment, however, Harve simply weighed Paramount's support against Roddenberry's criticism and, with deadlines approaching, plowed ahead. Ensuing drafts of the script, each trying out a brand-new twist or two, generally bore little resemblance to their predecessors. Still, through a process of trial and error, many of the plot points that would eventually make it into *Star Trek II: The Wrath of Khan* got thrown into the mix, along with an equal number that were ultimately discarded. In one draft Kirk gained a grown son named David, and romanced a beautiful redheaded (and, of course, doomed) fellow officer named O'Rourke. In another, the young female Vulcan named Saavik was introduced and began a rather steamy relationship with David. Finally, when the film's art director, Mike Minor, casually tossed out an off-the-cuff idea that perhaps the Federation had come up with a device that could actually speed up the evolutionary processes of previously uninhabitable planets, he was thrilled to find it immediately being incorporated into a new draft of the script entitled *Star Trek: The Genesis Project*.

However, as the clock continued to tick, Harve found himself generally pleased with a lot of the ideas that had been thrashed about, but nonetheless disheartened over the fact that no single storyline seemed quite capable of standing on its own merits, much less coalescing into a full-blown, full-length feature. With a lot of terrific but rather disjointed loose ends piling up all over his desk, Harve decided that it might be a good idea to bring in a *Star Trek* veteran or two in the hope

that they might be able to turn *Star Trek II* into something more than just the awkward sum of its mismatch-
ing parts.

After interviews with a solid half-dozen of the series'
most talented writers, Harve invited Sam Peeples,
whose pilot "Where No Man Has Gone Before" initially
sold the series, to read the various scripts, then rework
whatever aspects appealed to him in writing his own
version of the script. Peeples did just that, and several
weeks later, he returned to Harve's office, offering up a
screenplay that bore absolutely no resemblance to any
previous draft.

Khan had been tossed from the story, as had Saavik,
Kirk's son, David, and nearly every existing aspect of
Harve's initial storyline. The Genesis Project was
Peeples's sole survivor, but it had now become a mere
subplot amid a rather strange storyline focusing upon a
formless, unfathomable and extremely powerful pair of
villains from another dimension. Upon reading this re-
re-re-revised screenplay, Harve, like Roddenberry
before him, was beginning to sweat. And then, thanks
to a couple of pounds of ground chuck, he and *Star Trek*
both got lucky.

Across town, over a hasty hamburger cookout, the
man who is arguably most responsible for jump-starting
Star Trek and propelling it toward cinematic success
was about to enter the picture. His name is Nick Meyer.
He is a tremendously talented writer and director, and
he tells his story below:

I have a friend named Karen Moore, who used to
work at Paramount. She began as Louis Malle's
assistant on *Pretty Baby*, and she worked so well
with the studio that when the film wrapped, they

hired her. I've known her since she was twelve years old, and she's just terrific.

Anyway, I had recently directed *Time After Time*, and it had been very well received, so as a follow-up, I wanted to do something really special. With that in mind, I was turning down jobs and passing on projects, and basically not doing much of anything. That's where Karen and the hamburgers come into the story.

Karen was up at my house in Laurel Canyon one night and while I was burning the burgers and complaining about the studios, she let me have it. She just sat there, rolled her eyes, and said, "How long are you going to sit up here like an infant waiting for them to do what you want to do? If you want to learn how to be a director, you've got to direct." Now if my mother had said this to me I don't know that I would have been capable of taking it in, but you know, this is a friend, and it was around barbecued hamburgers. I asked her, "What are you getting at?" And she said, "Well, there's a guy you ought to meet at Paramount. His name is Harve Bennett and he's gonna do the second *Star Trek* movie. I think that you and he would get along."

I said, "I don't know anything about *Star Trek*, I've never even seen it. Although I *did* know a guy in Iowa who watched it, dropping LSD, for fifty-four days straight in college, at the end of which time his wife left him. So, I don't know . . . maybe there is something there."

So Karen had snapped me to attention, and I went to see Harve. We got along and he said, "Draft five of the script should be done in about ten days. I'll send you a copy, and if you like it, maybe you would consider doing it." So I said, "Great!" By this time I had seen *Star Wars*, and I thought, "Okay, let's make a space fantasy. That sounds like fun." And then I didn't hear from him.

Two weeks went by. I woke up one morning and I thought, "What ever happened to Harve Bennett and draft five?" So I called him up and Harve just said, "Oy," or words to that effect, "oy, am I embarrassed." He said, "We have real problems here." He said, "If I were you, I'd forget about this project." I said, "What happened? What do you mean, forget it? I can't forget it, I've been looking at old *Star Trek* episodes, and I'm all stoked up. What specifically is wrong?" And he said, "The script stinks, it's a hundred and eighty pages of nothing." So I said, "No, send it up, let me take a look at it." He said, "No way, I'm too embarrassed."

So we had this whole conversation, a real tug-of-war, at the end of which Harve sent me the script, I read it, and indeed it was not very good. I said, "Maybe you should show me draft four." And he said, "Look, Nick, you don't understand, draft four is a totally different attempt at *Star Trek II*, and draft three is yet another totally different attempt. They're not drafts of the same story." This was all news to me, and I said, "Well, then, send them all up to me. Let me read them all." Harve sent a messenger, and I had all five scripts about an hour later.

Nick read them all, thought about them for a while, made a few notes, and then called Harve, asking if he and the film's newly hired producer, Bob Sallin, would come up to his place and have a chat. When they got there, Nick greeted them at the front door by saying, "I have an idea." He ushered the men onto the nearest sofa, pulled out a legal pad and said, "Let's make a list of all the things we like in these five drafts. It could be a line of dialogue, it could be a character, it could be a scene, it could be a plot, it could be a subplot, anything." He continued, "Once we've finished that, I'll write a *new* screenplay in which we'll incorporate all the things we liked in the other drafts." As Nick explains, this unusual behavior virtually blindsided his guests.

Harve and Bob just kind of blinked at each other for a minute or two, until finally Bob said, "Well . . . we have a big problem." I said, "What problem?" They said, "Well, our special effects house is ILM and they say that if they don't have a script in twelve days, they can't guarantee that our special effects will be ready by the time we're done shooting." I, being very young and very stupid, then said, "Oh, that's okay, I can write this in twelve days." And Harve looked at me like I was crazy and said, "We couldn't even make your deal in twelve days."

Then I did something for which I've always felt very strange. I said, "Forget about my deal, forget about my writing credit, because if nobody else does this, there's not gonna be any movie. I'm writing it for nothing. You decide whose name goes on the credits later." Later that day I told my agent what I had done, and I really thought he was gonna kill me.

And I was in analysis at the time, so I discussed this endlessly with my shrink, and ultimately came to the conclusion that this insane

NICK MEYER, THE TWELVE DAY
WONDER, MEETS HIS FIRST VULCAN

gesture wasn't entirely altruistic. It was really a way of taking the pressure off of me, if the script that I wrote didn't work. You know, by avoiding the proper channels, some part of my brain could believe that none of this was really happening. My name wasn't really on it, so if it stunk, it didn't make any difference. If I had known how well it was actually gonna turn out, I certainly wouldn't have done it that way.

And I *really* wanted this to happen. I had totally gotten stoked on the idea of doing Captain Horatio Hornblower in outer space. So Bob said, "Are you really serious about this?" And I said, "Yeah, I'm dead serious. I've got the pad here." So we went through everything. We decided that we wanted Kirk to meet his son, so that became one definite component, the Genesis planet became another, Khan was another, Spock's death was another, the *Kobayashi Maru* simulator sequence, which was actually in the middle of one of the earliest drafts, got thrown in there as well, and that afternoon we made a whole list. That evening, I started writing a screenplay.

First I made an outline, and my outlines usually operate like the headlights you see in cars at night, with each idea illuminating enough of the road to get to the next curve and then you go on. In this case, however, I really had to work backward, toward a set of predetermined circumstances that could combine all of the dramatic threads Harve and Bob and I had spoken about. Kirk meets his son, the Genesis planet gets introduced, Khan shows up, Spock dies, and at the same time, some of the film's thematic content, friendship, old age, death, started seeping through the narrative, coating it with some meaning. As it evolved, I found myself playing more and more into that.

And at some point in there, I decided that since Captain Kirk is supposed to be a history buff, it might be kind of interesting to give him a book. I looked at my bookshelf, and spotted Dickens's *A Tale of Two Cities*. I stopped right there, because it just seemed to tie in so beautifully with this film. At the same time, it's the only book I can think of where just about everybody knows the first line and the last line: "It was the best of times, It was the worst of times," and "It is a far, far better thing I do than I have ever done before, a far better resting place I go to than I have ever known . . . " Those two lines went on to sort of bracket the whole movie.

And be that as it may, the screenplay that came out in twelve days was fairly indestructible. Still, it took a couple of tries.

Surprisingly, Nick's instant script, the building block for one of the best *Star Trek* films of them all, was not immediately embraced by the cast. George Takei actually quit the film for a time, over his feeling that Sulu wandered through the entire movie as a sort of living, breathing prop. De Kelley nearly went the same route, concerned that the script was just too busy, overstuffed with storylines that basically neglected the character of Bones. Leonard, still tentatively hoping for the best while expecting the worst, was similarly troubled:

When we made my deal for *Star Trek II* with Paramount, it included two non–*Star Trek* pay-or-play projects for me. This was important. I would get my fee for doing *Star Trek II* and they would guarantee me two other pay-or-play assignments. And when I was discussing the details of that deal with the studio, Harve stepped right into the breach and said, "I can give you one of those two roles right now. I'm currently producing a miniseries entitled *A Woman Called Golda* and I'd like you to play her husband."

So I went to Israel, and while I was there, we were still waiting to see the first draft of the script for *Star Trek II*. When it came, I did not like it, and I said so. Spock's death took place about midway through the film, but that didn't bother me. I was more concerned about Spock's function in the story. I didn't want to see him just standing around the bridge waiting to be killed off. I spoke to Harve about it, and we agreed that I'd come back to L.A. on my upcoming week off from shooting.

I flew back, and I was gonna be in L.A. for six days. I met with Harve, and he introduced me to Nick Meyer, who was a breath of fresh air, totally refreshing. He walked in, sat down and made a lot of flattering comments. He told me, "I'm a great fan of Sherlock Holmes, and I saw you play him on the stage. I think it was the best Holmes I've ever seen." He was really blowing the smoke up my ass, saying all the right things, and then he took it a step further.

He said, "I understand you have some problems with the script." I said, "Yes, I do, specifically because of 'A,' 'B,' and 'C' plot points, the use of Spock, his function in regard to the story, things of that nature."

KIRK LOOKS FOR PICTURES IN *A TALE OF TWO CITIES*

He surprised me by saying, "I agree, and furthermore, how long are you going to be in town?" I said, "Not long, I have to leave Saturday." With that, Nick said, "You'll have a revised draft of the script before you leave." I was impressed, and I thought to myself, *If this guy can deliver a script by Friday that has all of the merit we've been talking about, this film just might be okay.*

Friday came, I got the script, and I was absolutely delighted. I called Harve and said, "You guys really did it! This really works!"

Before I go any further, I must admit that upon first glance, I, too, was rather unimpressed with Nick's four-star, two-thumbs-up classic-in-the-making. In fact, I may have protested louder than the rest of the cast combined. Today, with the benefit of twenty-twenty hindsight, I think my rather vociferous unhappiness with the script had almost nothing to do with the actual script in hand. Instead, having been so badly burned by *Star Trek: The Motion Picture*, I most likely scrutinized this new script with a real chip on my shoulder and an overwhelming attitude of "You won't fool me again. This time I'm not filming anything until I'm one hundred percent thrilled with the script." Nick's script probably had two strikes against it before I'd even opened the plastic cover.

At any rate, I came away from that first draft feeling like it had some major problems, so I called Harve and set up a meeting wherein he, Nick and I could go over the script and talk about the stuff I wasn't happy with. Simple, right? Wrong, because as I came into Harve's office and we began the meeting, I couldn't help but be amazed by the inexplicable fact that Nick kept jumping up and going to the bathroom, literally every five minutes. I couldn't understand it, and it was making me nuts. However, in researching this book, when Nick finally explained himself, it all made sense . . . almost. He said:

It was the most embarrassing meeting of my life. I had finished the first draft of the script, made a few changes, and most people were pretty happy with it, so I was now up at ILM having a preliminary meeting about the film's special effects. And the phone rings, and it's Harve. He says, "We have a problem, Bill is not happy, Bill is really not happy." And because I was still the new kid on the block, I was really intimidated. I went back into my effects meeting thinking, That's it, it's not happening, there's no movie.

Over the course of the next several hours, Nick allowed himself to obsess over this upcoming meeting to the point where, by the time it got under way, he was smack in the middle of a rather sizable anxiety attack. I almost immediately made things worse by avoiding pleasantries entirely, starting the proceedings with my high-volume opinion that "This script is a total DISASTER!" This would have been a very poor choice of words under *any* circumstances, but with Nick falling apart at the seams, they were, well . . . disastrous. Nick remembers, "It was terrible. I was so distressed that I literally could not control my bladder. I didn't agree that the script was a 'disaster,' but at that point in time there was no way I could say, 'Wake up, Bill! You're out of your mind! Your problems with this script are actually rather cosmetic and fixable. I can fix them in forty-eight hours.' So I just kept excusing myself, going to the bathroom, and once I was in there, I was able to calm down and distill what you were saying from *how* you were saying it."

Now, I absolutely have to go on record saying that Nick did not fix the script in forty-eight hours . . . he did it in thirty-six. I mean, I got back a "revised" draft of Nick's script so quickly that I felt sure he'd just made a couple of halfassed attempts at window dressing to shut me up. However, when I grudgingly read it, expecting the worst, it was terrific! So I called Nick, his machine picked up, so I left a message, something to the effect of, "You, sir, are a genius, I don't know how you did it, but you did it. This script is fantastic."

But that's how Nick worked: "Got a problem? Give me ten minutes and I'll fix it." However, he's quick to point out that his ability to rework and revise the script for *Star Trek II* was aided greatly by the very structure of the script itself. "It was just one of those things," he says, "that was so largely 'right' that you could kind of stretch it and pull it in a lot of ways without hurting it. Khan, the Genesis project, the death of Spock, these are gigantic elements that could lend themselves to anything. We could segue and move, always picking out the best elements of the five previous scripts. I was able to accommodate the 'Shatner' changes the same way I'd made the 'Nimoy' changes when I heard, 'Leonard isn't happy.' This script was really flexible, and kind of like the U.S. Constitution in that I could amend it fairly easily, without ever altering any of the really big ideas." Still, Nick wasn't quite out of the woods.

About ten days later, while Nick continued polishing his Teflon-coated script, a strange and rather sticky situation flared up, and it nearly stopped the film's rapidly accelerating creative momentum dead in its tracks. Harve Bennett came into his office one morning and was horrified to find that despite extremely tight security, news of Spock's impending doom had already managed to sneak off the lot and into *Star Trek* fanzines all over the country. As a result, Paramount was now being deluged with poison-pen letters from thousands of *Star Trek's* most rabid fans, all of them furious over the anticipated murder of their favorite Vulcan. Knees jerked, emergency meetings were called, and suddenly, all over the Paramount lot, aspirin was being consumed like candy. Harve Bennett explains:

When the news leaked, I immediately began looking for the person responsible, and I ultimately came up with enough evidence to indicate that it was Roddenberry. It was obvious in reading these hastily published negative statements about Spock's death that they had all originated from a single source: same ideas, same verbiage, same voice. In effect, these fanzine and newsletter people were publishing the inside information and opinions that Gene was supplying. He was the source of the leaks, I really think so. Now, this is not to say that he was making these people do what they didn't want to do. He was simply tapping into the energy of a very unusual group of people whose very loyalty made them powerful.

The issue became very clear, and the reason I'm daring to say this on the record is because there was a memo that went out only to seven people. And this memo was a preliminary rundown of our storyline that basically said, "This is the film we're gonna do." It was about ten pages long, and it was the first written notice that Spock would die. In fact, in that particular version, as it was in *Psycho*, Spock would have died about a half-hour into the movie. It would have been a real shock. Within hours, Gene wrote an ardent memo back, saying, "You cannot do this!!!"

Within three days, the letters from the fans began arriving. Now, I rest my case, Your Honor.

Would Michael Eisner have orchestrated this? No. Would Barry Diller? I doubt it. There was absolutely no one on that list who had anything to gain by blowing this secret except Gene, who'd been opposed to the idea from day one. It was a very interesting time for me because I suddenly identified with those in Washington who suffer from leaks.

At first I tried to ignore it, but when the letters started flooding the executives, they became nervous, because the power of the fans is very real. I ultimately came to realize that *Star Trek*'s fandom is divided into several cores. The smallest circle was the inner hard core, the letter writers. Then there was a slightly less intense outer rim, and finally a broad circle of people who would always be there, but who weren't that passionate. And in terms of the uproar over Spock's death, the inner cult seemed to really frighten Paramount management. They read this sudden outpouring of "don't kill Spock" letters to be the will of the people, or more specifically, the will of the paying audience. And so in that sense, Gene and these fans had succeeded.

So then we had a big meeting. "What are you gonna do about all this protest?" they asked me. "Well," I said, "why do we have to do *anything*? Isn't protest good for business? Isn't that the way it works?" You know, since the secret's out and there's nothing I can do to change that, I've got to rationalize it. And as I sat there thinking about it, I came to the conclusion that even though we would have loved to surprise people at the top of the film, by the time this thing gets into theaters and the first group of people have seen it, the secret would be out anyway.

"So what's the plan?" they asked, and I said, "Well, Leonard committed to be in the picture on the basis of Spock's dying. The whole picture falls apart if we don't do it, but there may be a benefit here. Instead of surprising people, why don't we make the whole movie about it and let's climax the movie with the death of Spock?" In retrospect, that was a blessing. Because if this had not happened, we would have simply written ourselves into a corner. We'd have had this monumental shock, and the picture would have stopped one-third of the way through. People would have been very moved, very upset, and their reaction would have basically served to trivialize the last two-thirds of the movie. I was too blind to see that. So, in a perverse way, who did I owe a debt of gratitude? Gene Roddenberry. He basically slid us sideways into a much better film.

Harve and Nick Meyer hooked up almost immediately after this meeting and began remolding Nick's Silly Putty script one more time, hoping that it would remain flexible enough to allow them to push Spock's demise a lot closer to the end. At the same time, Nick had been putting the finishing touches on the film's opening "flight simulator" scene. In it, Spock's training a group of Starfleet cadets in the proper procedures to be employed during an all-out attack. Today's lesson, however, plunges the students into a hypothetical battle scenario which, as designed, is entirely unwinnable . . . the *Kobayashi Maru*. Battling their computerized and extremely realistic opponents upon a fully functional mock-up of the *Enterprise* bridge, the students are tested as to their probable mental, physical and emotional reactions in the face of such an incredibly difficult situation.

Faced with the Paramount-instigated revisions, Nick joked that "We ought to kill Spock off right here in the first scene just to freak them out."

"At that," says Meyer, "Harve turned around wide-eyed and said, 'Jesus Christ! Nick, that's incredible! That's perfect!'"

"I never even realized it," Nick continues,

I was just sort of mumbling and joking around, and the next thing you know we've got a new

THE *ENTERPRISE*'S ENGINEERING SECTION TAKES A HIT

improved opening for the movie. We'd "kill" Spock in the first three minutes, expose his death as merely part of a training exercise, then move on with the story. Later, when the audience had gotten swept away by Khan and the Genesis project and so forth, we could sneak Spock's death back into the action as a genuine surprise. We basically just reorganized our strongest material.

I should also add that at this point in time, Spock's death was a lot more final, a lot more clear-cut, than it would ultimately become. The "remember" exchange between Spock and McCoy didn't exist yet, nor did the notion that Spock's casket would land upon the Genesis planet. All of that would come much later.

At any rate, as the script continued flexing its muscles, the creatives also began contemplating the new film's visual effects. Having learned a valuable lesson from the mistakes of *Star Trek: The Motion Picture*, and bearing only a fraction of the first film's effects budget, Harve, Nick and Bob Sallin were unanimous in their "less is more" philosophy. This time around, there was absolutely no way our storyline would be overwhelmed by its technological wizardry. No one wanted that, and even if they had, they couldn't afford it.

At the same time, Harve and Nick began casting. Merritt Butrick, fresh from his role on the cult-classic sitcom *Square Pegs*, was hired to play Kirk's son, David. Bibi Besch came aboard as his mother, and when Kim Cattrall proved unavailable, Nick Meyer provided Kirstie Alley with her screen debut in the role of the Vulcan Saavik. Most notable, however, is the fact that at this point in the story, Ricardo Montalban enters from the wings, reprising his role as the genetically engineered superman/madman Khan Noonian Singh.

In the weeks and months ahead, he would provide this film with one of the greatest screen villains ever. Montalban tells his story:

Let me go back to *Star Trek* the TV series. All of a sudden I am offered a role in an episode of *Star Trek* entitled "Space Seed." I was familiar with the show, and I really thought it was something special. Also, the role of Khan was very different. This was not your standard cardboard villain. Khan had depth, intelligence, and he wasn't entirely evil. Indeed, some of his ideas were genuinely noble. His villainy really sprang from an overwhelming appetite for omnipotence. When I first read the script, I liked it very much and I thought to myself, *I hope I can do a good job with this thing. I hope I can be evil.*

Years later, I'm halfway through the fifth season of *Fantasy Island*, and I was feeling very grateful. I loved our crew and having new actors come in every week—that was wonderful. But as an actor, I was beginning to get a little bit nervous, due to the fact that I was playing a character that could never actually become emotionally involved in any of our storylines. My job was to play the perfect host, always in control, and that's not an easy role to play. I was always doing exposition. You know, "'Who's that, boss?' 'Well, Tattoo, her fantasy is that she would like to . . . '" And "'What's that, boss?' 'Why is that, boss?'" and so on. It's all exposition and as an actor it's the most difficult thing you can do. The best you can do is to try and inject some vitality and energy in the hope you'll be able to keep it interesting. So

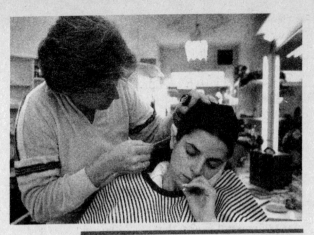

PRE-WAKEUP MAKEUP FOR KIRSTIE ALLEY

after five years I was beginning to thirst for something that I could be really passionate about.

When I was offered *Star Trek II*, which later became *The Wrath of Khan*, I read the script and thought it was very good. And the part of Khan was interesting, because you couldn't help but wonder, "What's happened to that man who was expelled all those years ago?" But at the same time, having been on *Fantasy Island* for five years, I visualized myself as being somehow beckoned by Hollywood on the strength of a hit series. Because of that, I foolishly, I admit, and unrealistically, wanted a more important role. Khan's role at first glance is fairly small.

But then I read the script a bit more closely, and said to myself, "Wait a minute, even when Khan is not on the screen, the other characters are talking about him. He is the driving force behind their adventure. His every scene has some real impact." So that changed my mind. I accepted the role, and then had a meeting with Nick Meyer, who I thought was an intelligent young man and a brilliant filmmaker.

So now I take my script home and I began to work on it. Until now, I'd never actually articulated Khan's words. It would have been premature. I started working on a scene and almost immediately, I said things to myself like, "Oh my God, I sound like Mr. Roarke. I'm moving like Mr. Roarke and the audiences are not going to take it seriously . . . Come now, am I not a professional actor? . . . Just shut up and do it." That's the kind of thing I put myself through. I had cold feet, and I was sure I'd be laughed off the screen.

So I went to Harve Bennett and asked, "Do you think I could have a copy of 'Space Seed'?" He got that for me, and when I played it for the first time, I started going back in time and I could once again remember the set, the lighting, Gene Roddenberry, and I started to remember what I did as an actor back then, less mature than I am now, and over time, Khan began returning to me. I realized that while he is still the same guy, he has now become consumed with an overwhelming passion. His superior strength and intelligence are now overwrought with a burning passion for revenge against this man he blames for the death of his wife.

Therefore, Khan is not insane, but obsessed, out of control. Nick Meyer also gave me a copy of *Moby Dick*, because he felt that Khan should be consumed by his quest for revenge in the way that Ahab had been consumed by his quest for the whale.

When I had properly digested all of that, I opened my script once more and started reading. To my great satisfaction, Mr. Roarke had disappeared: The only way I could bring this character to life was to do it with passion, totally obsessed, bigger than life, taking him right to the edge, to the brink of becoming ludicrous. I knew that if I didn't take that risk, Khan was going to seem small and insignificant.

Meanwhile, the standard preliminary chaos was beginning to run wild all over the Paramount lot and beyond. Costumers were hastily pinning and sewing Starfleet uniforms by the score, construction crews were once again pounding upon the seemingly indestructible sets originally built for the *Star Trek: Phase II* television series, and immediately in their wake came a horde of scenic artists, prop guys and effects men who'd paint and dress and light up the plywood shells of the *Enterprise* interiors until they seemed genuinely flightworthy. In San Raphael, California, the special effects wizards at ILM were equally frantic. Having been flatly refused even the slightest guidance and assistance from Douglas Trumbull and his Entertainment Effects Group, who'd handled the bulk of the work on the first film, an entire creative team was unsuccessfully, even disastrously trying to figure out how they'd ever make the bulky miniature *Enterprise* take flight. Still, despite the hectic pace, and perhaps even because of it, a real sense of enthusiasm was beginning to wash over everyone involved in the project.

Heightening the adrenaline rush was the fact that Nick Meyer's script was now just about at the "final draft" stages. However, several last-minute details had yet to be attended to. For example, at this juncture, and ultimately in the finished film, although Khan and Kirk spend the better part of the movie engaged in a merciless battle of wits, there is no face-to-face confrontation between them. I found that to be a bit unfulfilling, as did Montalban, as did Meyer, as did Harve Bennett. With that in mind, I recall Harve, Nick and me locking ourselves into Harve's office and trying to come up with a great hand-to-hand fight to the death between Khan and Kirk.

Finally, with a lot of broad gesturing, demonstrations and abuse to Harve's office furniture, we came up with the idea that maybe Khan would come into this battle stacking the odds in his favor with a long metallic whip. With each crack, this whip would rip into Kirk's flesh while undergoing any number of horrifying telepathic metamorphoses: it would assume the form of an eagle's claw, a lion's head, a snake and so on. Kirk would be cornered. Khan would torture him. Kirk would then scramble and fight dirty, destroying Khan's whip and bringing the battle down to the level of vicious hand-to-hand combat.

As scripted, it would have been a glorious twist upon the standard screen fight between villain and hero, but we ultimately didn't have the money to shoot it. After the financial debacle of the first *Star Trek* film, there was just no way this film was going to be allowed to bust its eleven-million-dollar budget, and this wonderful but ultimately nonessential fight got yanked from the script at the eleventh hour. I'm still a bit disappointed about that.

I made out a little better in regard to Spock's death. Several days later, as Harve Bennett and I talked through the final script in his office, we'd made it as far as Spock's death when Harve asked me, "How do you see Spock dying?" and I thought about it for a minute, looked over some of the preliminary set sketches, noticed the glass doors, and was suddenly struck with the notion that Spock and Kirk should say their final good-byes while separated by this invisible glass barrier. Unable to save Spock, unable to even embrace or comfort his old friend, the glass doors allowed Kirk's overwhelming grief and frustration to grow even stronger, Spock's suffering a bit more upsetting, a bit more poignant. The glass would also act as a sort of physical representation of Spock's lifelong self-imposed emotional distance.

I acted out the scene in Harve's office, playing both Kirk and Spock, while running through some rough, ad-libbed dialogue that ultimately made it into the film. When I had finished, I looked up from the carpet, asking, "Well, whattya think?" Harve's eyebrows nearly hit his hairline. "That's great!" he laughed, and after we'd talked it through a couple more times, he kicked me out of his office and immediately set about putting the wheels into motion that would carry my spur-of-the-moment idea onto celluloid. With that, having thrown my two cents into the pot, I went home feeling like a million bucks. However, down the hall right now in Nick Meyer's office, things weren't nearly that pleasant.

Nick's finished script, which was practically still hot out of the Xerox machine, was about to set off what would become the first in a series of skirmishes between Nick Meyer and Paramount. This time, it was over the film's title. Nick tells his story:

My original title for *Star Trek II* was *Star Trek II: The Undiscovered Country*. This was a reference that came from Hamlet's "To be, or not to be" speech, and it tied in nicely with the fact that Spock dies.

But then I come into my office one day, and my assistant says to me, very timidly, "You know, I think they changed the title of the movie." I said "What?!" She kind of cringed and said, "Yeah, I heard it through the office grapevine that Frank Mancuso," who was then working out of New York as Paramount's head of marketing, "has changed the title to *Star Trek II: The Vengeance of Khan*." I said again, "What?!" I said, "That can't be!" And she said, "It's done already." So I said, "But he hasn't even seen the movie!!" So then, even though I didn't know the man, I called New York and I said, "I'd like to speak to Mr. Mancuso." They put me through.

I said, "Mr. Mancuso, this is Mr. Meyer, I am the writer/director of *Star Trek II: The Undiscovered Country*." He said, "Oh yes, Mr. Meyer, how are you?" I said, "Is it true that you've changed the title of my movie?" He says, "Yes, I have, it's going to be called *The Vengeance of Khan*." And I said, "But you haven't seen the movie! I know you haven't seen the movie because I haven't even shot it yet!"

He said, "I know that." I said, "Do you think that it was polite to do this without even consulting with me as the writer and director of the movie?" I should explain, I guess, that this was one of my earliest confrontations with the studio, and I hadn't yet learned that everybody puts their pants on one leg at a time, so I was being overly polite.

Now Frank Mancuso is also a very courteous man, so this was turning into one of the most well-mannered arguments in the history of the film industry. And then, after listening to my side of things, Mancuso said, with infinite patience,

"Mr. Meyer, I must tell you that I'm only doing what's best for the movie." So I protested that remark on my best behavior, and he countered me in very courteous terms and we really must've just sounded like crazy people.

And finally, I just said, "I think this new title is wholly inappropriate and I know for a fact that right now George Lucas is making a sequel to *Star Wars* called *The Revenge of the Jedi*. Do you honestly think he's going to let you use *The Vengeance of Khan*? I don't THINK so."

And Mancuso paused for a second, and then said, "Oh, I believe he will. That shouldn't present any problem." One week later I learned that we'd backed away from *The Vengeance of Khan* and we were now going to be known as *Star Trek II: The Wrath of Khan*.

Later on, I remember being called into a sort of marketing strategy meeting in Barry Diller's office, where in a rage he said, "Nobody knows what the word 'Wrath' is! How the HELL did we wind up with this ridiculous, stupid title!! The Wrath, The Wrath, The Wrath." He just kept saying, "*The Wrath of Khan*?" and looking at me as though I were in some way responsible for this. I mean, I wasn't too happy with *The Wrath of Khan* either, but I didn't make a big deal of it, because my theory of film is that nobody cares what the name of the movie is, nobody cares what the movie's about, and nobody cares who's in the movie, they only care about one thing, "Is the movie good?"

To make a long story short, despite the fact that Lucas's *Revenge of the Jedi* was eventually renamed *Return of the Jedi* and despite Barry Diller's objections, *Star Trek II* would now remain *The Wrath of Khan*. At any rate, now that the film had a title, Bennett, Meyer and crew could attend to the finer details, like shooting, lighting, acting, editing, special effects, scoring and distribution. Meyer, in particular, could finally stop obsessing over his script and start obsessing about the look of his new film:

Conceptually, the one really important thing about *Star Trek II* was a notion that came to me very early in the process. I'd come to the conclusion that this would be the adventures of Captain Horatio Hornblower, in outer space. And when I told you about that, you got very excited as well, and said, "Oh yeah, Gene Roddenberry always said that, too." That made me feel even better about the idea, and I decided that since the chances of my getting to make a real Captain Hornblower movie were remote, this was gonna be it.

So, starting from that idea, I kept the characters as they were, but I redesigned everything in the movie that I could get my hands on, beginning with the costumes, to make things more nautical. In my mind, the *Enterprise* was going to be some combination of the submarine from *Run Silent, Run Deep* and one of those eighteenth-century galleons with cannons blasting away. If you look at *II* you can see a lot of the obvious comparisons. We had crewmen running out the guns, we had torpedoes, and all of that gave the film a style which I loved, but which frequently flew in the face of a lot of Roddenberry dicta.

This *Star Trek* was a lot more militaristic than Gene's. He was a utopian, he believed in the perfectibility of man. I don't. That always put me at odds with Gene, but as far as I was concerned, except for *Star Trek: The Motion Picture*, Gene was never really involved in the movies. You'd just go in and meet with him and then get back to work. In fact, on *Star Trek II*, I barely met him. He was more involved on *VI*.

I think the reason for that was that at the time we were shooting *II*, Gene's clout was sort of at low ebb. There was no *Star Trek: The Next Generation* or *Deep Space Nine* or *Voyager* and there seemed to be a feeling among the higher-ups that *Star Trek: The Motion Picture* was his creation and that he was responsible for taking it up a wrong path someplace. So what I had, rightly or wrongly, was a very clear vision of what I wanted, and the freedom to make it happen. So I made Captain Hornblower in outer space, an adventure movie that was about friendship, old age and death. It was very clear to me.

On November 11, 1981, studio lights were fired up for the first time, cameras rolled, Nick Meyer took up his usual position standing upon a ladder while sucking down the first of a thousand foul-smelling cigars, and *Star Trek II: The Wrath of Khan* officially began production. However, I wasn't there, nor was Leonard, De, George, Walter, Nichelle or Jimmy. We wouldn't have to show up for about ten more days. Instead, the first days of shooting were almost entirely devoted to scenes involving Khan and his crew aboard their hijacked ship, the U.S.S. *Reliant*.

From the start, production moved quickly, assuredly

and extremely cost-effectively. With a mere eleven million bucks to spread over the production of an entire feature-length film, pennies got pinched harder than ever before. In fact, so knotted were the purse strings that the U.S.S. *Reliant* didn't even exist. Instead, prop guys merely rearranged the furniture on the bridge of the *Enterprise*, made a couple of additional cosmetic changes, and started shooting. It was cheap, it looked great, and the switch has always gone unnoticed by even the most hard-core *Trek* fans, until now. Harve Bennett confesses, "That was a lesson I brought in from television, and a quick way to save a lot of money. After forty-five blanking million dollars, that made the studio very happy."

Still, despite our puny budget, you couldn't help but feel really good about this film. Everyone loved the script, Nick Meyer was full of energy and good ideas, and before long a genuine feeling of enthusiasm spread over everyone involved in the film. The result was a pleasant, relaxed working atmosphere that made acting in this film one of the best working experiences I can recall. Nick Meyer shares similar feelings.

I started feeling good about the film shortly after you had said, "This is a disaster." I went back to work, gave you a revised script, you read it again, and I guess you had gotten up out of a different side of bed that morning or something because suddenly you were very excited. You suddenly "got it" and when I came home, there was this message on my machine from you saying, "You're a genius, I don't know how you did this and blah, blah, blah, blah, blah," and I took that tape, and said I'm never getting rid of this.

So after a shaky start, you and I got along almost immediately, and eventually, as we started production, the other actors made me feel welcome, too. At the same time, Harve trusted me, and we got along like a house on fire, so I was basically just allowed to do the job and do the work and everybody was very helpful. The crew was great, the actors were helpful and supportive, and everybody liked the script. We'd make little changes here and there, you know, "My character wouldn't say this line . . . " kinda stuff, but all over the set you could tell that the people involved with this film really wanted to do it, really wanted to be there.

So my attitude was, "This is gonna be fun." I was very bowed up. And there were a few moments where I goofed, one of which came when Leonard, who's a real tough guy, looked at Spock's cabin for the first time and said, "This looks like a Sparklett's water truck." He was right, and he was also very disappointed and bent out of shape. but we got past it, and for the most part things on that shoot were terrific.

Still, I'm not sure if I was aware of how good a time I was having while we actually made the movie. Making a film requires a hundred percent of your attention on any given decision, whether it's an actor, a line of dialogue, a prop, even a studio executive on the telephone. It is a mosaic of intensity that prevents you from standing back and saying, I'm having a good time, I'm having a bad time, my confidence is here. There's not a lot of time for introspection. About the best you can hope for is that if things are going really well, when you finally get home at night and hit the hay, you're so tired that you don't lie awake staring at the ceiling and wondering, *How's this going*?

Ricardo Montalban, who stood at center stage during those first days of production, wasn't quite that confident, at least not at first:

I came onto the set scared to death, feeling almost out of place in surroundings that were unfamiliar, and quite different from those I'd grown so comfortable with on *Fantasy Island*. But all of that began to fade as I started getting into Khan's full makeup and hair and costumes for the first time. It's amazing how that helps you—I could now look at myself in the mirror and confidently say, I'm not Roarke, not at all. I am Khan.

Later, when I got to the set, which struck me as rather impressive, I could hear laughter, and when I turned around to see what was so funny, I watched a little toy robot, maybe three feet tall, rolling onto the set on four tiny wheels, guided by a remote control. And as it got closer to me, I recognized the robot's face as Tattoo. These guys had made this thing for me, and they had put Tattoo's face on one side of the thing, and Mr. Roarke's on the other. And I looked at that, laughed out loud, and I said, "I'm home."

Turns out that Nick Meyer had put them up to it, and throughout the filming, I have to say that he was absolutely wonderful. Some of the direction that he gave me was very insightful. He's one of the best directors I have ever worked with.

I felt especially lucky to have him on the set, because due to the fact that we shot my scenes

ABOVE AND BELOW: MONTALBAN MEETS ROBO-TATTOO AND THE GUY BEHIND THE GAG

aboard the *Reliant* very early in the production, a week or so before the rest of you had even begun your scenes, I had to deliver my lines to Kirk blind. We were supposed to be having a heated dialogue back and forth across our ships' viewscreens, but as we started shooting, there was nothing to look at except the stage. So while Khan's threatening Kirk, I'm just looking at the camera and the crew guys.

So I tried to visualize you talking to me, but with the script girl reading Kirk's lines to me, as talented as she might be, it wasn't easy. Still, I have never skirted challenges. And I told myself, "That's Bill Shatner's voice. That's Captain Kirk's voice." You know what I mean? As an actor, Captain Kirk would *always* be Captain Kirk, no matter the voice.

While Montalban was alone on the set saying things like, "I will kill you, Ki-i-i-irk," Kirk was off on a horse someplace enjoying his last few days off before he had to start shooting. Several weeks later, when the bridge of the *Reliant* had once again been redressed and transformed back into the more familiar confines of the U.S.S. *Enterprise*, I was able to afford myself the luxury of watching Ricardo's performance, gearing my own toward the great stuff he'd given me to work with. Once again, though it's virtually impossible to gauge whether or not a film is going to be any good while you're still shooting it, this time I really felt like we were onto something special.

Somehow, with the help of a fast-paced, action-packed story and a terrific screenplay, our characters seemed alive again, perhaps more vibrant than ever before. Our exchanges seemed more genuine, less formal, less preachy, and humor for the first time in a long time was given its due as one of the truly important elements of the best of *Star Trek*. In short, we were having a lot of fun, and I swear you can see that in the final product. Leonard, however, although he was enjoying this experience at least as much as the rest of us, had backed himself into a corner. He explains:

We had a great time making this movie. It was theatrical. It was fun. It had a nice little edge to it. It had Montalban. I felt that the cohesion of the characters was working again, and that we really knew who we were again. I was having such a good time that when we were getting ready to start shooting Spock's death scene, I thought, *I may have made a big mistake*. I was really experiencing a great feeling of loss.

I think the worst of it began as we were shooting Spock's reaction to Kirk's line "Scotty, you've got three minutes to get us out of here or we're all dead." Knowing what was coming, I got really emotional, very uptight, even scared of having to shoot this death scene. I started looking for any way out, any excuse to start an argument. I really just wanted to leave, to go home and hide. I had no idea that this thing would ever cook again, but here it was, going on all four burners, and I had backed Spock right out of the franchise.

When it came time to shoot Spock's death scene, emotions were running high all over the set. Naturally Leonard was having a hard time, as was I, in preparing for this incredibly emotional final farewell, but most of the crew were equally misty, running around the set,

ABOVE AND OPPOSITE: Kʜᴀɴ—ᴀʟʟ
ɢᴏʀᴇᴅ ᴜᴘ ᴡɪᴛʜ ɴᴏ ᴘʟᴀᴄᴇ ᴛᴏ ɢᴏ

Kleenex in hand, sniffling and wiping their eyes as they'd rig lights or load film, whatever. It was unbelievable. Never before and never since have I seen anything that could compare. Still, despite the difficulty of the scene, we were all a bit exhilarated through our tears by this concrete proof as to the power of this film, and especially of this scene. The following afternoon, when the dailies of Spock's death were screened for the first time, the same thing happened all over again.

Shown out of order, one shot at a time, and without music, the scene still packed enough of an emotional wallop to reduce an entire screening room full of cast, crew, creatives and executives into a quivering mass of weepy-eyed, runny-nosed Jell-O. Up in the booth, even our projectionist, a hulking, thick-biceped, thick-necked monster, got so moved by the scene that we had to pause momentarily while he removed, cleaned and reinserted his contact lenses. His tears had blurred his vision so badly that he couldn't properly handle the film.

In the weeks ahead, with just a short break for the Christmas and New Year's holidays, production continued forward rather smoothly. However, Nick Meyer had suddenly found himself faced with an extremely unpleasant holiday surprise. He explains:

As you know, this was only the second film I'd ever directed, so it never occurred to me to ask when the movie was supposed to be released. And the studio procrastinated with the start date for shooting, as they usually do, forever, forever, forever procrastinating, and they had already booked this film into umpteen hundred theaters for the twelfth of June, 1982. We didn't even start shooting until halfway into November, and I think we shot for like twelve weeks, so when I finally did the math, I said, "This is insane, there's no time to edit this movie!"

When I made *Time After Time*, I had about five

months to edit the film. On *Star Wars*, George Lucas took about a year. *I* would have had a month. At that point, they'd have had just about enough time to put in the special effects, put in the music, make their hundreds of prints and get them to the multiplexes on schedule.

So, to buy myself a little more time, and the way we finally got the movie made, was for me to spend the next seven weeks never seeing the sun. I would just rise before dawn, work all morning shooting on the set, eat lunch in the screening room while I watched the previous day's dailies, then go back to the set all afternoon, then into an editing room where I'd work until ten or eleven P.M. It got to the point where I really thought I was gonna collapse just getting it done. I had no time to experiment, no time to play with the film, and ever since then, the first question I ask when I'm directing a picture is, "Have you booked this film into theaters yet?"

Despite the grueling pace, Nick finished his first rough cut just about on schedule. Without special effects, without music, and lacking polish, he viewed the film for the first time alone in a screening room with Michael Eisner and Jeffrey Katzenberg. Nick remembers:

They really liked this film, and they were quite excited. The only change they requested was to ask for one set of reshoots, back on the Genesis planet, which had to do with clarifying the detail of whether Kirk knew that he had a son or never knew that he had a son. So we went back into the Genesis cave, and while Kirk's talking with Carol

Marcus, we added his line about "I did what you wanted . . . I stayed away . . . Why didn't you tell him?" and her reply was something like "How can you ask me that question? Were we together? Were we going to be? You had your world and I had mine. I wanted him in mine . . . not chasing through the universe with his father."

We made that change in a half-day shoot, and that was it. The visual effects started coming in from ILM, looking great, and Nick even managed to save a few bucks by cannibalizing and reusing a few effects shots from the first film. At the same time, he'd also won a battle to upgrade our musical score from synthesizer to full-blown orchestra, and the results were amazing. James Horner's score, grand, vaguely nautical and reminiscent of the classic pirate films of the forties and fifties, beautifully supported the look and feel of the new film in a way that no synthesizer ever could. Finally, with the film approaching its "final" status (although Spock's death was indeed still a death), Nick invited Eisner, Katzenberg and Barry Diller along with Harve Bennett into an executive screening room for a look at his newly polished film. It was a can of worms that he'd soon regret opening. Nick recalls:

Very late in the business, maybe nine weeks before the picture was due to open, Barry Diller saw the movie for the first time. And when it was over, he said, "Wait a minute, I didn't know this movie was about the death of Spock. You can't kill Spock!!" And I said, "What? You had the script, it's a multimillion-dollar movie, you must have known." Oh, he was real bent out of shape.

And I said, "Look, it's not about whether or not you kill Spock, it's about whether you kill him well. If this death is perceived as organic and coming out of the movie, the substance and plot and the theme of things, then it'll be fine. If it's perceived as just the dumb enactment of some agent's clause in a contract, they'll throw things at the screen and they'll be right." And Diller looked at me unhappily and he said, "Okay, all right. Now let's talk about this father and son." He said, "That scene at the end of the film where Kirk and David embrace has got to be cut out of the movie." He says, "It stinks!"

I said, "Why does it stink?!" And he says, "Because this kid should be enraged with his father. If it were my father I would go into his cabin and say where the fuck were you all my

JUST A LITTLE FATHER-SON CHAT

life?!" And again, he says, "It stinks!" I said, "In your opinion!" At that point, I noticed that the other people in the room were all sort of looking at the ceiling, trying not to get in the middle of this thing.

So now I'm thinking that I'm about to heave because this is the guy in charge, you know? And he says, "Well, look. I can say it to you nicely or I can say it to you not nicely, but the scene stinks and it's coming out!" And I looked at the floor and then back at him and I said, "Everybody likes this movie. You asked me for a reshoot, I did the reshoot. You've given me editing notes and I've followed those notes. I've now done all the reshooting and all the recutting I'm going to do. If you want to take the movie out of my hands and do *more* reshooting and do more recutting you can, but you'll do it without me. And *IF* you do it without me, I'll take out full-page ads in the trade papers and tell everybody what you've done. I'll picket the movie when it opens in Westwood and if that's the kind of atmosphere you'd like to advertise for directors who might come onto this lot and work for you, that's your business." And then Diller stared at me and said, "Well, if you feel that strongly about it, it's your fucking movie!" and he walked out. We kept the father/son embrace intact and that is how the movie got into the theaters.

But it was strange, you know? All of a sudden in that screening room all of my support sort of faded away until it was just me and Barry Diller. After it was all over, I said to Harve, "Don't let them tell you things like that. You're the boss-man."

Somewhere, someone once said, "Where ignorance is bliss, 'tis folly to be wise." And I think they were talking about me. I was very, very ignorant. I had the *courage* of ignorance, and that's what empowered me to stand up and fight and say, "Wait a minute, this is *our* movie. Let's make it the way we want!" And in defense of Harve, and in the words of Harve, he said to me, "Listen, I agree with what you're saying but you have to understand one thing, you may be the squadron leader, but I'm the wing commander, and when you've gone on to your next film, I'll still be here. I'll have to find a way to live with these people. I have an overall contract with Paramount Pictures." I understand now what he was saying.

Nine days after this private screening, *Star Trek II: The Wrath of Khan* was seen by the public for the very first time. The setting was a small theater on the Paramount lot, and the audience was made up entirely of people who'd been invited in from the local supermarket. It was terribly exciting. There were real people here. We were no longer just dealing with suits sitting in packs of three or four, or alone watching dailies in a large, empty projection room. In short, it was time to put up or shut up. But now, with my bowels a bit unsteady, I watched as this room filled to capacity, with strangers. At that point, a small round man in small round glasses went to the front of the room and called for attention. "Ladies and gentlemen," he began, "you have been asked here this evening to view the new *Star Trek* film." That's all they needed to hear. Cheering and clapping for what seemed like an eternity, this crowd became absolutely insane with delight. Sneaking into the back row as the lights dimmed, I knew that this was one screening I was going to enjoy. Harve Bennett continues:

I'm now absolutely thrilled, and I'm thinking, "Oh boy, we've got friendlies here." A shiver of anticipation ran down my back, and it was a real moment of connection for me—with all of you who had gone before. You know, Harve Bennett now had his own place in the *Star Trek* tradition of fifteen or sixteen years. I was on the team. I was officially part of the team. I was part of *Star Trek*. Ta-da! It was a very powerful feeling.

As the opening credits started running, I noted with interest that while there was a lot of applause for the regular names, I didn't get any. But that was appropriate because they didn't quite know who I was yet. I was still the newcomer in town, so they said, "Uh-huh . . . we'll see." But as the picture played out, it became an amazing experience.

The audience was responding just as I had hoped. It was very gratifying. You know, you start with the blank page and through every step of the way, at every moment, you're making decisions, thousands of decisions. And now, for the first time, the fruits of those decisions are being tested by a live audience, and they really seemed to like it. I would say that 90 to 95 percent of all the choices we made were being saluted by these people. They were laughing at jokes that had long since become stale in the cutting room to me. They were deeply touched and moved where we'd hoped, and at the top of the film, where we dealt with their fears about the death of Spock by apparently killing him off in the first two minutes, they were shocked. Spock is dead! And then, when they realized it was just a simulation, just a trick, a palpable wave of relief came over this audience. This diversion allowed them to say, "I'm glad that's over, now let's see the picture." What it restored to the end of the film was that wonderful shock when they realized Spock really had been overcome in the chamber. And that moment and their response to it were indelible. They were weeping openly, you couldn't hear the soundtrack for the weeping.

Nick Meyer was also in the theater:

So now we get to the point in this movie where the audience is suddenly reminded of something that they have been led to forget. By killing Spock off in the simulator at the beginning of the movie, we kind of got the whole issue of his death off everybody's mind, and we turned it into a joke, when Kirk's first words to Spock are, "Aren't you dead?"

Later, when we got to the shot where Kirk is in the command chair and Bones comes on the intercom and says, "You better get down here," I said to myself, "If they're gonna throw things at the screen, this is the moment." But of course that didn't happen. People wept, they wept at the good-bye scene between these men, and the movie went through the roof that night. In fact, as I was walking out, I bumped into Barry Diller, who'd been at the screening, too, and he sees me, he looks at me, and he says, "I know what I'm supposed to say, but I still don't think it works." At that point I replied, "It doesn't matter what you think. It doesn't matter what I think. The only thing that means anything is what *they* think."

Still, despite the fact that the film had gone over so well, and perhaps even *because* it had done so, there would ultimately be one more round of creative discussions, arguments, decisions and revisions. Harve Bennett, who was in the eye of the hurricane, explains:

At that first screening, the film played very well, but at the end of the picture, with Spock dead, DEAD dead, it really affected the crowd. You could practically hear the heavy, funereal silence. That bothered me. It bothered me a lot, bothered the suits, too. And the reason it bothered me was partially my commercial sense, partially my simple dedication to the *Star Trek* franchise. I didn't want to be the guy who dropped a lead weight on it all, and eliminated all hope for a *Star Trek III*. And also, curiously enough, our friend Leonard had a pretty joyful experience making that movie. I was killing someone who may have originally been very happy to be killed off, but who now might want to come back and do another one.

Later, we had a long conference with Mike Eisner, Gary Nardino, who was the head of Paramount's television division, Jeff Katzenberg, Nick, me, and maybe a half-dozen other people. Basically, we all just got together and said, "What do we do about this ending?" Nick, the purist, resisted to the end that we should do a, quote, "contrived happy ending." But I had learned from watching seventy-nine episodes. I said, "I think we're missing something and what we're missing is, Spock has said repeatedly, 'There are always possibilities.'" That's a coda for him. And I think if we leave the audience with that thought—and it's a valid thought—that they will not walk out of the theater feeling it's over. If nothing else, it's a spiritual ending. You know, those who believe in heaven will at least accept it as a religious ending. He may be happier someplace else. And those who do not and those who want to believe he's coming back have something to hang on to.

What emerged from that meeting was an idea that grew out of one of Michael Eisner's insights. "What we don't have here is resurrection," he said, when "we have the death scene, we have Good Friday, but we don't have Easter morning. We need the garden of Gethsemane." From that starting point, it was ultimately decided that perhaps we should find that Spock's coffin, jettisoned from the Enterprise, has somehow managed to come to rest in the middle of the intergalactic miracle that is the Genesis planet. Unanimously embraced by Harve and the suits, the idea was nonetheless vehemently opposed by Nick Meyer. In fact, when I asked him how that scene got into the film, he told me:

Over my dead body is how it went in. Because I tried everything to stop it. It was done without me and put in without me. I thought it was wrong. They said, "Oh, we can't just kill off a main character, audiences won't go for that." So I said, "You're absolutely wrong. Beginning with Romeo and Juliet, they *do* go for it, all that matters is whether or not you do it well. And with Spock, I think we've done it well." So the open ending was an upstairs decision and I don't know why they made it. All I know is that the original movie played great. While I was sitting there in that first public screening, it played great. I remember all that stuff. And in retrospect, while I think their decision worked well in setting up the movies that followed, in terms of *Star Trek II: The Wrath of Khan*, I don't think it made a difference.

Harve Bennett would disagree, and as producer of the film, he had the final say. With that in mind, and despite Nick's objections, Harve and a production crew from ILM immediately got to work bringing Spock's coffin to the Genesis planet. Harve explains:

We began three days of shooting in which Nicholas did not wish to participate, but later, when he saw what we'd done, he very fairly said, "This is good." These three days of shooting were at Golden Gate Park in San Francisco where we had contrived to see the casket after it had landed upon the newly reformed Genesis planet. In those frenzied days we also shot a simple insert of Spock's hand mind-melding with Bones back on the Enterprise, and we got Leonard to do a voice-over which said, "Remember." Because already the foundation for the next movie was forming in my head—we had to go back and get him, and the means to do that were self-evident within the format of the entire *Star Trek* legend. Spock had mind-melded with Bones, and all we had to do was say he put his soul on someone else's terms and it was retrievable. And Lord knows, intuition or blind luck had led us to the Genesis planet, a place which we said was reformed, newly reborn. The whole concept of that planet lent itself to the fact that anything could happen there.

I asked Leonard for *his* take on Spock's scripted reprieve:

Certainly I was having mixed feelings about Spock's dying, especially in the face of our recent reinvigoration, but the idea behind "Remember" was Harve's. He came to me and said, "Leonard, let's talk about something. What can you do or say in this scene that will suggest that there's some remnant of Spock, some kind of implant that still retains the most basic being of the character?" And we discussed it, came up with the "Remember" business, but there was never any discussion about actually reviving the character. I mean, there were a lot of ways Harve could've used that. There could have been some way of reincarnating Spock's brain or something.

So he didn't go so far as to invite me back. He was really just looking for a vague handle, one that foreshadows that something might happen in the future. I knew that it created an opportunity to come back, but at the same time, it opened up the gates for Harve and the studio to do whatever they wanted. And I went along for the ride because I was having a good time on this film.

While all that was being put together, we also did one additional reshoot, this time back aboard the *Enterprise*, revising the film's final scene, in which Kirk, Bones and Carol Marcus gaze upon the rapidly evolving Genesis planet. Harve had now revised Kirk's original monologue, which spoke about Spock's great sacrifice, and turned it into a much more uplifting internal voice-over. "All is well," says Kirk, "and yet I can't help wondering about the friend I've left behind. 'There are always possibilities,' Spock said, and if Genesis is indeed life from death, I must return to this place again." Bones then continues foreshadowing Spock's resurrection with the line, "You know, he's really not dead, as long as we remember him." Those few simple lines gave the end of the picture an entirely different feeling, one that allowed audiences to begin pondering what might happen in the future. From there, the scene continued as scripted, through Kirk's reciting of the last line of A *Tale of Two Cities* and into a final pan through space.

As originally scripted, the end credits would have rolled shortly thereafter. However, in an effort to provide even more hope for Spock's return, we now moved down upon the surface of the Genesis planet, dollying through its lush greenery and ultimately discovering that Spock's sarcophagus hasn't disintegrated in space, hasn't been destroyed in a crash landing, but has instead touched down upon the surface of this extraordinary planet quite safely. Spock's "possibilities" were rapidly becoming more numerous.

By now, the test audience had gone from mourning Spock's death, to hoping he might return, to basically *expecting* same. Yanking the final nail from Spock's coffin, it is Leonard who provides the film's closing voice-over narration of "Space, the final frontier . . . " Spock's

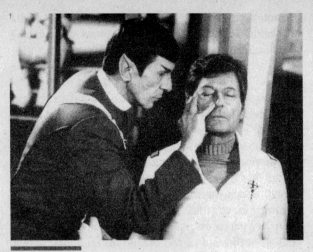

"REMEMBER."

voice, sepulchral and slightly filtered, allows Spock to seal the film with his spiritual stamp. In the minds of the audience, he's basically saying, "Come get me."

With these changes in place, Harve Bennett held a final preview of the film, once again at the Paramount studio theater. He recalls:

The film was now completed, exactly as it was released. We played it for this audience, and it was maybe one of the most joyful events of my life. Just as before, they loved the first 90 percent of the picture, but now, when we got to Spock's death, there was at first weeping, but as things progressed and they saw Spock's coffin on the surface of the Genesis planet, the weeping became almost joyful. And then, as the credits rolled, there was raucous applause, which had not been there before. These people stood and they cheered because we had given them back their hope.

After the film, I walked out into the alley and Mike Eisner was there with his children. He was standing there waiting for his car, and while I love Mike and it was fun working for him, he can sometimes get fixated on minor details. He'd had a problem with a certain matte shot inside the subterranean area of the Genesis planet—which I'd be the first to say was never right—and he ultimately got so fixated on that that when I asked him, "What'd ya think?" he just said, "That matte shot is terrible, you've got to fix that thing or it will ruin the picture."

So, having walked out into the alley that night with the applause of the crowd still echoing in my ears, I got a little crazy. It was the only time in my life I've ever had that kind of crazy chutzpah, you know, with a guy I'm working for. I'm usually very respectful, but like Rumpelstiltskin, I stomped my foot into the pavement of that cobblestone street outside the theater and I said, "Goddamnit, what about the *picture*!?"

"Oh," he said, "the picture's great!"

Eisner was right, and his opinion was ultimately shared by critics and moviegoers all over the planet. *Star Trek*, really for the first time since the second season of our prime time run, was back on track. We'd finally found the creative footing that had previously proven so elusive, and additionally, the chemistry and camaraderie between our characters were back in abundance. In the end, Khan was dead, Spock was iffy, *The Wrath of Khan* opened with the biggest weekend gross in the history of the movies up to that time, further sequels were assured, and we all lived happily ever after. There are, however, a couple of terrific footnotes that I've got to add.

The first takes place just after *Star Trek II*'s opening weekend, when Nick Meyer disguises his voice and changes the outgoing message on his answering machine. It ran as follows: "Hello, this is Michael Eisner. In order to make up for the rather shabby way that Paramount Pictures treated Nick Meyer throughout the production of *Star Trek II: The Wrath of Khan*, I'm gonna be answering Nick's phone from now on. So please leave your name, live long and prosper."

The one thing that had never occurred to Nick was that Michael Eisner might actually phone. "He had never called me in my whole life," explains Meyer, "why would I think he'd call me now? Because in its first week, *Star Trek II* had made umpteen millions of dollars, and experienced the biggest opening weekend in the history of the movies. When that happens, these guys don't have their secretaries place the call." So now Nick comes home, sees the red light blinking, and hits his PLAY MESSAGES button. At that point he hears a beep, then a long pause, then Michael Eisner's voice saying, "Nick, this is Mike . . . uh . . . I think this is funny, but Frank Mancuso didn't." Meyer recalls that his first thought was, "Oh, shit! You've done it again, Meyer. You've shot yourself in the foot, maybe you should just go in the shower and hang yourself right now."

While Nick was contemplating suicide, Harve Bennett was receiving a phone call that was equally surprising, though much more pleasant. Harve recalls:

Sylvia, my secretary, was a wonderful lady. She was a cranky, wonderful person and one day she grumbled in to me on the intercom and said, "There's some lunatic named Charlie calling you from his car phone. You know any Charlies with a car phone?" I said, "Charlie on a car phone? . . . No, I don't think so." She said, "Want me to get rid of him?" I said, "No, put him on, let's see who it is." So I pick up the phone, I say, "Hello?" and I hear a man with an Austrian accent say, "Harve, this is Charlie!" I say, "Oh, Mr. Bluhdorn!" Sylvia turns white.

I said, "Where are you, Charlie?" He says, "I'm in my airplane. I'm somewhere over the Dominican Republic. I just saw *Star Trek II*. Congratulations! It's great! It's gonna be a big hit! And listen, kid, we're gonna make a lotta movies together. Bye!"

I hung up the phone thinking, "I've done it, I made a movie for P. T. Barnum and P. T. Barnum says, 'We're gonna be in the movie business together.'" That high carried me through three more films, all the way to 1990.

As the whole world knows, *Star Trek II: The Wrath of Khan* was hugely successful, both creatively and at the box office. The sour taste of the failed second series and the embarrassment of *Star Trek: The Motion Picture* were put to bed and forgotten once and for all. In their place, *Star Trek* was now seen as a solid and highly profitable creative franchise. In fact, so enthusiastic were Paramount's execs that even before *Khan* had finished out its theatrical release, the wheels had already been set into motion for a sequel that would find the crew of the *Enterprise* stretched to the limit while facing a whole new set of challenges.

Leonard Nimoy would do likewise.

STAR TREK III:
THE PERCH FOR SPOCK

n October 1982, while Khan Noonian Singh continued blowing up twice nightly at drive-ins and second-run movie theaters all across America, Paramount made it official. *Star Trek III* was a go. As the days wore on, it also became clear that the studio, hoping to strike while the iron might still be at least lukewarm, was looking to get this new film shot, edited and into theaters as quickly and painlessly as possible. With that in mind, the wheels began turning rather rapidly.

By week's end, Harve Bennett had already begun getting exploratory phone calls asking if he might be interested in producing the new film. He jumped at the chance. At the same time, back in Laurel Canyon, Nick Meyer was getting similar calls, asking if he'd consider returning to the director's chair. Still a bit ambivalent about the whole idea of bringing Spock back from the dead, Nick passed. Shortly thereafter, Leonard, De, Nichelle, George, Walter, Jimmy and I all found ourselves being courted once more by the Paramount suits, in the hope that we'd fall into place quickly, with a minimum of fuss and delay. With all of us still reveling in Khan's afterglow, that came to pass . . . almost.

With the exception of Leonard Nimoy, we crew members of the Starship Enterprise practically danced back onto the bridge. Leonard, on the other hand, ultimately decided to boldly go where no Star Trek actor had gone before, and his story, his education and his ultimate success make up the real story behind this film. Leonard begins:

When I saw II for the first time, it was a very emotional experience. The picture was fun and fast-paced, and I was really moved by the death scene, and what was happening there between Kirk and Spock. I thought it worked extremely well, and when I saw that black tube laying there on the Genesis planet, I thought, Wow, this could go anyplace.

And then, when the film came out and did so well, I expected that I'd probably be getting a call in regard to a third film, but at the same time, they really could have gone off in any number of new directions. Some young kid could come popping out of that tube saying, "Hi guys. It's me, Spock! I'm back, only now I'm thirteen years old," so while I was assuming they'd call, I also knew it wasn't a lock.

Anyway, not too long after the release of II, I did get the call about III. Gary Nardino had already been penciled in as the film's executive producer and he requested that my agent and I come down to his office and talk about my participation in the new film. And one of the things that has always concerned me, and for that matter *every* member of the Star Trek cast, is the ability to springboard out of these *Star Trek* projects and into other non-*Trek*-related roles.

So I came in to the lot with the idea in my head that "Okay, I'll do your *Star Trek* picture, but what are you going to do for me in return?" It wasn't a matter of money, it was more a matter of my feeling like "Here I go again" and hoping that I might be able to find some additional pay-or-play project to get involved with, as I had on *II* with *A Woman Called Golda*. So my agent and I met at Gary's office, both of us baffled about what we might ask for, and as we sat in his outer office, I happened to pick up a glowing review of *Star Trek II*, and as I sat there reading, a thought suddenly occurred to me: *Why not empower yourself for the first time? Why not ask to direct this feature? You can do it.* It was an entirely spur-of-the-moment idea.

So I told Nardino what I had in mind, that I'd like to direct the next picture, and he smiled and said, "Oh, I think that's terrific, I've been thinking about that myself! You'd be great!" and we left. A few days later, Gary calls me and asks if I'll come in again, this time to meet with Michael Eisner. I said, "Sure." So now I come back in to the studio, I go to Gary's office, we say our hellos, and then we start walking together down the hall toward Eisner's. This turned out to be an interesting event, and it taught me a lot about how a skilled operator like Nardino maneuvers in these situations.

As we're walking, side by side, it occurs to me to ask Nardino, "Does Michael know what I have in mind?" Nardino turns toward me without breaking stride and says, "Absolutely not. He has

ABOVE: INSIDE *STAR TREK II*'S GENESIS CAVE
BELOW: ON LOCATION IN YOSEMITE DURING THE
PRODUCTION OF *STAR TREK V: THE FINAL FRONTIER*

ABOVE AND RIGHT: THE REALITY AND THE ILLUSION OF KIRK'S "FINAL FRONTIER," ROCK CLIMBING

BELOW: GRAPPLING WITH A PARTICULARLY COLOR-
FUL CELLMATE IN *STAR TREK VI*

ABOVE: FROM *STAR TREK VI*: IN SPACE, NO ONE CAN
HEAR YOU BLEED

ABOVE: FROM *STAR TREK V*: RE-CREATING KIRK'S FALL FROM A MOUNTAIN AMID THE AIR-CONDITIONED COMFORT AND SAFETY OF A PARAMOUNT BLUE-SCREEN STUDIO

SEVERAL OF NILO RODIS'S REMARKABLE SET AND
WARDROBE DESIGNS FROM *THE FINAL FRONTIER*

FIGHT

BREATHING MASK

VANS?
BREATHING
MASK

DEFLECTOR
SHIELD

ZP

ASSAULT TEAM
ST 8
10.82

SFS 4?
BSD-MP

ABOVE: FROM *STAR TREK V*: CHOREOGRAPHING THE "SYBOK SHUFFLE"
BELOW: FROM *STAR TREK III*: "YOUR NAME . . . IS JIM."

no idea. I have not told him a thing. You are going to do that right now." It was funny to see how these upper-echelon people were having their own little political chess game.

You know, Gary Nardino doesn't just go to Michael Eisner and say, "Leonard Nimoy wants to direct *Star Trek III* and I think it's a great idea." Instead, he sits back, waits for Eisner to ask, "What's going on with *Star Trek III*?" and says something safe like "We're working on it, and we're bringing in Leonard Nimoy. He wants to talk to you." That way, no matter what Eisner's reaction is, Nardino's in solid with both of us. He's told ME, "*I've* been thinking you should direct the film, too!" and yet as far as Eisner's concerned, Nardino hasn't committed himself to the idea. He has successfully avoided going out onto any limb that stands a chance of breaking off underneath him.

So now my blood is running cold. I'm being delivered to the studio's head man without any foreplay. We get to Eisner's office, we walk in, and the entire meeting lasts maybe seven minutes. I gave him a three- or four-minute preamble about my experiences with *Star Trek*, my history, my knowledge, my vision of why the first film wasn't very good, my feelings about what made *The Wrath of Khan* so much better, and I summed it all up by saying that in my opinion I could be and *should* be his first choice to direct *Star Trek III*.

You know what he said? "What a great idea! Leonard Nimoy directs *The Search for Spock*. What a fantastic idea. What a great hook! Marketing will LOVE that!" He said, "Mancuso will LOVE it, and the publicity and promotions guys will love it too!"

In the chess game, it's now Eisner's move, and he realizes that when he brings this idea to the table in a meeting at Paramount's New York headquarters, the people at the next level of management will say, "Oh, that's a great idea. We can really sell that." Meanwhile, I'm standing there thinking, "Wow, that was too easy. This is terrific. It's like I've tapped a gold mine here." Then Eisner asked me, "Do you want to write it as well?" I said, "No, Harve and I have discussed the script, and I'd like to work with him." I didn't want to undermine Harve in any way, because he'd been through the ropes, and I felt like I'd really need his help. I really wanted him to produce.

So now the seven minutes are up, I walk out of the office, and . . . I don't hear anything for six weeks. Drove me nuts. I walked out of that office thinking I'd probably get a call from Business Affairs before the day was over, asking, "What do you want? When do you want to start?" That kind of stuff. Instead, I got silence. They wouldn't return my agent's calls, they didn't call me and say, "Let's make a deal," and over time I started getting nervous, I could see this thing starting to drift away. I'm calling Harve. My agent is calling Nardino. Nothing. Nobody has any idea what's going on.

And then I started hearing rumors that Barry Diller had put the kibosh on it; that everybody in New York had loved the idea, but that Diller ultimately said, "No, this is too frivolous. We're not going to have a first-time director behind the camera on an important franchise movie." When I heard that, I immediately called Nardino and asked, "Do you think I should call Barry Diller myself?" He said, "Oh no, you'll only embarrass yourself." The game player, the politician, said, "Don't embarrass yourself." I said, "Okay," because it sounded like solid advice.

Several weeks went by, I still hadn't heard anything, and I was getting more and more frustrated, until I finally said to myself and my agent at the same time, "You know, Michael Eisner is the man who originally told me that I could do this. Why aren't we calling *him*?" So I called Eisner's office. He took my call, and I said to him, "What's going on? Weeks ago, we had this great meeting, and now I can't even get anyone to answer the phone. Business Affairs won't talk to us, and nobody seems to know what's going on. Do you?"

He said, "Leonard," and he sighed, "there's a problem. I just don't feel comfortable hiring a guy to direct a *Star Trek* feature when that guy hates *Star Trek* so much he insisted upon being killed off just to get out. It really bothers me that you insisted they put that in your contract." I was dumbfounded, and I said, "That's not true at all. I never 'insisted' on that. Spock dying wasn't even my idea, and I *certainly* never had it written into my contract for *II*." To this day, I have absolutely no idea how Michael came up with that notion, and I don't think I ever quite succeeded in talking him out of it.

He said, "It wasn't in your contract?" And I said, "Michael, the contracts for *Star Trek II* are with you in your office building. Why don't you have someone go and pull them for you? You'll see for yourself that's not true. It's just some dumb rumor. Listen," I said, "this conversation is far too important for some dumb three-minute phone call. Can I come in and see you?" He said, "Come in tomorrow."

Leonard was dumbfounded. Had Nardino bad-mouthed him? Diller? Bennett? Roddenberry? Shatner? Had Eisner's bubbling support merely been bullshit all along? Leonard had no idea. That evening, with nowhere else to turn, Leonard made an awkward phone call, seeking advice and assistance from the last man to ride the *Star Trek* director's chair, Nick Meyer. Nick recalls:

When Leonard told the suits, "I'll be in *Star Trek III* if I can direct it," Harve Bennett and Michael Eisner and everybody else with any authority immediately began trying to talk him out of it. And they were feeding him lines like, "You know, Leonard, it can be very difficult for actors directing themselves, and blah, blah, blah." So while all of this is going on, Leonard would consult with me every night on the phone. And I said to him, "This is actually a very simple dilemma, and what it all boils down to is this: Are you prepared to let this ship sail without you?" And Leonard said, "Absolutely." So I told him, "Sit tight, hold firm, tell them, 'No directing, no movie' and you'll direct it."

The following morning, Leonard woke up early and nauseous, preparing for his meeting with Eisner and running endless potential scenarios through his head. Finally, after hours of hand-wringing, 10:00 A.M. made like *High Noon*, and Leonard had his showdown:

went in at ten o'clock and Eisner and I had a very dramatic confrontation that lasted close to an hour. I told him about how I got involved in *Star Trek II*, about how the idea of Spock's death had originally been presented to me, and I reiterated the fact that I had never insisted upon it being part of my contract. I told him that the rumor he'd been hearing was probably just something that the press or some fans had created. I told him, "You and I are having a very important meeting here. This might be the last time we ever speak to each other. We're either going to start working together on something fresh, or we're literally down to the final moments of our relationship. I have a strong idea about what this movie should be. I know how to shoot it, I know what the story should feel like emotionally. I know how to do this. I know how to execute it," and again, I laid out the general plotline of the film.

Finally I just said, "Michael, we need to make a decision about this, because I have to get on with my life and you need to get on with your business. You want to make *Star Trek III*, and you want me involved, that's *really* what this is all about." I was trying hard to be nonconfrontational but threatening at the same time. I said to him, "The way I see it, you have *two* problems. You want Leonard Nimoy to play Spock in *Star Trek III*, *and* you need a director for this movie. I can provide you with the solution to both of those problems, or neither. It's that simple." We left it at that, but I wasn't very optimistic.

Later, while we were actually shooting the film, I was told by someone who claims to have been in the room that when Eisner and Katzenberg finally went to New York for their big meeting with Paramount's heads of marketing and distribution and sales and so forth, Frank Mancuso asked Eisner, "So what's going on with *Star Trek III*?" Eisner apparently said, "Oh, we have a big problem . . . Leonard Nimoy wants to direct." Mancuso then says, ". . . and . . . what's the problem?" I don't know what transpired from there, all I know is that shortly thereafter, I got the call that I was in, and suddenly everyone at the studio was telling me that they were "behind me one hundred percent" . . . you know, now that I'd gotten the official stamp of approval, it was safe to be my friend.

By April 1983, Leonard and Harve were already working together on the Paramount lot, hashing through some rough creative ideas in regard to the new film's storyline. They put together a basic outline, revised it a dozen times, and experimented until they felt satisfied to the point where Harve used it as his blueprint for first-drafting the script. Harve explains the scripting process:

It was the easiest writing job I've ever had. *Star Trek III* literally picked up the action where *Khan* left off, and the basic elements of the story were already in place. Spock's casket was sitting down on the Genesis planet. We *had* to go get him. Spock had already said, "Remember," and performed some sort of strange mind-meld on Doctor McCoy, so we had to find out what *that* was all about. And at the same time, the whole idea of the Genesis planet and the fact that the

NIMOY AND BENNETT, A MATCH MADE IN HOLLYWOOD

same technology that could now create life from lifelessness could also destroy every living thing on existing planets made me wonder, "What would happen if the Klingons found out about this?" All of that stuff seemed obvious, and using it as a springboard made this writing job fairly simple. I just kind of worked from rough outlines and intuition and I had the whole thing first-drafted in six weeks. It was a real pleasure after the way we'd agonized over *Star Trek II*.

What emerged from Harve's six-week writing binge was a basic script dealing with friendship, sacrifice and loss. Its initial storyline, which found the crew of the *Enterprise* battling time, the elements and a crew of Klingons that ranked as perhaps the most ruthless ever seen, all in an effort to rescue their favorite Vulcan, would ultimately prove fairly indestructible, although it was by no means unanimously embraced. Among its most vocal detractors was . . . me.

Certainly, I had no problem with the script's basic premise, *that* was a given. Having not just fallen off the turnip truck, I fully understood that the underlying thrust of this film would basically have to find the crew of the *Enterprise* traveling back to the Genesis planet, rescuing Spock and somehow restoring him to the bridge safe and sound, just in time to continue our moviemaking franchise. However, I was hoping that around this predetermined and fairly obvious storyline, we'd be able to concoct a ballsy and exciting adventure about whatever obstacles might stand in our way. That wasn't the case.

When I read the script for the first time, I liked a lot of its elements. The death of Kirk's son, David, really took me by surprise, the scuttling of the *Enterprise* did likewise, and I liked Kruge, our over-the-top gung-ho/psycho Klingon power junkie, a lot. However, I was also disappointed that Captain Kirk and company were really just sort of wandering aimlessly through this script, being dragged through a tepid adventure by a series of unrelated external circumstances. In effect, it didn't seem to me like we were so much "searching" for Spock as stumbling upon him. Once we'd been reunited, we would have then found ourselves scrambling for our lives through a Klingon battle that sneaked up on us from behind. The lack of forward thrust reminded me immediately of our first film, and I had no intention of making that mistake again. In fact, when I had worked myself into a sufficient state of anxiety, I even went so far as to consult a lawyer about whether or not I'd be able to demand, as opposed to "asking for," certain script changes.

With all that in mind, I phoned Harve and asked if he and Leonard might be able to meet with me and discuss the script. Harve remembers it like this:

When we sent you the first draft of the script, you called back and when I picked up the phone I made the mistake of saying "Well, what do you think?" You just said, "Uhhhhh . . . maybe we should have a meeting." That was it, I knew there was trouble. Leonard and I ended up going to your house that weekend, and when we got there, I was kind of amazed to find your agent, your lawyer and a couple of big guys who looked like maybe they were stunt cops from T. J. *Hooker* or something all standing around the living room frowning at us. For a moment there I really thought I might lose a kneecap before the day was over.

I need to break into Harve's story to swear, upon a stack of old *Starlog* magazines, that the only person I had with me that day was that lawyer. I wanted him to be available should Harve and Leonard simply tell me to shut up, report to work and read my lines as written. I did not expect that, but at the same time, I was sufficiently unhappy with this script that if the changes hadn't been made, I'd have been perfectly happy to walk away. Luckily, however, we never got to that point. Harve continues:

You then asked us, "So, are you guys happy with this . . . script?" At which point Leonard said, "Absolutely, it holds a lot of promise." And I chimed in with, "Well, I wrote it, so of course *I* like it."

You replied by saying, "I'm sorry, but I just can't be a part of this." And as the little hairs on the back of my neck began standing on end, I said, "Well, then, let's go through this thing scene by scene, and talk about specifics." With that, you smiled, sent the agent and the lawyer and the Cro-Magnons home, and we all felt a little bit better. We then spent the better part of the next six hours performing a point-by-point dissection of the script.

You wanted to expand the scene wherein Kirk finds out about his son's death, making sure we got a chance to focus upon the captain's grief. We said, "Great idea!" You wanted Kirk to get in the middle of the "remember" scenes between Bones and Spock. We said, "No way, that's De's moment." And we went back and forth like that through the script, agreeing, disagreeing and compromising, really quite pleasantly, until we'd hammered through each of your script problems.

It was funny, because at one point I even said to you, "Bill, you *know* you're the quarterback on this team, but the problem is you want to call the play, take the snap from center, block the defensive lineman, backpedal into the pocket, toss the perfect spiral, run downfield, catch the pass, fake out a free safety or two, score the touchdown, do the victory dance and captain the cheerleading squad all at the same time."

With that, I grabbed Harve, squeezed him into a bear hug and said, "You're absolutely right, but I can't handle the cheerleaders all by myself." We said our good-byes, still smiling, and I found myself feeling very gratified and very lucky to be working with such talented, flexible friends. Still, my objections were by no means the only obstacles that Harve and Leonard would have to overcome.

From his office on the Paramount lot, Gene Roddenberry was now drafting memos more negative and numerous than ever before. Gene didn't like the script for Star Trek III at all, and he practically burst a blood vessel railing about Harve's plans to whack the Enterprise. Again, as he had done on Khan, Roddenberry proposed dumping Bennett's script in favor of his own (now slightly revised) time-traveling story in which the Enterprise ends up back in the early sixties mixing and mingling with . . . you guessed it, John F. Kennedy. This time, it would seem, the climactic moments of the film would find Spock, standing on a grassy knoll in Dallas, firing that infamous "phantom shot" as a way of ensuring Kennedy's death and thereby guaranteeing a brighter future for all of mankind.

Undeterred, Bennett continued forward with The Search for Spock, while battling Roddenberry over the terminal status of the Enterprise at every turn. Almost immediately (and this time more directly traceable to Roddenberry's instigation), fan letters began once again drowning Paramount under a sea of hastily penned righteous indignation. This time, however, having previously watched the "Don't kill Spock!" furor explode into a high-profile media sensation/free advertisement, Paramount's powers-that-were simply sat back, smiled and rode the wave, milking the controversy for every sound bite they could wring out.

Still, despite the familiarity of the Enterprise, and despite its position as the main setting for almost every Star Trek adventure ever written, I could never really understand Gene's objections. To me, the death of the Enterprise merely provided a great bit of cinematic drama, a wonderful, exciting and unexpected plot twist in light of a seemingly unwinnable situation. In short, it made the film better. Gene's criticisms on the subject were for the most part dismissed without much discussion. However, when I recently spoke with Roddenberry's longtime friend and business associate Richard Arnold, I got a whole new perspective. Arnold explains:

Harve fought any input from Gene from the beginning, and it hurt him, it really did, but the more Harve fought Gene's input, the more Gene *demanded* attention. Y'know, with K*han*, Harve and Nick Meyer had made some rather drastic structural and thematic changes to Gene's original vision of *Star Trek*, and he was now just fighting as hard as he could to preserve what was left.

Nick, Harve, Leonard, the suits, *everybody* suddenly seemed like they wanted to "improve" *Star Trek* and to make it their own. So when the idea of blowing up the *Enterprise*, which lies at the very heart of the "Gene Roddenberry School of *Star Trek*," came about, Gene had a really tough time.

I think the best way to explain their difference of opinion is to mention that Harve Bennett's military experience came in helicopters over Korea, while Gene came out of World War II. When Gene was flying these great big airships, they had names, they were referred to as "she." If the plane was damaged, "she" was "wounded." He had a very similar attitude about the *Enterprise*.

Harve's perspective was entirely different. You know, in his mind, if you crashed your helicopter and walked away from it, it was still a good landing. You just went out and got another chopper. There wasn't any real attachment to the equipment. That explains, in part, why Gene was so hurt by Harve's destruction of the

Enterprise. It also explains why Harve never really understood that.

Additionally, once the *Enterprise* was gone, Harve originally wanted to forget about building any sort of new ship and simply transplant everybody into the *Excelsior* . . . a Harve Bennett creation. That just made things worse, and Gene's take on it was a feeling that Harve was now attempting to revise and rewrite *all* of *Star Trek* in an effort to make it his own. That feeling ultimately fueled a lot of disagreements.

Still, despite the fan uproar and the poison-typewriter memos that were now streaming from Gene Roddenberry's desk, Harve and Leonard continued forward. However, just when they thought the worst was behind them, the pair ran into one more script problem. This time it came from a very unexpected source, George Takei. George explains:

The script came. I was reading it, and I really liked it, and when I got to the scene where Kirk and Sulu break McCoy out of the hospital I was pleased to find that my character had a really nice bit of business. Sulu enters the scene, and when he sees that the security guard on duty is half-asleep with his feet up on the desk, he asks the guy, "Keepin' ya busy?" At that point the big guy replies, "Don't get smart, Tiny." And later, as we're making our escape, Sulu ends up shoulder-tossing this guy to the ground and saying, "Don't call me Tiny."

I have to admit, I just didn't get it. I mean, I had never imagined Sulu as being tiny. So I got

on the phone right away with Harve and I said: Harve, it's a wonderful script, I love it, except I think we need to rewrite this one scene where Sulu throws the big guy—I think it's a great bit of business, but this reference to Sulu as "Tiny" just doesn't make sense. And now Harve says, "Well, I don't know what you mean." And I said: "C'mon, Sulu is not a tiny man." And Harve says, "Of course not, but what you've got to understand is that this security guard is a giant, I mean, he's a Viking."

And I said, "Well, that may be, but Harve, I know how the fans see Sulu. They don't see Sulu as tiny—he's a hero and he mustn't be referred to as tiny." Oh boy, my ego was now really invested in this, so I strenuously tried to talk him out of that tiny reference. On the other end of the phone, Harve is now saying, "I can't believe this! I can't believe what I'm hearing! George, it's a charming, delightful scene and you come off fantastically. You're the activator in this scene." And

I said, "Yes, I know, I know, and I understand all that. I don't think you're quite hearing what I'm saying. This reference to Sulu as tiny. Fans will not buy it, they will not accept it. Believe me, Harve, I go to ten zillion *Star Trek* conventions and I know the fans. I'm speaking for them, they will not buy that!"

Well, the long and short of it is we did it. Harve says, "Can we make a compromise? Let's shoot it both ways and see how it plays, will you grant me that?" And I said, "Well, Harve, I'll tell you all right. I will grant you that, but when you guys get into the editing room, I know which one you're going to use, and believe me, in a million years, you're not going to want to use that one with 'Tiny,' it will fall flat on its face, the fans will not like that, but all right, we'll shoot it." That just goes to show you how much *I* know.

When I first found out that the "Tiny" scene was actually going into the finished film, I was angry, upset, and I told Harve again, "The audience won't go for this; you've made a big mistake." But then, when I first saw the film with an audience, I was amazed, because as Sulu flipped the guard and said, "Don't call me Tiny," a raucous cheer went up inside the theater. Until that point, I was still absolutely convinced that Harve was wrong.

And when that cheer went up in that theater, I knew I was going to have to give Harve credit. So I called him once more, and I said, "Hello, Harve, you know what I'm doing right now? I'm eating crow, and it tastes delicious."

I should interject here to explain that even though George's tale may sound a bit strange, it's easily explained. Takei, you see, is nuts. It's that simple. Even as far back as "The Naked Time," when George turned a simple scene with an epée into my near disemboweling, it's been obvious that he can get a bit . . . shall we say . . . carried away? Quite simply, he is far and away the most enthusiastic Trekker among us Star Trekkers. For example, limiting myself to just Star Trek III, George accompanied his battle to erase Sulu's diminutive nickname by personally leading groups of tourists through our Star Trek III sets, hugging almost every cast and crew member at least once a day throughout our production, and ultimately demanding work as an extra during the film's climactic Vulcan ritual scene. The reason for this wasn't money or screen time. George merely couldn't pass up the chance to wear a "genuine Vulcan ceremonial robe, at least once." Still, despite the occasional manic behavior, George's goodwill and unshakable on-set ebullience make him a joy to work with, and just plain fun to be around.

By week's end, back in Harve Bennett's office, the script for *Star Trek III* had now officially been beaten into submission, achieving final-draft status. Now it was time for Harve and Leonard to begin casting. As with any new working relationship, they'd suffer a few growing pains. Leonard remembers:

Harve's a good producer, and by that I mean he has the tools to entice people, to cajole people, to coerce people, to manipulate people, and he is quite good at it. He and I didn't always see eye to eye over taste or ethics, and we had our differences about the script, and shooting scenes, and casting, but he was always capable.

The biggest issue we had on *III* was in regard

to the casting of our Klingon heavy. We had talked about a lot of people, we had auditioned a lot of people, and when they read the part, it just didn't seem to come to life. It didn't work. They just couldn't grasp the character somehow. Then one day I showed Harve a tape of Edward James Olmos. This was before *Miami Vice* and Eddie was looking for work. So Harve watched the tape, and his response was, "Well, he's not bad, but he's small, a quarterback. I think what we need in this role is a defensive tackle." I said, "Well, that may be, but let's bring him in and find out."

Then, I don't know why, but I decided to meet with Eddie on a Sunday, at my house. I asked Harve to come, too, but he either couldn't or wouldn't for whatever reason, and he told me, "You make the call, I'll be guided by your judgment." So

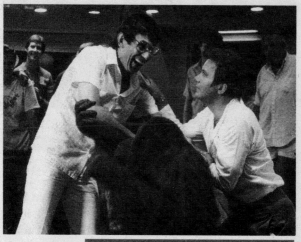

LEONARD ALWAYS SAID EVEN A
MONKEY COULD PLAY THE CAPTAIN

I saw Eddie and he's a really intense, interesting guy, and I felt he would do a terrific job. I felt that we could skirt the issue of his size, because his character would've spent the better part of the film sitting alone in his command chair on the Klingon ship. His actual face-to-face confrontation with

Kirk was the only time we'd have to fake it. I thought that with creative angles, camera work and elevating Eddie on boxes, we could've done that fairly easily. Before the day was over, I had more or less committed to Eddie, and as we said good-bye I told him, "This is gonna be great."

But somehow Harve was still very concerned that this character seem a lot bigger than Kirk, and very threatening. I told him, "I agree with that, and I really think I can achieve it on film." We went around and around on the issue, getting nowhere, until Harve said, "Well, let's have him come in and read for it." And I said, "But I DID that already. He read at my house yesterday, he was fantastic, and you said you'd be guided by my judgment."

Harve said, "Well, I don't know if I can sell that to the suits." So now I'm thinking to myself, *Geez, this is getting a little strange. They're going to retest the guy that I've already decided I want in the role. It's getting embarrassing.*

So Eddie came in, read for Harve, and it went quite well. There was no way he could argue that Eddie wasn't perfect. Instead, he said, "Would you mind coming back one more time and scaring the hell out of a management person here at the studio?" Eddie agreed, and meanwhile I'm thinking, *What the hell is this?*

The "management person" turned out to be Gary Nardino, who'd been given the title of executive producer on this movie. I went along with the gag, basically because this was my first picture and I really didn't know what my limitations were. I was still unsure of myself and feeling my way around. I was worried about taking a stand here, worried that they might just say "fuck you."

So Eddie came back one more time, read for Nardino, and by the time he'd finished and left the room, I knew he was dead. Nardino said, "I don't get it at all. To me, this is a character who should be 'to the manor born.' He's a sophisticated, Terence Stamp kind of guy." I said, "I don't think that at all. I think he's a bright, intense, gung-ho, threatening kind of bad guy." But for all intents and purposes, it was now two against one, and Eddie was gone.

Obviously, somewhere in the middle of that gray area determining the comparative authority between a producer and director, a real power struggle was beginning to brew between the two men. That's not at all uncommon, in fact, it occurs to at least some degree on virtually every movie set in Hollywood, with the currents of power ebbing, flowing and changing direction as governed by any number of circumstances. Who's got the bigger reputation, the louder voice, the more dynamic personality? Who's got the most experience? Who's coming off a hit? All of these political elements enter into ultimately deciding who emerges as top dog on the set. That title is almost always up for grabs as a picture begins coming together, and experienced people almost always make the most of those situations, jockeying against one another for position and ultimately grabbing hold of the dominant role. Once that pecking order gets established, it almost always remains intact, simply becoming a pattern of habit. Leonard and Harve were obviously engaged in just such a battle.

Leonard, with unquestionable *Star Trek* experience, was nonetheless a novice when it came to directing feature films and battling behind the scenes. Harve's reputation, his status as a master tactician of studio politics and the fact that he was still riding the momentum of *Star Trek II* combined to put him at the top of the food chain. Leonard recently explained the situation perfectly by saying, "It all comes down to a matter of confidence both in your judgment and in your position. It's a matter of who's got the confidence to say, 'You are absolutely wrong. I know I'm right, and I refuse to give in.' I didn't have that confidence on *Star Trek III*." Leonard continues:

You know, when Gene Roddenberry was first informed that I'd been hired to direct this picture, his reaction was to say, "Well, you've hired a director that you can't fire." That wasn't very supportive, but I realized it was absolutely valid, and in a way, I took that to heart, and it empowered me to stand up for myself a bit more than I probably would have in a situation with less leverage. Still, I didn't have enough experience under my belt to feel comfortable saying, "Get off my case, Harve, don't fuck around here." That came on *Star Trek IV*.

But on *The Search for Spock*, I came to understand that Harve, because of his intense television background, saw his project's director as a sort of field sergeant whose job it was to get a lot of coverage, shooting every scene from a lot of different perspectives, and then delivering those scenes to Harve's desk. On a television project, the director would then have gone home and Harve would have been free to construct the film himself. Because of that, he had absolutely no compunction about saying to me, "This scene won't cut right. You should go back and get a shot of such and such." He did that three or four times throughout the shooting of the film, and I pretty much went back and shot whatever he thought we'd need. I can't fault him for that, and as a rule, Harve's eye is pretty sharp. I learned a lot from him on this film, about some of the technical aspects of filmmaking, about covering scenes as a director, and especially about editing.

In the middle of all this, I should add that while completing casting on this film, Leonard was able to pull off a real coup. Suddenly, from out of nowhere, we heard that Dame Judith Anderson, perhaps the most revered actress on the planet, had consented to play our high Vulcan priestess, T'Lar. I couldn't believe it. Nimoy had somehow convinced a truly legendary actress to join our cast, and I had absolutely no idea how he'd managed to pull it off. Leonard, however, can supply all the details:

I t *is* an interesting story, and I think I'm going to stick my neck out here. When we made *Star Trek: The Motion Picture*, there was a scene early on wherein Spock is back on Vulcan, and he's about to complete the *kolinahr* ceremony. And a high priestess type is about to present him with this thing that's supposed to go on his head when suddenly he gets distracted by some unknown message . . . it was never fully realized and it wasn't well thought out . . . but that moment somehow causes Spock to decide that he has to give everything up and go to the *Enterprise*.

Anyway, when we shot this exterior Vulcan scene, Bob Wise had wanted to hire somebody of real stature to play the high priestess. They found somebody they liked, but whoever it was wanted $5,000. The fucking picture cost about $45 million, and they wouldn't spring for $5,000. Apparently they were just offering bargain-basement money, and because of that they ended up hiring some nice lady who had no stature, no size, couldn't say the dialogue . . . it was embarrassing. To me it was physically painful. And I was angry about it because I thought it demeaned Spock and it demeaned me.

So now, when *Star Trek III* rolls around and I'm doing the casting, I immediately became fixated on who we might be able to cast as T'Lar. I thought to myself, *We're finally going to get a woman with some stature here and you'll see what this is all about.* I was still carrying that anger. And off the top of my head I said let's get Dame Judith Anderson, the Medea of our generation. Somebody said, "Is she still alive?" I said, "Of course she's still alive, and she's still brilliant, too. Let's take a shot." Now I had to find her.

The first thing I did was to call a mutual friend, a man named Elliot Silverstein, who had directed Dame Judith in his terrific film *A Man Called Horse*. He arranged a meeting, and the following Sunday I ended up going to Santa Barbara to visit with her.

So we met, and she then had me drive us to a local restaurant for lunch. We got there at about noon. My agent, Sandy, was with me at the time, and so the three of us sat down at a table, and the waiter came by asking, "Anybody want a drink?" And now Dame Judith Anderson, who was less than five feet tall, and at that point eighty-five years old, says, "C'mon now, who's going to

have a drink with me?" Sandy just kind of smiled and said, "I don't drink," and I said, "Not me, thank you very much."

But she said, "Well, I'm going to have a drink, but I wish somebody would join me." So of course I said, "All right, if that's the case . . ." and we ordered Bloody Marys. The waiter left and I said, "Look, I love to drink but I consider myself at work here and I never drink when I'm working . . ." I then told her, " . . . but that all goes out the window when the curtain falls. When I'm working in the theater, the dressing room people always have instructions to have a drink ready for me when I come off the stage at the end of the performance. Just have it sitting there cold and waiting for me because that's the first thing I'm going to be looking for."

And she laughed and said, "I can do better than that. When I was doing *Medea*, at every curtain call, while I was taking my bows, I used to do this." And she showed me a dramatic little hand gesture in which she sort of twirled her right hand outward in a sort of half-wave/half-flourish kind of reaching out toward the wings.

She smiled at me with a twinkle in her eye and said, "Leonard, do you know what that gesture means? It means the play is over, where's my drink?" I laughed, she laughed, and it broke the ice.

Still, despite the fact that Leonard and Dame Judith had struck up a bit of a friendship, she actually declined to appear in the film, until a strange twist of fate changed her mind. At the time of the film's release, she explained the turnaround by saying, "I ultimately decided to appear in the film because of my nephew. He was an avid fan of Mr. Spock, and when he learned that I had actually lunched with Leonard Nimoy and discussed playing a part in *Star Trek III*, well, he went absolutely out of his mind with excitement. He just kept insisting that I *must* be in *Star Trek*. His enthusiasm is what really got me involved."

Further strengthening our cast was the addition of Christopher Lloyd, who'd been cast as that raging Klingon bastard Kruge. Hidden under gobs of makeup and one of those patented Klingon headpieces that always look sort of like big brown omelets, Lloyd was almost entirely unrecognizable as his small-screen persona of *Taxi*'s Reverend Jim, and he chewed the scenery with a tremendous amount of skill and enthusiasm (even going so far as to become fluent in the formal Klingonese language, invented by a doctoral student of linguistics). And while early on he admitted feeling like a bit of an outsider among the "family" of *Star Trek*, he quickly grew more than comfortable on the set and in his role. I can't say enough good things about him.

As a final casting note, after a brief monetary dispute,

Kirstie Alley gave up her role as the half-Vulcan, half-Romulan Saavik. Ask Alley about the situation and she'll tell you, "Paramount's offer came in very, very low; it was less than they'd offered me for Star Trek II, so I figured they weren't very interested in me playing the part." Ask Leonard Nimoy about the same situation, and he'll tell you that "We just couldn't afford her. She'd been paid a decent sum for Star Trek II for a beginner, and I think the studio was prepared to pay her more than twice that much for III." Either way, the numbers simply refused to add up, and Saavik got a facelift. Robin Curtis, who took over for Alley, came into the role early in August 1983 and ultimately gave a solid performance in a rather thankless role.

By the fifteenth of that month, we had all donned the maroon and black one more time and reported for duty back on the bridge of the Enterprise. However, I have to admit that this time it felt a little strange. Leonard, one of my best pals and my closest ally through seventeen years of battles against the guys in charge, over scripts and ideas and contracts and dressing rooms, had suddenly changed sides. My friend had abruptly become my boss. I couldn't help but feel awkward and alone.

On top of that, I was also apprehensive as to whether or not Leonard would actually be able to pull this thing off. I mean, at that point in my life I certainly didn't feel capable of directing a multimillion-dollar movie, so how in the world could Leonard, my friend,

my peer, the man whom I'd routinely pummeled at the card table, ever *hope* to succeed? The answer, of course, is that he triumphed without the slightest reservation. Leonard was absolutely great, kicked that picture's ass. He basically took an okay script and turned it into a really good film. I was shocked, I was impressed, and I was ultimately just proud to be working with him.

I should also add that my fears regarding Leonard's promotion turned out to be entirely unwarranted, and by the end of our first day's shooting, they'd almost entirely disappeared. To my surprise, Leonard *hadn't* become an asshole. He didn't suddenly sprout a goatee, or a pony-tail, or a beret. He wasn't smoking clove cigarettes while pontificating about the writings of André Bazin; didn't call me "Babe" or "Sport." Instead, throughout all of the chaos and insanity that run amok on virtually every movie set, he simply remained . . . Leonard.

Sporting an un-Vulcanly grin, and speaking in calm, measured, reassuring tones, Leonard approached his massive challenge calmly, systematically, and (pardon the pun) logically. Fighting off every first-time director's urge to reinvent the wheel and stockpile the film with incredible camera moves, complicated setups, massive sets, mind-blowing locations and gaudy special effects, Leonard simply stuck to what he knew best. He shot his scenes simply, moving his camera around our sets with a subtle grace and focusing his attention away from the technical complexities of moviemaking, concentrating much more intently upon what he knew best: the dramatic content of every scene.

He began working *very* closely with his actors, and whereas that would probably have seemed rather intru-sive were anyone else directing this film, Leonard's advice was always a welcome treat. Having worked with all of us for the better part of two decades, he knew every Star Trek character, and more important every Star Trek actor, like the back of his hand. He knew our strengths, our weaknesses, our idiosyncrasies, our superstitions, and for those reasons, he was able to consistently provide us with solid, accurate and insightful advice. The results were unmistakable. Leonard recalls:

Early on, I found that the cast was apparently very nervous about me directing this film. That really surprised me. I thought they knew me better than they actually did. Still, as soon as we got past the initial question of trust, the rest was easy. Once everyone realized that I'd rather *collaborate* than dictate, we started having a lot of fun. Everybody began feeling like a part of this film, they really had some creative input, they were no longer outsiders, and I think that really shows on-screen. I think we had some moments in this film that compare favorably even against the best of the original series, especially for Kirk.

You had scenes in this film in which you really had to reach down and dredge up very personal aspects of your character, aspects we'd never seen before. And when it came time to shoot those scenes, we just took our time, talked everything through, and in the end, I really think we were able to surpass anything you've ever done with the character.

More specifically, Leonard is referring to the scene in *Star Trek III* wherein Kirk first learns that his son, David, has been killed. It was an extremely well-written scene, very powerful, its emotion running much deeper than anything I'd ever had to do with this character before. And as we began rehearsing, I have to admit I was nervous as hell. I wasn't sure I could pull it off. At that point, having come to truly respect his advice, I went looking for Leonard.

We huddled up in one corner of the stage, sat down together, got very close, and Leonard surprised me. He said, "I can't tell you how to play this scene. I can't even give you any advice on how Kirk might react to the death of his son. It's just too personal, and it cuts too deeply. You're on your own here. You have to decide where you're going to take this, and how far. You have to decide the level of emotion and vulnerability that Kirk is capable of expressing, and you have to feel comfortable playing it." Leonard continues:

I felt as if this scene provided us a perfect opportunity, perhaps for the first time, to really wipe away some of Kirk's bravado, to knock the wind out of his sails, to forget about the untouchable, invincible hero for a moment, and expose the fallible, vulnerable human being underneath. You pulled it off beautifully, played it honestly and really conveyed the character's incredible emotional pain without reservation. I mean, when Kirk hears the news of David's death and falls backward, stumbling on the steps of the Enterprise bridge, it has a truly jarring impact. You just don't expect to see that. Kirk's pain really comes through very vividly. As a result, the scene turned out to be very moving, even upsetting.

In retrospect, I have to admit three things. First, I'm really proud of that scene. Second, I really believe it

ABOVE: "Now, Bill, that big black thing is the camera."

BELOW: Leonard once again thrilled with one of my suggestions

might actually represent Kirk's finest celluloid moment ever. And third, it came together by accident. Leonard and I had barely even begun blocking that scene for the first time when I came to the conclusion that Kirk's most likely move upon hearing such devastating news would be to retreat, taking a step backward in an effort to compose himself. Leonard seemed to agree, and upon our first run-through of the scene, I took my backward step, caught my heel on the front edge of the metal steps, and took a header so catastrophic that by the time I'd come to rest, crumpled into a heap, head over heels at the bottom rung, half the crew actually looked up from their newspapers and donuts to see if I'd died. Leonard now hovered over me, eyebrows even higher than normal, asking, "Oh my God, are you okay?"

"Sure," I replied, "think we can shoot that?" Leonard now lowered one eyebrow and performed an absolutely perfect Spock take. I actually half-expected him to utter the words "highly illogical." I then explained that in midtumble, I'd realized that for Kirk to actually stumble and fall might be a perfect way to play this scene. "What do you think?" I asked my pointy-eared director.

"Hmmmmm," he said for about four and a half

OPPOSITE: DAVID'S DEATH
ABOVE: AMID THE PLASTIC SNOW OF THE GENESIS PLANET
RIGHT: KIRK FOOLISHLY TRIES TO REASON WITH A KLINGON

minutes, "I think that's really good. Let's try it . . . just don't knock your brains out, you still have scenes to shoot." With that I began setting myself into a position in which three short backward steps would put me just at the lip of that treacherous first step. Once I had the technique worked out, I could then focus my attention inward, toward the motivations behind it all.

Finally, the cameras rolled and after about a half-dozen takes, not to mention at least that many baseball-sized bruises, we walked away feeling really good about the scene. Later, after we'd wrapped for the night, with my back and my legs just beginning to stiffen into knots any sailor would envy, I came back onto the set to find Leonard and compliment him on our day's work. However, he was nowhere to be found. When his dressing room proved similarly unoccupied, I gave up the search and headed back through the bowels of the *Enterprise* toward the exit closest to my car. That's when I heard it.

Snoring with a pitch and timbre reminiscent of perhaps . . . a gas-powered weedwhacker was our esteemed director. He was out cold, in Spock's quarters, appropriately enough, catching a quick power nap before heading off to scrutinize yesterday's footage.

As our days of production and Leonard's stamina both began winding down, *Star Trek III* continued moving forward rapidly and, for the most part, entirely successfully.

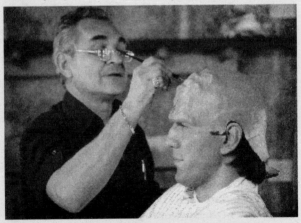

JUST ANOTHER DAY AT THE **KLINGON** FACTORY

There were, however, two small disasters that bear mention. First, the ultimate fight scene between Kirk and Kruge on the hastily disintegrating Genesis planet was originally supposed to be a lot more spectacular than it ultimately came off. Once again, as we had with K*han*, I locked myself into Harve's office and badly abused his office furniture, this time with Leonard at my side, and tried to come up with something that might make this screen fight a bit special, a bit more than just the industry standard of guys faking punches to one another's midsections while cheesily mouthing the word "OOOOF" into the nearest camera.

What we finally came up with was an ambitious plan that would have started with Kirk and Kruge pummeling one another upon the surface of the Genesis planet. However, early on in the proceedings, enormous boulders would have suddenly begun rising out of the planet's extremely unstable surface. At that point, Kirk and Kruge would have begun leaping from boulder to boulder while continuing their attempts to beat each other's brains in. However, that never came off.

This time around, while our budget held up, our set didn't. When it came time to actually shoot this scene, the boulders that would have literally provided the foundation upon which this fight was to have been carried out, and which had performed flawlessly throughout any number of rehearsals, simply couldn't rise to the occasion. Instead of booming powerfully from the planet's surface, they just sort of wobbled around flaccidly, looking for all the world like enormous fiberglass turds.

However, with the clock ticking and no real assurances that the rocks would ever again work as designed, we quickly went to Plan B, the fairly standard good-guy/bad-guy brawl. Watch closely, and you'll notice that in our haste to rework the scene I even managed to dredge up a few of Kirk's well-worn TV moves. The giant windup into a left-handed haymaker, the roundhouse kick, the two quick jabs to the stomach followed by a right to the jaw, they're all in there, and despite the fact that the scene ultimately plays fairly well on-screen, I still can't help but feel disappointed every time I see it.

And finally, on my second-to-last day of shooting, one of our sets caught fire. I had just finished shooting a scene on the *Enterprise* bridge, and as I began wandering back toward my dressing room, I suddenly heard a fire alarm blast. Jumping three feet in the air in surprise, I recomposed myself, chuckling that perhaps the Genesis planet had finally exploded. I then turned a corner and realized that New York City was burning down.

I watched as one of Paramount's most elaborate permanent sets, an entire city street made up of perhaps twenty building facades, rapidly began being cremated, laid out in front of me like an outtake from some Irwin Allen disaster film. The facades were made almost entirely of wood, and seasoned into a highly flammable accident waiting to happen beneath years of exposure to the California sun. I stood there marveling at how rapidly this fire was now spreading. The makeshift deli collapsed, the Chinese laundry fell over, and only as the rest of the set's half-inch plywood walls came tumbling down did I realize that Stage 15, which was attached to the back of the burning cityscape, was now burning as well. Wide-eyed, I recoiled in horror as I realized that inside Stage 15 was *Star Trek III*'s Genesis planet. I ran like hell.

By the time I'd reached the stage door, it too had begun burning. Luckily, however, the handful of special effects guys and scenic artists who'd been working inside had made it out in plenty of time. Relieved that no one had been hurt, I now began contemplating what this impending major disaster might do to Leonard's shooting schedule, and that's when I was struck by a highly illogical, highly disturbing thought. I was scheduled to shoot the last of my scenes for this film the next day . . . on Stage 15. Immediately following those scenes, I was going to have to report to the Columbia lot to begin shooting the new season's episodes of *T. J. Hooker*. Were I to be late, all hell would break loose. Were I to leave Paramount without completing my work as Kirk, even greater hell would break loose. With that in mind, I snapped and sprinted away, looking for the nearest fire hose.

I found one rather quickly, and with the assistance of two or three of the effects guys I started blasting. Standing there, schpritzing like mad, still decked out in Kirk's entire full-dress uniform, I must have looked like I'd completely lost my mind. Even worse, the effects guys had now climbed up onto the roof of the burning building, and while I continued squirting, they stood there cutting a hole in the roof of the stage, hoping to prevent a heat buildup, and simultaneously allowing some of my spray to drift downward onto their precious set.

Throughout the ensuing moments, we beat the flames back into a near stalemate, and by the time the fire engines arrived, the battle was just about over. Stage 15 remained intact. And although the entire city-side wall of the stage was blackened, at some points even burned right through, the Genesis planet had survived. Overnight, crews worked continuously, pumping water from the set while laborers hastily re-sided the structure. By morning, the job was far enough along to allow us to shoot our scenes as scheduled. In short, we'd saved the day, I got to *T. J. Hooker* on time, and *Star Trek III* remained on schedule. It would have made a hell of a segment on *Rescue 911*.

In the end, though all was well on the Paramount lot, we'd thoroughly screwed with the *Star Trek* universe. The *Enterprise* was gone, David was dead, Spock was back but a bit addled, and the crew of the Starship *Enterprise* had gone from heroes to outlaws, all in the course of 105 minutes. Even more amazing, *Star Trek III* officially wrapped production on October 15, 1983, one week ahead of schedule, and just slightly under budget. This kind of cost efficiency, *very* unusual in the business of filmmaking, virtually cemented Harve and Leonard back into their posts come *Star Trek IV*.

Star Trek III: The Search for Spock premiered on June 1, 1984, and ultimately became our second big-screen hit, racking up seventy-six million box-office bucks. Still, even with back-to-back megasuccesses under our belts, the future of our aging *Star Trek* franchise was once again a bit cloudy. Sequels, as any good market researcher could have told you, simply got less and less successful with every installment. That was an established fact, and before long rumors of our impending retirement began sounding rather credible.

With that in mind, I settled back into *T. J. Hooker*, smiling, grateful for its stability, grateful for the paycheck, and content to let James Tiberius Kirk fade out of my life once and for all. However, in the months ahead, as he'd done so often in the past, the captain would somehow manage to cheat death once more, this time performing an end run around the grim reaper and ultimately reaching unparalleled heights of success.

Stay tuned.

STAR TREK IV:
THE VOYAGE ROAMS

ith back-to-back blockbusters now bulging from our vest pockets, we of the Starship *Enterprise* suddenly found ourselves extremely popular around the Paramount lot, and throughout the summer of 1984, as *Star Trek III* continued gluttonously inhaling money out of box offices all over America, Paramount's executives threw their research out the window and decided rather quickly that the *Star Trek* franchise was an exception to their rule of progressively dwindling sequel returns. The suits quickly began taking *Star Trek*–themed power breakfasts, and shortly thereafter, car phones all over the southern half of California began buzzing in an attempt to get all of us back onto the silver screen as quickly as possible. However, although by now we all knew the drill, having waltzed with the studio on several occasions, this time around a lot of the dancing partners had changed.

We might as well start at the top. In September 1984, with *The Search for Spock* still hot at the box office, Barry

Diller left Paramount and took over the reins at Fox, ultimately heading up the fledgling Fox network. Ironically, the man who was behind Paramount's aborted attempt at creating a fourth network was now leaving the studio to do exactly that. Shortly thereafter, in fact just nine days later, Michael Eisner left, too, becoming Disney's chief executive officer. Ten days after that, just long enough to write up a solid contract, Jeffrey Katzenberg followed Eisner and began working for the mouse as well.

With that wave of defections, Paramount's power base shape-shifted quite rapidly. Martin Davis, a bottom-line-watching, no-nonsense businessman, now became head of Paramount, having replaced Charlie Bluhdorn, the energetic, enthusiastic bear who'd rescued the beached whale called *Star Trek* after our disappointing film debut. Bluhdorn, who would never have retired, ultimately succumbed to a heart attack supposedly while juggling business calls on two different phone lines aboard the company jet.

Frank Mancuso, the soft-spoken marketing and distribution man whom most people tend to view as a cross between Don Corleone and Mr. Rogers, was now playing chairman of the board. As president of the motion picture division we had the moody and tough Ned Tanen, and our new president of production was Dawn Steel. Reporting directly to the talented Ms. Steel was a pair of new creative executives named David Kirkpatrick and Teddy Zee. The icons in this hastily rearranged totem pole would continue to shift over the course of three ensuing sequels and a half-dozen years, and many of these names will show up throughout the rest of this book. For now, though, you've got your program, and I suggest you use it to identify the players.

Despite all the turmoil and upheaval, some things

hadn't changed a bit. By late 1984, Leonard Nimoy and Harve Bennett, now officially the golden boys of the Paramount lot, had already returned to their respective positions as director and producer and gotten down to business. Within days they'd formulated a few guidelines and general conclusions in regard to their brandnew challenge, with Leonard immediately deciding that this time around there would be "no dying, no fistfighting, no shooting, no photon torpedoes, no phaser blasts, no stereotypical 'bad guy.'" Instead, the *Star Trek* crew would be fighting time, circumstance and a seemingly unwinnable dilemma. As Leonard told me, "I wanted people to really have a great time watching this film, to really sit back, lose themselves and enjoy it. That was the main goal, and if somewhere in the mix we lobbed a couple of bigger ideas at them, well, then that would be even better."

With the broad strokes falling into place, it was time to start toying with some of the finer details that might flesh them out. Harve Bennett explains:

When Leonard and I had our conferences early on, we agreed that it would be great fun to do a time travel story and that we could really make it unique by bringing the crew of the *Enterprise* back to the present day and having them mix it up with modern-day Americans. On the old series, "City on the Edge of Forever" brought them back to the thirties, and "Tomorrow Is Yesterday" brought them back into the sixties, but almost from day one, we decided to go eighties contemporary. This was a marvelous thing to do, for three reasons.

First, while we knew that *Star Trek* fans clearly

LEONARD TAKES OFF HIS TRAINING WHEELS

loved time travel stories, we felt that a contemporary setting might lure a lot more non-*Star Trek* fans into the theaters. That notion, of course, ultimately proved itself absolutely true.

Second, both Leonard and I felt that there would be a wonderful quality of whimsy in depositing you guys on the streets of San Francisco, where you couldn't help but become fish out of water. The comedic possibilities would be endless.

And third, now speaking from a practical standpoint, we realized that by setting this thing in the present day we could really open this movie up. For the first time ever, we could shoot in ordinary locations and not spend all of our time on expensive and confining planetary or spaceship sets. We could get outside, move around, and shoot San Francisco as it is! The park and the aquarium and waterfront, all of those things really made the scope of this particular picture seem a lot larger than what we'd seen previously.

It was funny, too, because Gene Roddenberry's first memo on *Star Trek* IV said, "Well, that's more like it. Time travel *will* work on *Star Trek*, however, a far better story to tell is . . . " and he went right back into pitching his Kennedy assassination story. So that was the drummer we heard for five memos in a row.

Sidestepping Roddenberry's tale once more, Leonard and Harve now huddled together and tried to come up with a solid and exciting dramatic reason for the crew of the *Enterprise* to suddenly come wandering back to the eighties. Almost immediately, the pair hit upon the idea that perhaps there would be some sort of life-and-death dilemma threatening all of twenty-third-century mankind, and that the crew of the *Enterprise* would discover that the key to solving the crisis could be found only by traveling back to the late twentieth century.

At about the same time, Leonard had become fascinated by a book, *Biophilia*, authored by globally renowned biologist Edward Wilson. The book asserted that by the end of the twentieth century, thousands upon thousands of animal species on this planet will have become extinct even before scientists have gotten a chance to discover them or to begin understanding their species' purpose on the planet. Additionally, the author surmises that the loss of these species could prove devastating to life as we know it, destroying food chains and ultimately wreaking havoc on the ecosystems of the Earth. Synthesizing these ideas, Leonard came up with the notion of humpback whales, long extinct by the twenty-third century, becoming an absolutely integral ingredient in the rescue of all life in the universe.

As the lightbulb went on over Leonard's head, he called Harve, and within the day, the pair had come up with the basic equation for their new movie: A = whales needed to solve twenty-third-century crisis, B = whales extinct. A + B = C: *Enterprise* crew must return to the twentieth century, retrieve whales and carry them forward in time to head off impending disaster. Smiling and patting each other on the back, the pair felt as if they were on to something that could really pay off on screen. However, despite their creative sync, the professional relationship between Harve and Leonard was now beginning to deteriorate. Leonard explains:

In all fairness to Harve, I think we came into *Star Trek IV* having been given different signals. The signal I got was, "This is your picture. Do you want Harve Bennett to return?" At the same time, I think the signal *he* got was, "You're our guy. YOU'RE our guy." I think he may have been set up, put into a position wherein I wasn't going to be reporting to him.

While all that was going on, I was being "difficult," at least according to the studio. More specifically, citing the fact that our previous three films had earned the studio well over a quarter of a billion dollars, I was steadfastly refusing to sign on the dotted line for our new film, holding out in an effort to partially make up for two decades' worth of nonexistent residuals and merchandising revenues. In short, I was trying to get Leonard and me a well-deserved (at least in our opinion) raise.

I should explain that even though Leonard was directing this picture, and at face value it would seem that he and I should be at opposite sides of the fence on this issue, I was indeed working on our mutual behalf, and while that sounds a bit strange, it wasn't at all unusual. Years earlier, during the original run of the TV series, Leonard's lawyers and my lawyers actually got together and drew up a favored-nation clause, which remained in effect throughout all of our *Star Trek* projects, and basically stated that whatever Leonard got, I got, and vice versa. With that in mind, whenever one of us entered into *Star Trek* contract negotiations, the other was unknowingly dragged along for the ride, and in time, we both learned how to manipulate the situation pretty well.

For example, thanks to that favored-nation clause, there was just no need for *both* of us to hire a gaggle of attorneys and agents and jump into the lion's den with every new *Star Trek* project. Instead, we could simply play good-cop/bad-cop. One of us would take a hard stand with the studio, while the other just sort of smiled and said things like, "Well, *I'm* not looking to make any waves, but I think my friend is really going to take a hard stand this time. I think you're really going to have to give in to his demands." Ten minutes later, we'd of course call each other, offering advice and support, and conspiring as to the plan of action that would prove most successful in our quest. With each successive *Star Trek* film, we alternated as the troublemaker, and when *Star Trek IV* came around, it was simply my turn in the barrel. Additionally, although Leonard could never openly support my battle (and in this instance he even helped my cause by publicly feigning annoyance with my fight, urging the studio and me to come to terms with a minimum of delay), he was nonetheless fully aware and supportive of my efforts. He would ultimately return the favor on *Star Trek V*.

Meanwhile, while my lawyers and agents were reveling in an orgy of billable hours, Leonard was off in the library, researching whales, and toying with some very basic story ideas. And then a monkey wrench fell into the works. Eddie Murphy, one of the planet's most enthusiastic Trekkers, and still hot off his success in *Beverly Hills Cop*, had begun making himself very vocal around the Paramount lot, lobbying tirelessly in an attempt to get himself into the next *Trek* film. Of course, upon hearing that unexpected news, Harve and Leonard were immediately interested (you don't brush off the biggest star in Hollywood when he says he wants to work with you), and within days, Murphy and a passel of black-leather-clad bodyguards had taken over Leonard's office, watching Nimoy and Bennett pitch the basic idea that he and Leonard had concocted. When they'd finished, Murphy smiled and said, "That's REALLY good! Make sure you get me a script as soon as possible." With that, Eddie and company swept out of the office, and Harve and Leonard leapt into action. They had a script to write . . . fast.

By February 1985, having already interviewed dozens of writers, Leonard ultimately asked the team of Steve Meerson and Peter Krikes to write his Eddie Murphy–laden script for *Star Trek IV*. In dozens of creative meetings, Leonard, Harve, Meerson and Krikes hashed out any number of script ideas until a very basic throughline began taking shape, and certain story elements began falling into place.

As legend has it, Murphy was to play a rather eccentric college professor, one who firmly believed in the existence of extraterrestrials, ghosts, ESP and the like. His students, however, weren't nearly as open-minded, and they'd let him know that whenever he'd open up his classroom to discussions of such topics. Finally, after a series of embarrassing and very public false alarms, Murphy's job would have been hanging by a thread. And at that point, he would have gone to the Super Bowl.

Occupying the worst seats in the house on a typically foggy San Francisco afternoon, Murphy's professor character would have been enduring the game's stereotypically awful and overblown halftime show when he would have become one of about sixty thousand witnesses to the first appearance of a Klingon bird of prey in the twentieth century. He would also become the *only* witness to believe it to be real.

With low visibility, a shaky mastery of the Klingon controls, and no idea as to their exact location, the former crew of the *Enterprise* would have finally decloaked their beat-up, clunky Klingon ship about one hundred feet above the Super Bowl halftime show. At that point, an uproarious cheer would have risen from the stands as the crowd acknowledged what they believed to be a man-made special effect. Murphy, however, unlike his fellow 59,999 ticket holders, would be sure that what he was seeing was the extraterrestrials he'd believed in all along.

However, due to the character's reputation as a kook, his every attempt to convince anyone that genuine extraterrestrials had come to visit the Earth would prove fruitless. Later, when Murphy was alone in his classroom, listening to a series of recorded whale songs, the Klingon ship's computers would lock onto the sound, and shortly thereafter, Murphy would have found Kirk, Spock and company beaming into his classroom, asking directions, bidding him good day, and ultimately hightailing it away from their wide-eyed observer. Many plot-twisting scenes and about three centuries later, in the end, as the *Enterprise II* is unveiled, Murphy would have been seen in full Starfleet regalia, having joined the force and saluting his friends.

Seven months passed in the creation of that . . . uh . . . rather unusual storyline, and it was finished just in time for Eddie to drop out of the project. Depending on who you believe, Murphy backed away from the film for one of two reasons. Either he simply opted instead to make *The Golden Child*, or he was talked out of appearing in *Star Trek IV* by the Paramount suits, who most likely wanted no part of mixing their top two franchises. In short, with every Eddie Murphy film of that era potentially capable of drawing one hundred million dollars, and the *Trek* films consistently drawing just about eighty, mixing franchises, though it would have been wildly entertaining on screen, would have made absolutely no business sense. Either way, Murphy's withdrawal from the film left Leonard and Harve back at square one, with time beginning to get tight.

At that point, Leonard and Harve began formulating a plan that just might get them back on schedule. However, it would not be possible unless one very key player could be lured aboard. So Dawn Steel made a phone call, begged, pleaded, schmoozed and ultimately brought in a ringer, her friend . . . Nick Meyer. Nick explains:

One day I got a call from Dawn Steel saying, "We've got to start all over on *Star Trek IV*. Can you go in and see Harve and Leonard?" So I said, "Sure." And I went in to see them and I asked, "What's going on?" And they said, "Well, we have a basic story, and we hired two screenwriters to do the screenplay but they . . . well, it just didn't work out." I asked them, "Why didn't it work? Story problems? Writer problems?" And they said, "Well, we don't want to get into why." Only much later did I learn that they had written this thing for Eddie Murphy.

So then I asked Leonard, "What's this thing all about?" And I'll never forget Leonard's response, he said, "It's something nice. We're going to do something nice." And he and Harve started telling me about the whale story, I liked it, and they said, "We're a little bit under the gun now because our production date is closing in. Is that a problem for you?" And I said, "Hey, c'mon, 'Under the Gun' is my middle name! Remember me? I'm the twelve day wonder! I'm in!"

At that point, Harve said, "Great, here's what will happen. I'll write the bookends, I'll write Act One and Act Four, which is the stuff in space, and you write Act Two and Act Three, that's the stuff on Earth." I said, "Fine," but when I heard the story, I had to say, "Wait a minute. Wait, there is one problem here. This is just like *Time After Time*. I already *did* this. Can't they go to another city? Do they have to go to San Francisco, because that *really* is *Time After Time*. Can't we go to Paris? I've always wanted to go to Paris." They said, "Nope, sorry, we can't go to Paris because Starfleet is located in San Francisco and Paramount is located here in L.A." So I just said, "Well, okay. Maybe it's not such a big deal."

So we went through the story, talked about how it was really just a big scavenger hunt, fooled around with a couple of plot points, and had a long discussion about how time was of the essence. That didn't bother me at all, because I have a theory that certain kinds of art work best when they're done very fast. Cooking is one of those things, and you know Handel's *Messiah* was written in twenty-four days, so I don't mind being in that sort of pressure cooker. It just doesn't trouble me. I think it may actually be a positive part of the process.

Then I got to work, and because this was a scavenger hunt, and very much like *Time After Time*, God knows I had been in these vineyards before. So it came together quickly, and rather easily. I think that after we did it, there were really only a couple of minor revisions. And then you guys were off and running.

I stayed away from *III* because I didn't want to resurrect Spock, which somehow in my mind attacked the integrity and the authenticity of the feelings provoked by his death. However, by the time we got to *IV*, Spock was alive, it was a de facto thing, and on top of that, my friends were in trouble. I had a problem. Dawn was my friend, Leonard's my friend, Harve is my friend, you are my friend, so I thought, *Well shit, you know, be useful. These people were awfully good to you, awful good. You be good back.* So, I was quite happy playing the waiter. The most fun thing for me was getting to recycle moments that I'd had to cut out of *Time After Time*.

I should take a moment to explain that *Time After Time* is a terrific film that Nick directed in 1979. A romantic adventure-fantasy, the film mixes and matches elements of *The Time Machine* and *Jack the Ripper*. Basically, when Jack the Ripper successfully uses H. G. Wells's time-traveling device to escape Scotland Yard's best, Wells chases after the legendary bad guy, ending up in the San Francisco of the late seventies. With that in mind, you can understand Nick's ability to lift many of his unused ideas straight out of the plot of that film. Nick continues:

had a scene in the movie where H. G. Wells, who has already caused one traffic accident by not understanding streetlights, now walks up to a streetlight that says DON'T WALK and he stops and while he's standing there, a Chinese boy with a ghetto blaster pulls up next to him waiting for the light to change. And this ghetto blaster is blasting acid rock and you can see on Malcolm McDowell's face, "What is this?" and he'd like to move but the sign says DON'T WALK and he's taking that literally. Finally, after enduring the noise, the light changes and he is able to leave.

Subsequently, about three reels later in the movie he's having dinner with the love interest, Mary Steenburgen, and she says to him, "What kind of music do you like?" And he thinks about it for a moment and finally says, "Anything but Oriental." And while that always worked pretty well on paper, when we began having our previews, it just didn't work on screen at all. The punch line was just too far away from the setup.

THE SAN FRANCISCAN NERVE PINCH

So I cut out the punch line and left in the scene with the kid and the radio, but over the next couple of previews, it started to really bug me. I had overdirected the kid. He was bopping around in a very exaggerated style and it wasn't funny, so I ended up cutting it out.

However, when I got to write Star Trek IV I still wanted to trash rock music and that's when I put that guy in the bus.

I can even tell you exactly where I start and where I stop. First line of mine in the movie is, "Judging by the pollution content of the atmosphere we've reached the late twentieth century," and I go out right before the line about D. H. Lawrence and the whales. That was Harve's.

As they say in our business, "success has many fathers" and it bears mentioning that Leonard Nimoy also claims paternity for Spock's mass-transit pinch scene. As leonard tells it, he came up with the idea for the scene as a result of an encounter he had during a pleasant stroll in New York City. When a young man with a gigantic boom box disrupted the relative peace with his blaring, twin-speakered, bass-heavy noise, Leonard recalls, "I really wanted to pinch him into oblivion." Months later he'd get his revenge vicariously, on camera, through the fingers of Mr. Spock.

Either way, while Meyer was pounding a keyboard at home, Harve Bennett was whipping his half of the script into shape on the Paramount lot. Squirreling himself away for the better part of every day, he too found himself enjoying the process and making rapid progress. In fact, within three weeks, both Harve and Nick Meyer had completed their tasks, and when their scripts were finally paired up, attached, and read as a whole, it was obvious to all concerned that *Star Trek IV* had a real shot at being real good. With such highly seasoned *Trek*-experienced talent churning out our script, writing with an unparalleled ear for our characters' dialogue and a thorough understanding of the dynamics and interrelationships of the *Enterprise* crew, the script, even at first-draft stage, required very little polishing. In fact, it may very well have represented the finest portrayal of our crewmen ever penned. Leonard Nimoy, who was thrilled with the script, would certainly agree. Leonard explains:

I've always felt that the dynamic between Spock, Kirk and McCoy was an incredibly important driving force behind the best of *Star Trek*, and when I first read the script for *IV*, it became apparent that the characters were going to interact very well in this particular installment. One wonderful example takes place early in the film with Spock, Kirk and McCoy huddled around one of the ship's computers as it goes about deciphering our "mysterious incoming transmission." It tells us it's the song of the humpback whale, at which point Spock says something to the effect of, "As I suspected, we cannot reproduce this sound because it is made only by the humpback whale, which is extinct." Kirk then asks some leading questions, trying to figure out if it'd be possible to re-create the whale sounds, and Spock replies that while we could duplicate the noise, we'd have no ability to re-create the actual language or the thoughts of these whales. In effect, the synthetic re-creation would simply be speaking gibberish.

Kirk then asks, "Can we find these whales

elsewhere . . . perhaps on another planet?" Spock replies, "No, the species is indigenous only to the Earth of the twentieth century." Kirk takes a thoughtful pause, lets out a "Hmmmm . . . right," and at that point you can practically hear the wheels turning inside his head.

At the same time, McCoy's brow is beginning to furrow, it's obvious that he too knows Kirk's probable reply, and almost immediately he starts in with "Wait a minute, do you know what you're talking about?" Kirk then replies, "Spock, prepare your calculations for time warp," and he's off.

Physically and intellectually, Kirk is now in motion. He's gotten the information he needs, he's made his decision and he's now going to put it into action. The character's motivation is clear, precise and well-defined. His actions are therefore absolutely appropriate.

Kirk now begins walking down one of the ship's corridors, toward the bridge, intent on implementing his plan, and that allows McCoy to become the antagonist for a moment, saying, "Are you crazy? You say you're going to do A, B, C and D?"

Kirk says, "That is correct."

"And then you're going to do X, Y and Z?" says McCoy.

"That's right," says Kirk, "if you've got a better plan, now's the time." We get to the bridge and we continue forward. Kirk's closest allies have now provided him with information on both sides of the issue. He knows the possibilities, he knows the potential problems, and he's made his decision. That sort of back-and-forth dialogue created great opportunities for all of us. Kirk could assert

ABOVE: Overlooking the real *Enterprise* bridge
BELOW: Cranky ol' doctor versus stubborn ol' director

himself as the classic leading man, whose decisions drive the action of any given scene, Spock could play reflective, and McCoy could be the anguished, argumentative hand-wringer. McCoy could be the quibbler, which was great for De, and that allowed me to play, "Hmmmm . . . very interesting. Now how is this dilemma going to play out?"

Leonard, equally insistent that this film remain light, enjoyable and full of comic moments, was also quite happy with that aspect of the script:

Harve's sense of humor is a lot broader than mine. I tend to go for the "wink of an eye" kind of humor, and Harve tends more toward the banana peel. He constructs jokes. On *Star Trek III*, there's a moment that got a genuine laugh that's his joke. Scotty steps into the elevator of the *Excelsior* in a bad mood and hears a pompous elevator voice asking, "Level, please?" In fact, I did that voice. And Scotty says, "Engine room." The voice then says, "Thank . . . you," at which point Scotty replies with, "Up your shaft." Genuine laugh, but a constructed joke.

I shot that, and I used it in the film, but I much prefer to have the humor come from directly within the characters. Because of that, I much preferred the stuff that Nick Meyer wrote in *IV*: "Do you like Italian?" "Yes." "No." "Yes." "Yes." Chekov not understanding why nobody will tell him where the nuclear wessels are, or that wonderful moment when Kirk says to Gillian, "You'll have to forgive my friend. He was in school at Berkeley in the sixties, and I think he did too much LDS." Wonderful. Throwaway line, big laugh. That's the perfect example. Kirk is standing there fumbling, trying to say the right thing, obviously not trying to make a joke, but in trying to remember the name of this drug from the sixties that might help to explain away Spock's eccentricities, he comes up with LDS. I was very happy with all that.

Another moment that really seemed to work in the film wasn't scripted at all, and it turned out to be a really great moment. It really allowed us a moment wherein camaraderie could break loose out of rigidity and discipline and responsibility and tension. It was a moment wherein all of our principals were allowed to simply break loose, relax and have a good time.

It comes at the end of the film, and as we shot it, we were in the water, standing on the hull of the ship, and as far as the story's concerned, the storm's now over, the whales have been saved, and as we stood there, victorious upon the hull, I said to everybody, "Let's just have fun with this." And then I looked over at you, and I knew I'd made a mistake, because I knew exactly what you were going to do. I could see that evil gleam in your eyes, and I knew immediately that you were determined to tear me loose from that fucking thing and throw me in the water. I ended up getting soaked, but the spontaneity of that scene and the freedom worked beautifully. The audience really loved it.

As the script continued taking shape, Nimoy and Bennett continued to find themselves thoroughly pleased with the progress. Weeks later, as our first readthroughs and rehearsals began, the script was quickly and almost unanimously embraced as one of our very best. The only holdout was Gene Roddenberry. Memos initialed "G. R." quickly began piling up on Harve's desk, but by now, having dealt with similar objections on *Star Treks II* and *III*, Harve was much more adept at dealing with and dancing around Gene's input:

would just type out "Per your memo of . . . ," and then I would take all the positive stuff that was helpful and I would say, "Page two, line four, what a fantastic idea, let's do this 'n' this 'n' this," or "You say that this line is not appropriate for this character, and you're probably right. Why don't we revise it as follows?" And sometimes, when we were dealing with more than just lines, I'd write back, "You're absolutely right. We'll look into a fresh approach immediately." I simply found that the best way to deal with Gene was to accentuate the positive and forget about the rest.

Still, when all was said and done, the script for *Star Trek IV* fell into place beautifully. Eddie Murphy was gone, and in his place was Dr. Gillian Taylor, a beautiful young marine biologist, who just so happened to be attracted to a certain starship captain. Kirk chasing after a woman? Not exactly a novel concept, but because the poor guy had suffered through *Treks I*, *II* and *III* without a love interest, he'd basically spent the past seventeen years without a woman. Talk about cold turkey! Talk about withdrawal! And you wondered why he always looked so intense. Anyway, with Kirk back in the saddle and an exciting, well-written story ready to start shooting, everyone involved in this film was awaiting the start of our principal photography with a great deal of enthusiasm . . . except, of course, for the whales.

Whereas Jimmy Doohan had always been the largest mammal in our previous films, we now had George and Gracie, a pair of fully grown humpback whales, as two of our main characters. As you might expect, that posed a bit of a problem. How do you shoot whales? Find them in the wild? Shoot them in some theme

ABOVE: Vulcan overboard—almost
OPPOSITE: Spock prepares Kirk for his first
date in seventeen years

park? Animate them? Ultimately, we did none of those things, opting instead to try something entirely new, which leads me to reveal another previously unknown secret. There are no actual whales in *Star Trek IV*. Instead, the effects guys at Industrial Light and Magic made up a pair of mechanical humpbacks so incredibly lifelike, with movements so meticulously matched up with those of real whales, that when we ultimately got our plastic-and-rubber mammals into the water, they actually swam. Without wires, without bottom support, these things were so well made, with movements so incredibly similar to those of real whales, that when their creators let go of them underwater, they simply "swam" away. The on-screen results of their unbelievable wizardry fooled absolutely everyone. They were, and continue to be, the best in the business.

I should also mention that Leonard decided to shoot many of this film's seafaring scenes amid the briny blue of the . . . Paramount parking lot. While desperately trying to come up with some idea about how we might safely and realistically shoot our whales, special effects

ABOVE: Out for a sail in the Paramount parking lot
OPPOSITE: Giving birth to George and Gracie

man Mike Lanteri came across some old blueprints showing that underneath what was now the Paramount Studios visitors' parking lot there lay an absolutely enormous water tank, used primarily throughout the thirties and forties for pirate movies, water-follies-style musicals, World War II epics, and the like. When those films went the way of the Edsel, the tank was covered over, blacktopped, parked upon and forgotten about . . . until now. Calculating that unearthing the old tank, repairing it and refilling it would ultimately prove far cheaper than actually trying to shoot our whales in the sea, Leonard and Harve greenlighted the dig and were thrilled to find that once filled with water, the tank was still intact and functioning perfectly. In the end, they saved the film almost a million dollars.

As it turned out, that tank was by no means our only unusual shooting locale, as we also, for the first time in a long time, headed out into the street, into the fresh air and sunshine. I have to tell you that at every turn and every step of this production, our location shoots were uniformly enjoyable and almost always exhilarating. In short, we had a great time. As executive producer Ralph Winter can tell you, the fun began very early on:

On *Star Trek IV*, we were scouting a location in Oakland with Leonard, and when we'd finished, we went back to the parking lot to pick up our van and go home. So the car attendant goes and gets the van, and then he says to the driver, just as we're all piling into the car, "You know, my friend over there thinks that guy is Leonard Nimoy. Can you believe that? I mean Leonard's not as tall as that guy. Nimoy's real short, weird-looking, too. He doesn't look like that guy at all." We all just nodded, trying not to laugh. Meanwhile Leonard's maybe three feet away from this guy. It

CREW OF THE *ENTERPRISE* ON
THE STREETS OF SAN FRANCISCO

was really funny, we were holding our sides and crying as soon as we pulled out of there.

A few minutes later, on that same trip, we're on the freeway when our driver notices that the woman driving the car in front of us has a bumper sticker on the back of her car that reads BEAM ME UP, SCOTTY, so Leonard says to the driver, "Slow down, and pull up even with her car." He then rolls down his window, makes eye contact with the driver, listens to her yell "Oh my God!!" five or six times, then gives her the Vulcan "Live Long and Prosper" salute. She almost caused an accident swerving around the highway.

About a month later, as shooting began, we all Trekked up to Frisco, checked into our hotels, checked out the local . . . uh . . . libraries and museums, and started shooting. It was great. Somehow, to be shooting out in the open after years of being cooped up on some plywood and plastic starship revitalized us all. We *knew* we had a good script, we *knew* we were in the hands of a talented director, and with all that in mind, we relaxed, rolled with the flow, and our locations became looser than any I'd ever seen before. We experimented a lot with our scenes, and in fact at times we even made things up as we went along. For example, look closely at the scenes in which Chekov grills random passers-by as to how he might find the nearest "nuclear wessels," and you'll notice that he's most often soliciting that advice from real-live, unrehearsed, slightly shocked pedestrians. Their resultant looks of incredulity are quite genuine, as most of them just assumed that Walter was simply out of his mind.

I can clearly recall feeling, as I was standing on the sidelines while those scenes were shot, like this set was the most casual, relaxed, joyous production I'd ever had the pleasure of working on. In fact, as I spoke with my fellow castmates about this particular installment, nobody had a bad word to say about it . . . well, except for George Takei, whose struggle to beef up the part of Sulu nearly drove him to distraction. George explains:

I've always been an activist in my career as well as the political arena, so right from the beginning of the TV series, I started bombarding Gene Roddenberry with ideas and suggestions, the main thrust of them being to make Sulu's part bigger, give him more to do, flesh him out more, establish some relationship with the character. I'm relentless, and I just kept on going at him, and ultimately a lot of my ideas did appear on-screen.

I kept that up all through the series, and when we started making movies, I started back in right away. For example, during *The Wrath of Khan*, I started pushing for Sulu to finally get his captaincy. I pushed hard, and it finally got to the point where Harve was so sick and tired of my lobbying about the idea that we shot it. You know, I'd never give up, I'd just keep smiling, and whenever I could corner Harve in some social situation, I'd be telling him, "You know, 'Captain Sulu' has a nice ring to it, don't you think?" Sadly, in the end, it wound up on the cutting-room floor. A similar thing happened on *IV*, and it's a great story.

When I got my script for *IV*, I read it and was disappointed by the fact that Sulu was basically just being used as an animated prop again, but instead of just complaining about that, I came up with a plan. First, I phoned Harve and I said, "I've got some ideas that I want to talk to you about." And Harve, of course, being a real diplomat, always says something like, "Oh, that's great, I have some ideas too. Let's talk." So we got together and he had this notion about our going into a San Francisco sushi bar and when I heard it, I too had to be diplomatic because my first thought was, "Oh my God! That's a *load* of sushi!" It was so clichéd.

So I said, "Harve, we're going back in time many generations. Wouldn't it be fun if we made San Francisco Sulu's birthplace? Because if Sulu's birthplace was San Francisco, it's conceivable that his ancestors would be living there and wouldn't it be interesting if Sulu should bump into one of them? Wouldn't it be even *more* interesting if Sulu should meet his great-grandfather who just so happens to be a little boy at the time of their encounter?" And Harve said, "That's a GREAT idea! Let me think on it."

All the way into principal production, George heard nothing—and then one day, Harve rushed in:

He was just beaming. He had written it. He had written my scene. Sulu was going to meet his own great-grandfather. I read it and I said, "Harve, I could kiss you." And he said, "Why don't you?" So I did.

As it was written, McCoy and Scotty and I were walking down a busy city street in front of an old apartment building when this little lost Asian boy comes running up to us, and he hugs Sulu and smiles because he thinks I'm his uncle. Turns out

I look just like the guy. And when the kid finally realizes I'm *not* his uncle, we get into a conversation. I ask him his name and address, and that's how I come to the realization that he's my great-grandfather.

On the morning of the kid's "big scene," he arrived bright and early, had breakfast, got made up, and tried his best to keep smiling through all the chaos that was going on around him. At the same time, hovering around the kid on either side was one of the most over-the-top stage mothers ever created on this planet and an older brother who seemed to take particular delight in taunting his younger sibling. With all that, and adding into the mix that this kid was NOT a professional actor and had never been on a movie set before, you can understand how he very quickly grew rather intimidated. Sensing the tension in the air, George made a quick stop at the local five and ten, then paid a quick visit to the boy's trailer, smiling at him, introducing himself, and trying his best to buy the boy's friendship with a handful of dime-store candies. It seemed to be working. George continues:

He took the candy, and we started talking, but the mother was hovering all over this poor kid. You know, I'd ask him, "Do you like *Star Trek*?" and before he could even answer, she'd be going, "Oh YES! You've seen it, haven't you, honey? You know Mr. Sulu, don't you? You like Mr. Sulu, he's your favorite, isn't he?" And the kid would just sort of look down and nod.

I was already sensing that we had problems, so I tried to get this kid away from his mother, hoping that without her around, I might be able to establish some sort of relationship. I felt like it might be our only hope. This mom was extremely intense about the whole thing. Y'know, as far as she was concerned, this was her child's "big break," so throughout the day, in-between scenes, I just kept sprinting back to this kid, hoping that I might be able to make him a little more comfortable with me and the scene. But every time I came back, the kid just looked more upset.

And every time I tried to start a conversation about *Star Trek* with the kid, the mother was answering for him, and touting him. "Oh, he knows the lines backward and forward, he's done it many, many times now, you have nothing to worry about." She was really selling the kid. I asked her, "Can we practice?" And she answered, "Oh, yes, he's wonderful, he's very good, Mr. Takei." So I said, "Please, call me George." And she smiled and suggested, "*Uncle* George, we'll call you 'Uncle George.'" Then she turned to the kid and said, "Uncle George is going to work with you now. Do it exactly like I taught you, remember?" I saw that and immediately asked, "Uh, can we go off . . . alone?" And she frowned, but said, "Yes, of course."

So the boy and I went off together, but when I looked back over my shoulder I could see that the mother and brother were still hovering, maybe twenty feet away, listening to everything we were saying. "What do you do at school?" I asked him. "I don't know," he told me. He was being very shy. Now there's a tap on my shoulder.

Turns out it's the brother, and he's arrived as Mommy's emissary. "Mom says you should stop talking and practice the lines with Uncle George.

You did it at home, just do it like that." I sent him back to his mother. Then this kid and I picked up our conversation where we'd left off. I asked him, "What school do you go to?" and that stumped him for a moment, at which point the mother yells from twenty feet away, "He goes to Buchanan Avenue School!" At that point, I knew we needed to get the mother and brother further away. The kid was really starting to freeze up.

With several hours to kill before shooting his scene with the kid, George collared Leonard, explained the situation, and asked for his help. Several minutes later, at Leonard's request, two of our AD's arrived, distracting the kid's mom and the brother while ushering them toward our free coffee and donuts. At that point, while clad in the robe he wore throughout most of this film, Leonard got on his knees in front of the boy, smiled, then pointed at George, asking, "Do you know this man?" The kid grinned a little, nodded, and all three sides of the triangle started feeling a little better.

And now, right before their very eyes, Leonard miraculously transforms from curmudgeon to cheerleader. He starts bobbing up and down, smiling like crazy, tousling the kid's hair, trading high fives, and by the time he's called back to the set, Leonard's performance has left the kid laughing. From there, however, George's afternoon, and the kid's, progressed steadily . . . downhill. George continues:

I had been trying to spend some time alone with this kid all afternoon, but no matter how hard I tried, I just couldn't shake Mommy and big brother. Because of that, we were never able to

SULU, SPOCK AND THE KID

make any further progress, and the kid spent the better part of the afternoon getting progressively more tense and unhappy. Finally, I got called away to do a scene, and when I returned, I found the mom between two buildings, holding the script in one hand and spanking her kid with the other. It was just awful. So I went right in there and said, "Please don't do that. That's not helping the situation." I took the child with me, because it was now time for us to start shooting our scene. The kid's no longer smiling, no longer talking, basically he's just scowling, and trying hard not to cry. Perfect timing. Absolutely perfect.

Not surprisingly, when we got to the set, it quickly became obvious that this kid wasn't going to do ANYTHING. Leonard and I begged, pleaded, offered candy and presents, but still we got almost nothing, just a few random shots. Leonard turned the camera on the kid and had me squeeze right up next to it. We forgot about the script at that point, I improvised a bit while we got a few reaction shots from the kid. Then we lost the light. It had gotten too dark for us to continue shooting.

Sulu's big scene was now hanging by a thread, but I was not willing to give up. I said to Leonard, "We are going to come back, aren't we?" And Leonard said, "We'll see what we can do," you know, he doesn't make definitive statements, but I thought surely we'd come back the next day and make another attempt. So I went back with the kid and told him, "We don't have to do it anymore. We're finished for the day, so we can relax." And the kid instantly relaxed and said, "Oh, we're finished?" His energy level picked up immediately, and he then started into an animated conversation with me. On the way home, I actually began feeling pretty good about being able to get that back.

However, when I got to the set the next day, I found out the scene had been canceled. I was devastated, absolutely devastated. Immediately, I went to Leonard, and he said, "I'm sorry, George, we just don't have the time to go back and shoot the scene. We're going to have to move on." I said "But Leonard, it's such a charming, delightful and heartwarming scene—we need this in the movie." And Leonard said, "Yes, I know, I agree, but we're only here at this location for a very limited time, and we've just got to move on. Sorry, George."

I could have cried, but I didn't, because y'know, it's happened to me so often.

Still, despite George's disaster, the bulk of our shooting on *Star Trek IV* came off without a hitch. Once again we ran slightly ahead of schedule, and as far as Leonard was concerned, the training wheels were now off, and he commandeered the camera with a great deal of poise, confidence and enthusiasm. And though his relationship with Harve Bennett had now frozen stiff—the two men were not speaking to one another—our production ran like clockwork, finishing ahead of schedule, with a final price tag of $25 million, almost a full million under budget. Postproduction commenced almost immediately, and while it too ran rather well, Harve and Leonard's relationship became its sole casualty. Leonard explains:

I found on *IV*, because I'd gone head-to-head with Harve a couple of times during production, I had almost no problem with him in post. I was very happy with the way it was going. The previews had gone extraordinarily well, and I'd even won a couple of bets over certain scenes or jokes and whether or not they'd play. But there was one major complication, and Harve and I ended up having it out on the street again.

I became very angry with Harve, maybe unfairly, because Dawn Steel was concerned that audiences would be put off by not being able to understand the dialogue between the probe and the humpback whales. She thought we should spell out their conversation, but I said, "We are better off not explaining it. Let it be mysterious and magical. Let the audience retain its wonder, because if we reduce this thing to mundane dialogue, it's going to play funny and tacky, and we'll lose that magic."

She continued to be concerned about it, and

FOR TWO OLD PALS LIKE US, IT COMES NATURALLY

then one day, out of nowhere, up popped a memo from Harve, and circulated to myself and the studio executives, touting his ideas about the dialogue between the whales and the space probe. His suggestion was that during our opening shot, wherein the probe moves toward camera, making its sounds, we could add a subtitle saying "Where are you?" He also suggested that we add similar subtitles later on. I was furious, furious!

I said to him, "You should have come to me and discussed this rationally. I already had this discussion with David Kirkpatrick, who was sent to me by Dawn Steel." I then explained to him why I didn't like the idea, giving him the same pitch I'd used on Kirkpatrick. That's when it hit me. Dawn Steel may have been using Harve as a stalking horse. Harve's memo may have been ordered by Steel. It may simply have been a tool of political gamesmanship.

I took Harve to task over that, and I said, "I think this is really nasty. Putting out this memo for all to see puts me on the stand." Suddenly, I have to rejustify my position, because my producer writes a memo making it clear that he sides with management. That gives them ammunition. I knew they'd come back and say, "Look, Harve Bennett agrees with us, read his memo!" I was going to have to argue this thing through all over again. So I really raked him over the coals. Only later was I able to rationalize that because he worked for the studio, Harve was really just doing his job, and these people really do play these games.

Sadly, this flare-up became the straw that broke the camel's back, and the two men, who'd now been sporadically battling for the better part of four years, simply gave up the fight, going their separate directions without ever really healing the wounds they'd inflicted upon one another. Still, despite the personal turmoil, their co-creation, *Star Trek IV*, became an enormous success.

Star Trek IV, to employ a tired cliché, went where no *Star Trek* film had gone before, racking up critical raves and an amazing $109 million at the box office. As you might have guessed, rumored plans for an unprecedented fourth sequel surfaced almost immediately. No one was happier about that than I. And that leads me to one final plot twist.

During our final days of production on *Star Trek IV*, Leonard and I were sitting together at lunch one day, and halfway through a lasagna hard enough to hammer nails, he hit me with something from out of the blue. "You know," he told me, "I was thinking about something. Because of our favored-nation situation, if there's ever another *Star Trek* sequel, you *could* successfully demand to direct." All at once I got chills and grew just a bit queasy. It had nothing to do with the lasagna.

In the months that followed, as we finished shooting and went our separate ways, I just smiled, kept my mouth shut and started thinking about what ideas might make for a good *Star Trek V*. By November 1986, as we all reassembled for *Star Trek IV*'s world premiere, I had already come up with a pretty clear idea of what I'd like to do. All that had to happen now was for *The Voyage Home* to become a successful enough hit to merit a sequel.

That night, as the lights dimmed and people all over the theater began rapidly shushing one another, I sat there quietly rooting for Leonard's film to be a hit, and by the midpoint of the movie, I found myself smiling uncontrollably. With the crowd laughing and cheering enthusiastically on cue, it was clear that this film might very well turn out to be a smash. Later on that evening, at the swanky cocktail party following the film, as we all got progressively more uncomfortable in our tuxes and endlessly answered a series of uniformly dumb questions from the uniformly perky blond newspeople who'd converged upon the proceedings from every nook and cranny of the country, I made it a point to seek out studio chief Frank Mancuso. I caught him near the cheese puffs.

"Frank!" I yelled as I threw my arm around his shoulder, negating any chance he might have of escaping. "Wasn't that a great picture?"

"Oh yeah, terrific."

"And you'd have to guess that there's gonna have to be another sequel?"

"Uh . . . sure, I guess so," said Mancuso, squirming a bit in my grasp.

"Well, uh . . ." I stammered a bit ". . . what would you say if I told you I wanted to direct *Star Trek V*?"

"I'd say, 'By all means. Go right ahead.' I think that's

a great idea." He then smiled at me while sucking down an entire cheese puff in one bite. Immediately I found myself having to suppress an almost uncontrollable urge to turn cartwheels all across the banquet hall. I was beside myself with glee.

It was almost too simple. No yelling, no fighting, no threats, just one question and one answer, and a life-long dream was about to be fulfilled. I was going to direct a movie, and the crew of the *Enterprise* was about to meet God . . . after taking one short detour through hell.

STAR TREK V:
THE FRANTIC FRONTIER

By the time I'd been officially assigned the *Star Trek V* director's chair, I already had a story in mind. I got it from my TV set. See, right around the time I was seeking story inspiration, televangelists Jim and Tammy Faye Bakker were becoming an absolutely unavoidable national phenomenon. Night after night you'd see them on the news: Jim staring blankly through a shit-eating grin, Tammy weeping uncontrollably through a half-pound of putty-knife-applied, bargain-basement mascara. They were repulsive, strangely horrifying, and yet I became absolutely fascinated, for two reasons.

First, I was amazed by the idea that the Bakkers, the Robert Tiltons, or the Jimmy Swaggarts of the world could actually get up in public and espouse their theory that God, in his infinite wisdom, was now speaking directly into their heavily hairsprayed heads, demanding that they spread his word, demanding that *they* do his bidding. Was this the ultimate narcissism? A surefire money-grabbing scheme? Psychosis? I was now officially spellbound.

Even more astounding was the fact that these divinity-soaked telemarketing geniuses were almost uniformly getting rich through their wild storytelling, inexplicably convincing large numbers of outwardly sane people to believe in their blatantly transparent message. That ability stuck in my brain for weeks, and when I finally started toying around with some preliminary story ideas for *Star Trek V*, I couldn't help myself. Almost immediately, I sort of reengineered, softened and twisted all those TV evangelists into one character. He was Zar (though he'd soon be remonikered as Sybok), a holy man driven by a genuine belief that God was speaking to him, demanding that he accumulate as many followers as possible and provide a suitable vehicle with which the deity might better spread his teachings throughout the universe.

From that germ of an idea, it became a pretty natural assumption that the vehicle this guy would ultimately get hold of would be the hijacked Starship *Enterprise*, and using that plot point as a building block, while scribbling all over about a half-dozen yellow legal pads, the bulk of my preliminary story ideas laid themselves out quite nicely. The mountain-climbing at Yosemite, the campfire scene, Zar's abduction of Klingon, Romulan and human hostages in the failed desert boomtown of Paradise City—all of these ideas fell quickly into my blueprint, and ultimately survived into the finished film. However, from midpoint to finish, my original storyline bears almost no relation to that of the actual theatrical release.

In my rudimentary version, as in the film, Starfleet orders Kirk and company to rescue the hostages and apprehend Zar, but that's where the train leaves the tracks, because almost immediately, Spock surprises his shipmates by stating that he knew this renegade holy man back in Vulcan seminary. Surprise turns to shock when Spock makes it clear that he feels this man is indeed so brilliant, and so advanced, that he could *genuinely* be the Messiah.

Throughout the midsection of this tale, the crew of the *Enterprise* travels to Paradise City, battles with the forces of this holy man, and is ultimately overwhelmed by the sheer numbers within his command. In a last-ditch effort to regain control, Kirk sets a fatal trap for Zar but is defeated when Spock warns the holy man of the danger. Kirk is furious, and he is not mollified when Spock explains his actions by stating that he now truly believes Zar could be the Messiah, and with that in mind, he could not in good conscience allow any harm to come to the man. The end results of his actions find Kirk, Spock and McCoy at odds while locked up in the brig.

Later, as Zar pays a visit to his trio of prisoners, he lets them know that the rest of the crew is now solidly behind his cause. They believe in him, and through a series of mind-controlling exercises he soon convinces Spock and McCoy of his genuine divinity as well. In an attempt to heal each man's personal pain, he conjures up images of McCoy performing euthanasia upon his ailing, terminally ill father. He allows Spock to witness his own birth and immediate paternal rejection, and by the time he's finished, both Spock and Bones are believers. He then goes to work on Kirk.

He immediately speaks to Kirk's lack of family, and dredges up Kirk's self-imposed feelings of responsibility and guilt over the death of his son, David. Promising that a meeting with God will cure even such deeply embedded pain, Zar implores Kirk to believe in him as well. Feigning acceptance while remaining the sole

holdout against the powers of this man, Kirk joins Spock and Bones on the surface of God's planet.

The planet, located directly at the center of the universe, could have come from Dante's *Inferno*—a fiery, uninhabitable, completely barren wasteland. An awesome godlike image appears, surrounded by angels, and demands that the *Enterprise* transport him back toward more populated sections of the universe. Kirk then challenges "God," and an argument ensues. As it escalates, "God" begins showing his true colors, and his image begins to transform, ultimately becoming unmistakably satanic. The angels simultaneously change into hordes of gargoyles, the Furies of Hell.

At that point, Kirk, Spock and McCoy, still suffering the effects of their first real adversarial relationship, split up, with each man running in a separate direction. McCoy falls, breaking his leg, and is surrounded by the Furies, as is Spock. At the same time, however, Kirk has broken free, but even with a clear path toward escape, a last look back at the fates of his friends convinces Kirk to go back, risking his life in an effort to save them.

Spock is first, and when he's been successfully freed, the pair immediately joins forces in an attempt to save McCoy, who's already been carried away by the minions into Hell. Descending together into the river Styx, Spock and Kirk fight off their hideous attackers and save their injured friend, with Kirk carrying McCoy on his shoulders as they flee.

Essentially, I was trying to say that while man conceives God in his own image, that image changes from generation to generation, often allowing manmade gods, pretenders, their foothold. Additionally, since we had come face-to-face with the devil, we could infer that God does indeed exist, most tangibly and understandably within the heart of man.

I took that sketchy rough storyline to Paramount chairman Frank Mancuso, nervous that he'd be scared off by its rather weighty religious aspects, but to my surprise, he really liked the idea, asking that I now hire a writer to flesh this thing out into a full-blown story treatment. Immediately I knew who I wanted. His name was Eric Van Lustbader, a novelist whose work is uniformly mysterious, spiritual and unfalteringly beautiful. I called him, flew to New York, met him, liked him, he liked me, and by meeting's end we'd tentatively agreed to team up. However, as weeks passed, he and the studio couldn't agree over who'd own the rights to the published version of his story, their negotiations fell apart, and I found myself right back at square one.

Finally, when I just couldn't sit still any longer, I grabbed my tape recorder and dictated a full-blown version of the story myself. When it was typed up, I presented it to Paramount's reigning president of production, Ned Tanen, and waited for his input. At the same time, I had begun fighting an important uphill battle. I had to convince Harve Bennett to come back and work with me.

Since Harve had produced *Treks II*, *III* and *IV* while writing *III* and co-writing *IV*, I knew that there was no one on the planet more qualified to hold my hand while softening the bumps and bruises of my tenure on *Star Trek V*. Harve's experience and talent were irreplaceable, so I called him up, told him that I wanted to chat with him about producing *Star Trek V*, and invited him to come have lunch with me at the Equestrian Center near my home. "No," was his answer, "not on your turf. I want you to come to my house."

I had no idea what he was talking about, but because I like Harve a lot, and because I knew I really needed his help in making this picture, I was more than happy to meet at his place. Harve explains:

The reason I insisted upon you coming to my house was because of the pain I was still feeling from *Star Trek IV* and the fact that Leonard and I weren't on the best of terms by the end of that movie. Somewhere along the line, Leonard began to view me as an obstacle, as the guy who delighted in saying "No," as somebody constantly conspiring against him. When that happened, things got tense, and on one occasion it got really mean, mean from him to me, right on the stage. So I was still a bit shell-shocked.

Basically, there was just no way in hell I was going to allow myself to get into another situation where I would find myself getting deballed by Gene Roddenberry's memos and knocked around by a star/director at the same time. After my experience on *IV*, I really felt like I wasn't a family member after all, that maybe the stars had all the power, that everybody knew that, and that no one would accept any other situation. I felt like a tin soldier, a dog without teeth, and I felt I had *earned* the command authority, and I didn't want to be used. Those were my feelings going into it, and because of that, I wanted things on *my* turf. You had to come to me.

But you had no problem with that, and we ultimately spent the better part of an afternoon, at least four or five hours, holed up together at my bar, talking about my feelings, and about the stuff that happened between Leonard and me on *IV*, and my fears that the same shit could happen again on *V*. I wanted to make it very clear that if I found myself having a bad time, I'd quit. I said to you, "If you accept me as your producer, you've also got to accept my ability to say 'no' and my opinions in terms of the story." And as we talked, you ultimately seduced me with your honesty, your need, your enthusiasm and of course the good feeling that I had always had about you.

You said, "Harve, I really need your help," and I felt good about that. It's what actually convinced me that I would *not* have to go through another painful experience. As a result, we shook hands, and I came into *Star Trek V* with a lot of excitement. Of course, that didn't prevent us from arguing over the story.

I always had—and I expressed to you—a deep concern that the essential premise of the story you wanted to tell was like *Star Trek: The Motion Picture*, more of a tone poem than an adventure story, and at the same time, it was also saddled with problems not unlike Roddenberry's "Let's go back and save Jack Kennedy" story. Namely, no matter what happened in your first ninety minutes, you were still going to be stuck with a predictable, unsatisfying, unworkable solution at the end of your film.

You know, if you were to reduce your original story down to a TV *Guide* log line, "Tonight on *Star Trek* the *Enterprise* goes off in search of God," people would have said, "Well, that'll be a fruitless search," because they know from the history of literature and myth and movies that no one will ever find God. You just can't, because if you did, no matter how you depicted him, or her, you would ultimately just offend people. Since nobody can accurately and assuredly answer the question "What is God?" your climax becomes amorphous, and less than satisfying.

Harve's concerns were almost immediately echoed by the studio's latest round of feedback. Basically, while they liked the idea of my story, they were nonetheless concerned that the subject matter, as written, might prove a bit too heavy, too large for the average moviegoer, especially after the laughs and lightheartedness of *The Voyage Home*. Could we lighten our story a bit? Upon receiving those notes, I sighed, rolled with the punches and made the best of the situation. I grabbed ahold of Harve, and the two of us immediately locked ourselves into his office and began a period of self-imposed imprisonment, routinely spending ten to twelve hours a day, sleeves rolled up, reading glasses in place, endlessly hashing over every aspect of our story.

Our first days in Harve's shag-carpeted, climate-controlled jail cell were spent arguing over the film's most basic premise, the *Enterprise* crew's search for God. As you know, Harve was opposed to the idea from the start, and with the studio now feeling similarly shaky about the idea, Harve came up with a workable alternative. He explains:

Originally, almost from page one, we made it clear that this holy man believed that God was speaking directly to him, ordering him to travel the galaxy, to gather up a starship and to bring it to him. And as I thought about that, it struck me that in effect we'd taken all the suspense and surprise out of the film. What I proposed as an alternative was to hold that information back until much later in the story. You know, ultimately we had this guy overtaking the *Enterprise*, then plotting a course through this mysterious and highly dangerous "Great Barrier." Only at that point did we have Kirk ask him, "How do you know you'll get through?" and Sybok answers, "Because of the vision . . . the vision given to me by God. He waits for me on the other side."

Kirk then says, "You're mad!" and that puts the audience on his side. That had to be very clear, because if there were any gray area there, the audience would've simply been disappointed in Kirk, and they probably would've turned on him, at least subconsciously. We basically took a serious story that said, "We're going to find God" and flipped it over by positioning God as a surprise plot twist, the climax of a bizarre series of events.

Coming into this thing, I wasn't at all sure your storyline would ever really work, but I accepted that challenge, and as the weeks wore on and the delight of our relationship began to deepen, I'd say to myself, "Maybe we *can* make this work. Maybe we *can* pull this off." And my thesis in our discussions was, "Okay, we can go to find God if we make the trip interesting enough. If we can pull that off, no one is going to be sitting there thinking, Oh, c'mon, they'll never find God, but maybe there'll be some surprises here." So what we did as storytellers was to try and make this trip a real roller-coaster ride. Y'know, we wanted it to feel like, "Whoa, whee, wow, whoo!" And I think we succeeded in that.

While Harve and I argued about story structure, we were also duking it out over an even more basic issue. Basically, with Harve and the studio suits both worrying that my story, featuring appearances by both God and Satan, would more than likely offend a lot of moviegoers, Harve came up with the idea that perhaps we should alter the story and turn God and Satan into an evil alien pretending to be God for his own gain. This was a HUGE change, lightening the script considerably, and as I look at it now I can clearly see my acceptance of this most basic revision as my first mistake. Had this film remained true to its convictions and remained a story about God and the Devil, I think it would've played more vividly, packing a far more powerful dramatic punch. For now, though, I didn't see any of that, and walked away from that meeting satisfied that we'd just done something great, successfully eluding our biggest potential studio problem without a whole lot of headaches or wasted time. When we finally presented that revision to the studio, they were, as expected, thrilled with *Star Trek V* Lite, and we got the official thumbs-up. Immediately we began looking for a screenwriter.

With Eric Van Lustbader's withdrawal from the project, *both* Harve and I came up with the idea of approaching the franchise's genius-in-waiting, Nick Meyer. However, when he turned out to be knee-deep in directing another film, we began rapidly widening our search. Finally, perhaps a hundred scripts into the hunt, Harve came running into my office with a manuscript entitled *Flashback*, written by a guy I'd never heard of. His name was David Loughery, and when I read his script, I too felt like he might be our guy. His work was funny, edgy, cynical, full of sharp, clever dialogue and populated with well-drawn, well-intentioned characters. We screened a film he'd written and hated called *Dreamscape*, then hauled him into Harve's office to feel him out. To our surprise, he was genuinely enthused about the project, and perhaps one of the funniest men I'd ever interviewed.

That was important, in that a large percentage of Paramount's *Star Trek IV* research was pointing rather conclusively to the fact that one of the main reasons for that film's overwhelming crossover success had been its sense of humor. With that in mind, the studio was now becoming increasingly insistent that *Star Trek V* be peppered with comic moments as well.

Spitting out one-liners at every opportunity, David shook our hands, signed his contract, and immediately got down to the business at hand, fleshing out our bare-bones storyline into a sort of blueprint for his screenplay, always bearing in mind Harve's idea that for the script to work, we'd have to turn this thing into a runaway train ride, surprising our viewers at every turn. With David at the keyboard, a lot of the more specific twists and turns of our story began plopping formally into place.

Kirk's fall off that mountain, Kirk being saved at the last minute by Spock, the horseback storming of the pioneer city, the rescue of the hostages only to have them side with Sybok and against the crew, Sybok's pirating of the *Enterprise*, Spock's refusal to fire upon the man: all of these plot points worked well in keeping our audience off guard, having been consciously sculpted in an attempt to keep the picture moving forward rapidly. As a final kicker, we decided early on that Kirk's ultimate rescue from the rampaging minions of Hell would come in the highly unexpected form of a gun blast emanating from a Klingon bird of prey. Certain that he will be their next target, Kirk would scream at the ship, "Is it me that you want, you Klingon bastards? Come and get me!" At that point he would get beamed onto the bridge of the vessel only to find that manning the Klingon gun would be none other than Mr. Spock. With that, all animosity between the two men would have been shelved indefinitely.

As David began writing our first-draft script, the twists and turns of real life were also conspiring to put us in a bind. First, Gene Roddenberry, upon hearing our proposed storyline, was adamantly opposed to almost every bit of the idea. He was opposed to the idea of the *Enterprise* crew meeting God, and even more opposed to our representation of God in the familiar Western form. In Gene's mind, there would most likely be hundreds, even thousands of God images throughout the galaxy. He also objected to the idea that McCoy and Spock could actually become followers of Sybok. Richard Arnold, who was working in Roddenberry's office throughout all of this, sheds some light on Gene's specific objections:

Gene would have preferred avoiding the theme of God and man altogether, because he had already written it with *The God Thing*. And the studio had said, "You just can't make a movie this controversial. Absolutely not." Y'know, back in 1975, there was just no way they were going to let him tackle that subject matter. So when you came along, though it was years later, with very similar themes, and the studio gave you a green light, Gene was really hurt. I think it hurt Gene's ego that you were finally going to tell the story that he had wanted to tell ten years earlier. You were about to succeed where he had failed.

At the same time, Gene's secretary, Susan, was making matters worse by walking around the office saying things like "I can't believe it! He stole your idea. Bill's an asshole, Bill's a bastard." So that didn't help, and additionally, I know there was a fairly legitimate concern on Gene's part that your sense of humor was a little different than had ever been visualized before. His perception was that you were using the lesser characters for comic relief. Y'know, Chekov and Sulu lost in the woods, Scotty banging his head on a pipe, the lesser characters were to be laughed at, not with.

But most of all, Gene was bothered by the fact that nowhere in this script did anyone bother to question the very existence of God. What about alien races that have no religion? What about atheists? What about people with Eastern concepts of religion who don't believe in a god per se?

Finally, I can remember him saying, "Why, all of a sudden, is every single person on this ship betraying Captain Kirk to follow this Christ figure? There's got to be somebody on the ship who'd hold back: someone who'd say, 'Wait just a minute.'" Obviously, his concern was that people in the audience would ask, "Are we being told that in *Star Trek*'s future everybody is Christian?" Ultimately you guys smoothed over that point by having God say, "I have many faces." But Gene still wasn't happy, and I think a lot of it stemmed from the very basic fact that this was a story that he wanted to tell and hadn't been allowed to.

At about the same time, a pair of entirely unrelated events teamed up to delay this film's start date by about a year. First, the Writers Guild of America went on strike, forcing David to log out of his computer for the foreseeable future. And second, about a month into that strike, Leonard Nimoy accepted a job directing a film entitled *The Good Mother*. It was a duty that would keep him occupied for the next five months. At that point, well aware of the fact that even when the strike was over we still faced several months of script revisions, it became unavoidable that our front-burnered project was going to be delayed by about twelve months. "Hurry up, we've only got a year" became the newest catchphrase around the office, and throughout the ensuing months, while I relieved the boredom by writing a novel entitled *TekWar*, I also got together rather frequently with Harve, poking through our suspended story, looking for whatever ideas might need to be reworked.

First and foremost, it began to hit me that Zar (soon to officially become Sybok) was perhaps a bit too intense in his quest, a bit too close to the similarly driven Khan Noonian Singh. With that in mind, we softened the character significantly, making him less ruthless, less evil, more of a tortured soul. Shortly thereafter, as the Writers Guild settled their strike, David Loughery came back to work, and he ultimately redrafted our script rather quickly.

Quite pleased with the results, I did the logical thing and flew off to the Himalayas for a couple of weeks. Fulfilling a contractual obligation to a project entitled *Voice of the Planet*, I was gone just long enough to get stabbed in the back.

When I returned home from the shoot, late one Friday afternoon, I visited my office and was told by Harve that he and David had just revised the script and I was going to absolutely love it. "Terrific," I replied, "I'll read it tonight." I went home, sat down in my favorite corner of the sofa with the latest in a long line of Dobermans flopped over my lap, and began reading. I couldn't believe my eyes.

This script had almost *nothing* to do with anything that had preceded it. Now, instead of searching for God, the crew of the *Enterprise* was being led by Sybok to a land of great peace and contentment, a land where no one ever grows old. In short, Harve and David had revisited *Lost Horizon*, with Shangri-La now hiding beneath the cheesy pseudonym of Sha Ka Ree (a bastardization of "Sean Connery," who we all hoped might play Sybok).

The whole thing came as an unpleasant surprise to me, and as I sat there reading, I actually had tears in my eyes. I was that hurt. Harve and David and I had worked together for months, banging out a screenplay that dealt with my idea of searching for God, and now, at their first unsupervised opportunity, my fellow creatives were conspiring to yank that entire concept out from under me. I called a meeting for Monday morning, and spent the rest of the weekend guzzling Alka-Seltzer.

When the new work week finally dawned, I marched into Harve's office, sat down with him and David Loughery, and spent the better part of the next forty-eight hours trying to convince them that their new idea wasn't very good. It wasn't easy. Finally, I got Harve alone and asked him, "Why would Kirk, the great warrior of the galaxy, *ever* want to go to a place like Sha Ka Ree? Y'know, *Star Trek* was never about running away, or about finding peace, in fact it's always been about the exact opposite. These characters have now spent the better part of two decades fighting, standing up for what's right in the face of oppression, and trying to effect a positive change in the universe. We've never run away from anything!"

Finally, after a mind-numbingly lengthy exchange, Harve began to soften, and at that point, with the pair now effectively divided, I moved in to conquer. Cornering David and shotgunning him with the same argument, I ultimately won the battle, and we quickly returned to our original God concept. In a world where you've got to choose your headaches wisely, this truly merited the thumping skull.

Still, once all the arguing and the oppositional posturing had subsided, we did hang onto the notion of Sha Ka Ree. Transforming it from a place of ultimate peace into a land of ultimate knowledge, Sha Ka Ree now became the *place* Sybok was looking for, the *subject* of his vision from God, his Holy Grail. It actually made his quest a lot more understandable, much more clearly defined.

With that in place, we set about making our characters work better. First and foremost on our list was trying to find some dramatically believable reason why Spock would not shoot the mutineering Sybok when he had the chance, ultimately siding with him in traveling to Sha Ka Ree. From the very beginning, we had established that Spock and Sybok had become acquainted in the seminary, but that just didn't seem to be enough. This pair had to somehow be bonded to the point where Spock would believably betray Kirk to follow Sybok. Finally, just when it was beginning to appear that we'd all written ourselves into an inescapable corner, Harve lit up and yelled, "Ahhhhh, I've got it. There's only one way out of this, and that's to make Sybok Spock's brother."

I wadded up the sheet of paper I'd been making notes on and winged it off of Harve's forehead. I just didn't like the idea at all. To me, it seemed too easy, cheap, the kind of plot twist you'd find on a soap opera, but when Harve explained that such a strong relationship could immediately and believably translate to the big screen without a lot of clunky exposition, I skeptically challenged him to write it up and make it work. Three days later, he did just that.

I was convinced, David Loughery loved the idea, and when we sent our latest round of revisions to Roddenberry's office, he, too, was beginning to grow noticeably fonder of our show. However, just as we were beginning to see a light at the end of the tunnel, it turned out to be the headlamp of the onrushing Leonard Nimoy express.

Having now completed his stint behind the camera on *The Good Mother*, Leonard was beginning to concentrate on *Star Trek V*, and upon studying his script he had decided that Spock simply would not, under any circumstances, betray his good friend Kirk, especially in light of the sacrifices the captain had made for him in *Star Trek III*. That same day, we found out that De Kelley felt similarly about Bones. Finally, that same awful weekday marked the beginning of what would become a prolonged series of budgetary battles with the studio.

In reading our story, it seemed that the bean counters had poked away at their calculators and decided that as written, our film would most likely come in at slightly over our approved budgetary drop-dead figure of $31 million. We were told to make cuts right away, so Harve and I got out the red pencils and began chopping at a few of our favorite (and most costly) ideas. We lost the river of fire, cut down on our supply of gargoyles, and by the time I slunk out of my office, this awful weekday had forevermore become known as Black Thursday.

After dinner, a gutful of *agita*, and a fitful couple hours of sleep, I ventured back into the office and met with Leonard, determined that I could convince him to change his mind. He arrived just before lunch, and by the time the sun was setting, I was still begging, pleading, cajoling, massaging and going through whatever histrionics I thought might prove helpful to my cause. However, in the end I was thoroughly defeated. No matter what reasoning I could muster, Leonard simply refused to budge, because in his mind, Spock would never, *ever*, brother or no brother, pain or no pain, betray Captain Kirk.

In a situation like that, I simply could not win. I certainly couldn't pretend to understand Spock any better than Leonard, and I couldn't *demand* that Leonard perform the role as written. My only real option was to schmooze like hell, my only tools being passion and salesmanship. Turns out what I really needed was a pickax. Leonard held firm. Days later, De Kelley proved similarly unmovable.

With the clock now ticking away, I had no time to fight it out, and with that in mind, I caved, twice. I had to. Arguing with two guys whom I love, whom I have tremendous respect for, and who've been beside me throughout so many previous battles, I ended up trying to please everyone. I should also note that in discussing the script, I didn't entirely disagree with

Leonard and De, and with their prodding, I came to realize that if Kirk were ever penciled into betraying Bones and Spock, I too would most likely raise the roof. Fully cognizant of the fact that film is perhaps the most collaborative of all art forms, I had David rewrite the script. Right? Wrong? Better? Worse? I still don't know, although I would have loved to have seen the original scenario on-screen.

I think it would have been fascinating to watch Kirk, Spock and Bones going at each other, enduring their first real falling-out in the history of *Star Trek*. However, in appeasing the studio, my co-stars, my producer, my screenwriter and our all-powerful ledger sheets, I'd slowly but surely allowed my original story to become significantly diminished. God and the devil were gone, replaced by a mere cosmic pretender to the throne, and much of the inherent dramatic tension that would have crackled between our main characters throughout the second half of our film was now similarly diluted. No longer would there be any dissension among the ranks, and instead, the three of us would ultimately join hands, venturing down to Sha Ka Ree at film's end mostly out of curiosity. In retrospect, and twenty-twenty hindsight, that story solution weakened the dramatic tension of the film's climactic moments while flattening the buildup of tension throughout our story. For now, though, having accepted the compromises all around, I was busy accentuating the positive.

Determined to enjoy my moment at the point position on a thirty-million-dollar movie, I threw myself wholeheartedly into the revised storyline. Peering over David Loughery's shoulder as he reworked the script, I invoked some self-imposed spin control, and found myself feeling that even though this new version of the script had begun to stray wildly from the course I'd originally conceived, it was still good, and full of solid dramatic moments. Within a week, Loughery handed in his revised script, and at that point, Gene Roddenberry, Leonard and De all gave it their official thumbs-up. The only folks who remained unhappy with our progress were the studio pencil pushers.

Combing through our latest version of the script, they'd now upgraded their suspicions and become convinced that Star Trek V, as written, was still going to come in significantly over budget. More cuts were ordered, and the first place to take a hit was our special-effects-laden climax, basically the film's final ten minutes. With erasers and red pencils flying at warp factor eight, I lost my band of angels, lost the resultant horde of gargoyles, and in their place, we concocted a mere handful of monsters, made of solid stone, which would become animate upon "God's" command, rising up out of the planet's rocky surface. It certainly was a notch less amazing then transforming packs of cherubim, but we could have done a lot worse. By afternoon's end, I had ordered up six Rockmen.

However, as the days passed and our costume designers began formulating a plan as to how they might actually create believable men of rock, we got back the horrifying news that our half-dozen Rockmen would run us just a shade over $300,000. Moments later, as I lifted my jaw back up from the carpet, I amended my order and figured that maybe three hulking Rockmen could seem just as menacing and terrifying as six.

"No way," said the studio, "you're not spending one hundred and fifty grand on three costumes that will be seen on-screen for only a couple of minutes. Not a chance. You can have one Rockman . . . no more." Crossing my fingers that my lone Rockman would ultimately prove up to the task, I was now beginning to build up a tolerance to aspirin.

With our square peg of a script, hammered upon for months, now beginning to squeeze down into its round hole, I could finally begin thinking about a million other details: casting, production, scheduling, special effects, costumes, music. First and foremost, however, came the *look* of the new film.

I knew from the beginning that I wanted this picture to have a real epic stature, large and impressive, and I had planned on visualizing that through a series of unusually broad, sweeping camera shots. For example, in the first scene of the film, I wanted viewers to find Sybok laughing, at which point we'd tilt up into the sun,* widening out, continuing to stretch our perspective almost exponentially, until the sun was far off in the galaxy. At that point, I wanted the camera to turn slowly toward a small planet in the distance and begin magnifying its focus, each time by a power of ten, until the planet became recognizable as Earth. As the zoom continued, we'd have seen America, then California, then a giant mountain with a small speck of a being on it, then a hand grasping the side of that mountain, which of course would have ultimately revealed itself as Kirk's.

I had planned similarly grand visuals in several other spots throughout the film, and in further cementing our epic status, I desperately wanted large *Lawrence of Arabia*–sized bands of soldiers/extras to come sweeping in from the desert and storm our Paradise City. However, with our production already treading shaky budgetary ground, those shots were now hanging by a thread. When we began finalizing our special effects work, that thread got cut . . . fast.

Having begun our search for magic at ILM, we were dismayed to find that most of that firm's best

ABOVE: Finally, I'm at the real helm
BELOW: My daughter Melanie takes my advice—
at last!

technicians, the A team, were already hard at work on
the Spielberg/Lucas collaboration *Indiana Jones and the
Last Crusade*. At the same time, a good portion of the B
guys were putting together the effects for *Ghostbusters II*.
We knew that the best ILM could offer us simply wasn't

their best, and for that reason, we tested the water by asking a number of companies all over Hollywood to audition for the job on *Star Trek V*, fronting each of them $10,000 and asking that they do their best to create a striking and unusual image of God. We found our winner in . . . Hoboken, New Jersey.

The birthplace of Frank Sinatra and the best homemade mozzarella on the planet Earth, Hoboken is about as far removed from Hollywood as you can possibly get. Still, tucked away in a grubby little corner of the Mile Square City, we found the special effects shop of a man named Bran Ferren, who'd done some rather remarkable effects work on a large number of television commercials. A bit of a long shot coming into the festivities, Ferren nonetheless beat out the more formidable competition, winning himself the job from inside a fish tank.

Traveling to Ferren's studio, he almost immediately dispensed with the small talk and dragged us into his workshop. Once inside, he showed us that without complicated opticals, lenses, or computer-generated graphics, he could conjure up effects that were truly magical. With a small centrifuge whooshing amid a large aquarium-style tank, a whirlpool quickly developed, ultimately running almost perpendicularly through the center of the redesigned guppy house. Now adding a few chemicals to the tank while smiling broadly, not unlike the Sorcerer's Apprentice, Ferren clicked on a few lights, creating a blinding column of light, and held us enthralled in his low-tech wizardry. We signed him on the spot.

In the days that followed, Ferren took a closer look at our script, worked up some preliminary figures, sent them in, and forced us all to realize that once again, we were going to be over budget. At that point, I officially

money, you wanted stuff that would take time. My job was to keep your enthusiasm and your appetites from going over a line of practicality.

You were coming up with idea after idea and I was into circuit overload. And the ideas were, in and of themselves, fantastic, but strung out as a necklace of ideas, they would've become *Intolerance* or *Greed*, some eight-hour movie. So I think I conned you a lot about the specifics, making up stories and talking you out of the things I could see looming as potential problems. So when we started cutting back on the budget, it didn't bother me at all to see some of those things go away.

As the scope of my script atrophied, our cast got bigger. I had found my Sybok. When Sean Connery proved unavailable (he'd signed on to play Indiana Jones's father in *The Last Crusade*), Harve and I drew up a long list of candidates for the role, loaded with solid, talented actors. We ultimately avoided them altogether, in favor of a man I just happened to catch on PBS that evening. Flopping down in my living room and piloting the remote, I channel-surfed into a one-man play entitled L.B.J. Obviously about Lyndon Baines Johnson, the play itself was rather ordinary, but elevated significantly by the captivating performance of its leading man, heavily made up for the role, so I had no idea who I was watching. However, he had an exuberance and vitality that cut right through a cathode tube, and I knew that I'd found our Sybok. At play's end, squinting at the credits, I found that I'd been so thoroughly impressed by a man named Larry Luckinbill. I called him and offered him the role, he accepted, and we moved forward. It may have marked the last truly easy task on the film.

By week's end we'd begun searching out many of the desert locations that we'd be using in the film, and almost immediately I was simultaneously thrilled and horrified by what we'd found: In the Ridgecrest section of Yosemite National Park, we found several ideal locations. There was Owens Lake, actually a dry lake bed, which laid itself out beautifully to become our Paradise City; Trona Peaks, full of gnarled, jutting rock formations that would be absolutely perfect for Sha Ka Ree; and in a place called Cuddy Bank, we found the dry desert hellhole uninhabitable enough to form the basis of our film's opening shots in which Sybok makes his entrance, riding triumphantly through the desert.

However, despite the beauty of the locations, it was immediately obvious that the high desert heat and hardships could very well drive us all nuts. We knew that, but at the same time, our only realistic alternative would be to fake virtually everything, squeezing the film into soundstages, where we would have greater comfort but a lot less to look at. As we sat down to eat at one of the only restaurants for miles around, the idea of wimping out on a soundstage garnered only a moment's discussion, with Harve and I united in our assertion that we'd be more than happy to stick it out for the good of the picture. We then spent the better part of our meal discussing the weirder aspects of the local landscape, and as it turned out, one of them was sitting at the next table.

With my mouth full of the local cuisine, I was less than thrilled to feel an inordinately large hand grasping my left shoulder blade. "Mr. Shatner?" gasped the inordinately large voice attached to the hand. "Can I have your autograph?"

Not wanting to offend the Sasquatch, I simply smiled and replied, "Uh, sure, do you have a piece of paper?"

Now he's rustling around in his overalls, digging through grimy pockets and pulling out all sorts of trash. Finally, in the chest front pocket, he pulls out a business card and hands it over. "Thanks," I reply, glancing down at the card, reading his name, and noticing that underneath that name was the word *sawyer*.

"What's a sawyer?" I asked him.

"Lemme show you," he replied, heading back over to his table and digging through a green army surplus duffle bag for what seemed like an eternity. Finally, he pulled out a handsaw and strode back toward the table. Fearing the worst, I was ready to hit the deck, until I noticed that in his other hand he was cradling the tip of a long violin-type bow. "You see," he chimed merrily, "a sawyer is a guy who plays the saw." At that point, looking not unlike one of those big furry animatronic bears that sing and dance for patrons at Disney World's

SYBOK AND HIS BAND OF MERRY MARAUDERS

Country Bear Jamboree, this big moose sat down on the nearest stool, closed his eyes, and, as a look of overwhelming peace transformed and softened his face, proceeded to play a bit of Chopin so stunningly beautifully that we all just sat there, enraptured, unable to divert our eyes or ears from his musical mastery. Grime-covered and sweat-soaked in a greasy-spoon diner miles from the nearest paved road, we all forgot about our own discomfort and were swept away. It was quite a welcome.

In the weeks that followed, while we tweaked at our script amid the air-conditioned luxury of the Paramount lot, large crews of carpenters began descending upon our harsh Yosemite location, erecting our sets at a feverish pace. Polaroids Fed-Exed from the location each afternoon kept us up to date on their progress, and we were never less than thrilled. At the same time, scattered about the Paramount lot, *Star Trek V*'s costumes, makeup effects, props and casting were all just about nearing completion. I was beginning to get really excited.

Star Trek V officially began production on October 11, 1988, amid a mixture of enthusiasm, excitement and nausea. Sitting aboard a small aircraft bound for Yosemite, I couldn't help but notice a steady ridge of black clouds along the horizon and the turbulence they'd left in their wake. As we continued forward, with visions of rainstorms and mudslides washing away everything we'd worked for, I just crossed my fingers, crossed my toes, and hoped like hell we might get lucky. Meanwhile, down on the ground, things were getting rather tense as well.

Less than a month before we were to begin our location shooting, Hollywood's Teamsters' union had gone out on strike. These guys, despite their reputation for standing around all day reading the paper while guzzling coffee, smoking Camel unfiltereds and sucking down bagels by the dozen, are actually quite indispensable in the grand scheme of moviemaking, especially on location. Basically, they are your ride, responsible for the loading, transportation and care of all production vehicles to and from any and all locations. Without them, in theory, your cameras, lights, actors and props would never even make it to the show. Your entire production would grind to a dead stop.

However, with the union on strike and the start of our principal photography approaching rather rapidly, we had no other option than to assemble a nonunion crew of drivers to take the Teamsters' place. As you might expect, this did not sit well with the Teamsters, a union not known to be particularly gentlemanly in their protestations.

While our associate producers tried their best to round up any number of able-bodied drivers willing to cross a picket line and drive our caravan of production vehicles to location, we had begun hearing rumors that the union might start playing hardball at any moment. The feeling around our offices was that violent retribution might be a possibility: They might sabotage our equipment or threaten the safety of our substitute drivers. Another possibility, sporadically employed by several Hollywood unions in the past, would have found the strikers hiring a few small airplanes to simply fly over our location in circles all day long, effectively negating our ability to record any sound at all. Helicopters too have been known to rise up unexpectedly out of the horizon and then sit contentedly over a disputed production site for hours at a time, blades chopping loudly, wind whipping madly, successfully shutting down any sort of film shoot.

And then, two days before we were to head out, one of the camera trucks earmarked for our trip mysteriously blew up in the studio parking lot. It was empty at the time, but it shook all of us to the point where several of our substitute drivers hastily backed away from the project, and we ultimately ordered our entire fleet of drivers to begin their trek toward Yosemite in the middle of the night, sneaking them off the lot in an effort to get on the road as quickly and as unnoticed as humanly possible. Still, even with all these precautions, our drivers were almost immediately tailgated along the highway by cars full of masked men shouting threats. Only when our production manager orchestrated a full police escort did the harassment stop. And while we never actually confirmed the source of the harassment, it certainly made for a less than auspicious beginning.

Things, however, got a lot more pleasant when we finally arrived at Yosemite. After hours of darkness and threatening skies, as our caravan of production trucks, vans and trailers was just coming into sight, the sun poked through the clouds for the first time all day. As if having been cued by some big stage manager in the sky, the clouds then quickly dissipated, leaving behind some of the most brilliant, most beautiful sunbeams I'd ever seen. Dancing off the foliage and rock formations of the park, the sights were an absolute joy to behold, and as we all hooked up for the last leg of the trip, in through the park gates and up to our accommodations, you couldn't help but get goosebumps, you couldn't help but feel like this film was gonna turn out just fine.

Later that evening, I found that just about everyone else involved in the film had now begun feeling similarly energized. Leonard was on-site already, as he and

I were scheduled to shoot our rock-climbing scenes first thing the next morning, as were George and Walter, who'd be spending part of the next week pretending to be lost in the woods. Harve and almost all of our key crew members had arrived as well, and as the sun set, we all lifted our champagne glasses high, wishing each other good luck and looking forward to the task at hand. By 9:00 P.M., I'd gone to bed.

My wake-up call came in earlier than the sun's, and, riding an adrenaline rush as big as El Capitan, I soon found myself wide awake, showered, dressed and out the front door of the hotel, breathing in the crisp, cold air and running the day's events through my head maybe six or seven hundred times each. In my left hand, I held a small note that I'd found tucked into my door. Hastily scribbled on hotel stationery, the message was from Leonard, sent to wish me luck on the project. It touched me deeply, and I carried those good wishes with me throughout the day. As it turned out, I'd be needing them.

Our first day of shooting was going to be busy. Kirk was going to climb his mountain, and while he was up there, Spock was going to use his nifty new jetboots to fly up and have a chat with the man. Of course, this being *Star Trek*, nothing was as it seemed.

First of all, weeks before we'd even ventured out toward Yosemite, I began preparing for these scenes by doing some mountain-climbing along the majestic peaks of the Paramount lot. Calling in a pair of experts, I learned how to climb a mountain by clumsily scaling a makeshift wooden replica over and over again while big guys in plaid flannel shirts and down vests (even in L.A.) yelled things at me like, "Go for it" and "Be one with the climb." Meanwhile, because I was deathly afraid of heights, and far too vain to let my instructors know this, I spent the better part of my time on the wall trying desperately not to lose my grasp or my lunch. In time, however, I got to the point where if I really tried hard not to look down or to think about my precarious perch (I found that math problems inside my head made a nice alternative), I could ascend the face of my prototype Alp without so much as a single misstep. From there, I graduated to the real thing.

At my instructors' urging, we got into a truck and four-wheeled it up to the middle of nowhere, about an hour north of L.A. "You won't look like you're really climbing a mountain on-screen unless you've actually done it," they told me, and although I wasn't sure I believed them, I just sat there smiling, trying my best to hide the terror now burning within my chest. Finally the truck slid to a stop, and amid a pile of tumbleweeds and desert dust, the guys stood smiling and pointing. Off in the distance, the target of their forefingers was staring at me.

Rising ominously, straight up, perhaps two hundred and fifty feet out of the ground, stood my probable cause of death; at least that's what I thought. Swallowing hard, I listened to my instructors' advice on my best approach to the climb, all the while trying my best to keep my eyeballs from rolling up into my head. However, upon hearing the words "You know, if you don't feel comfortable, you don't *have* to do this," I was absolutely astonished to hear myself say, "What? No way! No problem! I can do this." It's consistently amazing what an X and a Y chromosome can conspire to pull off.

At any rate, after a tentative start and a series of distracting fractional equations, I found myself fairly adept at not falling to my death. "Keep going," I was encouraged from the relative safety below, "don't get scared.

Don't lose your edge!" they continued yelling. Finally, when I could stand it no more, I took a quick peek down at the dirt and couldn't believe my eyes. I must have been one hundred feet up. "Wow!" I said out loud, thoroughly impressed with my accomplishment. "Holy shit!" I yelled immediately afterward, horrified that I could do something so crazy.

Needless to say, I made it back down the mountain in one piece, thankful for my continued existence and even more thankful that off in one of the Paramount lot's least noticeable warehouses, a crew of scenic artists was busy building me a better mountain. Working in fiberglass from some preliminary shots of Yosemite's El Capitan, scenic artists built me a dead ringer for a section of the mountain that was perhaps 175 feet above the ground, even going so far as to match the cracks and color of the rock exactly. As shooting began, we'd bring this faux mountain with us to Yosemite, lugging it up to the park's highest-altitude parking lot, then placing it so as to make it appear on camera as the genuine rock formation. That way, while it would appear that Kirk and Spock were conversing perhaps several hundred feet above the jagged rocks below, there would be absolutely no chance that either one of us could end up splattered all over the lush green beauty of America's favorite national park. Instead, throughout the Kirk/Spock chat, neither man is ever really more than ten feet off the ground. As an added bonus, my fiberglass mountain came complete with hidden safety handles.

I was safe and relatively comfortable, which is more than I can say for the levitating Leonard. His discomfort actually began about a month earlier, as effects technicians made a fiberglass body cast from Leonard's chest down to about knee level. With that accomplished, they then attached a piece of pipe to what they were now calling "the flying suit," and come shoot day, they crammed Leonard in there, attached the pipe, then hooked both of them into a special slot in my fake mountain. Once they'd done that, through a series of high-tech hydraulic thingies and doodads, they could

WHICH WAY IS REALLY UP?

lift Leonard off the ground at will safely, and with a great deal of realism as far as the camera was concerned. Later in the day, as we shot Spock's reaction to Kirk's slip from the wall, Leonard's rigging was rearranged so that he could flip over on command. Once that was in effect, we shot Leonard's facial reaction to Kirk's fall, and then watched as his head left the frame and his jet boots took its place. As the day progressed, things went surprisingly smoothly, Leonard and I survived, and although my Vulcan pal *did* manage to spend the better part of the afternoon hovering upside down as I laughed at him, the only real casualty was Leonard's dignity.

Despite the fact that our first day's shooting was going rather well, I hadn't yet gotten comfortable in the director's chair. I learned this by midmorning when our soundman offered me some unsolicited advice. "Excuse me, Bill," he said, tapping the back of my left thigh as I clung tightly to my fiberglass mountain.

I'M SURE IT WAS THE LACK OF OXYGEN

"Huh?" I answered. "What is it?"

"Listen," he said, "I know that for me to give you advice on your line readings is a little weird, but I think you're rushing all your lines. Kirk sounds like he's late for work."

I thought about that for a second, and realized he was absolutely right. I was so excited about directing this thing, so riddled with adrenaline, and so overwhelmingly concerned about staying ahead of schedule that I was racing through my scenes, damaging my final product in an attempt to remain punctual. It made no sense, I knew that, and though Leonard too called me on my sweaty-palmed rapid delivery, and I'd fight that tendency over the ensuing weeks, I still had a hard time relaxing and moving ahead at a comfortable, as opposed to rushed, pace.

I was not nearly as happy nor as comfortable with a shot that I was absolutely convinced would add a tremendous amount of realism to our opening rock climb. "What better way," I wondered, "to prove that you're hundreds of feet above the valley floor than to actually *be* hundreds of feet above the valley floor, hanging onto the side of the mountain with the camera's perspective aimed right down over your head?" With that in mind, I demanded to hang from the side of the real mountain. Working hard not to pass out, I simply told myself that the shot was in the best interest of my film, and that I could do it. Harve nearly had a coronary, our executive producer, Ralph Winter, was ready to kill me, but finally I prevailed. However, on the day we finally shot the scene, I just wished I had kept my big mouth shut.

With only a small metallic cable running up my arm and onto the side of the mountain to catch me should I fall, I wriggled feet-first down the side of El Capitan, feeling that I'd ultimately get one of two things: killed, or an absolutely spectacular shot for the top of my film. In the end, we got neither.

Hanging onto solid rock, and trying my best to gaze bravely at the scenery below, I was almost immediately disgusted by the fact that a row of huge white puffy clouds had just rolled in over the sun. That meant two things. First, due to exacting photographic requirements, we had now lost the light that would have allowed the valley to seem truly distant beneath my feet. Instead, amid the shadows caused by the clouds, the background of this particular scene now risked being so dark that it would just appear muddy, obscuring the detail below, screwing up our depth of field and making the purpose of the entire shot moot. Second, as the clouds rolled in, I knew I'd have to simply hang there, horrified, hoping they'd pass quickly.

Twenty minutes later, there I hung, turning red damning the accursed clouds, then white with fear. Finally, as our production schedule began running behind, and as Harve Bennett began having a hard time looking at me without puking over the side of the mountain, we decided that our only hope of getting this shot would be to simply roll the camera, while crossing our fingers and hoping we might get lucky. That's exactly what we did, and when it was all over, they hauled me back up to safety, unhooked my cable and brought me back to the hotel promising that just after dinner, we'd look at the dailies of our two days of shooting. When we'd seen them, I found myself seriously considering traveling back up to the summit of El Capitan and leaping.

First of all, throughout Kirk's phony-mountain dialogue with Spock, it became immediately apparent that just off in the extreme right of the frame, we had allowed the top of a medium-sized pine tree to enter our composition. The effect was horrifying, as now, amid Kirk and Spock's high-altitude aerial conversation, there stood unshakable, evergreen proof that we had indeed faked the whole thing. I was crushed.

Second, and less unexpected, was the fact that our shot down into the valley below El Capitan, with me hanging on for dear life in the foreground, had turned out very badly. The clouds had killed us, and the result was a shot of Kirk climbing something that appears to be about twenty feet aboveground, in front of a grayish, blurry, indistinguishable background. It actually looked a lot more fake than our fiberglass climb.

I was officially scared to death. Would every day be this tough? Would every shot be a struggle? Would I ever be able to relax? In the days to come I began getting my answers, which were not always the ones I'd hoped for.

Throughout the ensuing days in the desert, communications and equipment breakdowns seemed to dog us at every turn. For example, when we got ready to shoot Sybok's gallop through the desert, we found our horseman, his costume and a full-sized prop tree missing. "How the hell do you lose a tree?" I wondered aloud. Turns out our stuntman had been stranded at his hotel, and our tree had been sent to a different location. At that point, in one of the most bizarre moments I've ever witnessed on a film set, our art director, Nilo Rodis, ran off in search of a new tree that we might quickly substitute for our missing-in-action elm. As he ran off into the brush, he was immediately and rather loudly warned by a park ranger to keep an eye out for rattlesnakes. He came to a dead stop.

"What do I do if I see one?" asked the now terrified Rodis.

"Your best hope is to make a lot of noise," said the stiff-lipped ranger.

Five minutes later, while we all stood there, handcuffed by the slings, arrows and miscues of the day, we listened intently and could not help laughing as Nilo wandered up into the hills singing Filipino folk songs at the top of his lungs.

Thankfully, both my fuse and our luck held out, and our stuntman and prop tree both arrived just in time to save the day. We got the shot, and in a rare moment of perfect luck, the gods conspired to make things easy on us. The shot came off absolutely beautifully. Still, despite the good fortune, I was becoming increasingly concerned that due to our inexperienced drivers and the communication gaffes that were steadily bogging us down, I was really going to have to get more involved in this film's nuts and bolts. That nearly drove everybody crazy.

By morning, back in the desert location, the sun was broiling with a new intensity, and though we'd so far been able to smile through the desert's adversities, to do so at 110 degrees is a whole other story. Sometime during that awful morning, amid the dust, heat, bugs and various technical difficulties, I cracked, yelling at Harve, loudly berating my head electrician, and ignoring my cinematographer's pleas for additional prep time. The results? A pissed-off producer, a generator man who'd been insulted in front of his crew, and a cinematographer whose talents had been publicly challenged. I was now officially pushing too hard. Ralph Winter explains:

That day in the desert marked the point where you had officially crossed over the line, where you had stopped pushing and begun shoving. It was too much, too intense. You had a tremendous passion for the project which was obvious and contagious on our set, but you were walking a very thin line, and by pushing that hard and second-guessing the people around you, the mood you were creating could very well have wiped out all the good feelings you'd already earned from these guys. You know, panic could've set in. Ultimately, you found that you had to sit back a little bit and let these people do their jobs. Getting overly intense doesn't solve anything, it just creates additional problems.

You know, that day you had four different cameras running simultaneously. Setting that up takes time, and if we ended up going a little long or a day over our schedule, who cares? You just have to do it. You can't rush a great film.

The ensuing days on location, as Sybok and his mini-hordes of soldiers stormed into Paradise City, were easily the most complex and potentially stressful so far, but taking the words of Harve, and Leonard, and Andy Laszlo, our cinematographer, and Ralph Winter, to heart, I spent the day taking a lot of deep breaths, determined to avoid complicating matters and try to have some fun. By midafternoon, the plan was working rather well.

After a truly horrendous morning of desert shots and continued miscommunication we had finished Sybok's close-ups and were just about to change locations and begin shooting our crowd scenes. As I looked west, I could see that the sun was now *maybe* four fingers above the horizon. Time was really going to be tight, but barring disaster, we just might make it. Ten seconds later we had our first disaster. No one had shown up to drive us over to the next location.

So there we sat, a skeleton crew of filmmakers, stranded in the desert, alone, while hundreds of thousands of dollars' worth of equipment and extras waited for us in the hot sun several miles down the road. Try remaining stress-free in THAT situation. Actually, have you ever seen the classic *Honeymooners* episode where Ralph Kramden ends up vainly trying to keep his cool while growling through a smile, "Pins and needles, needles and pins, a happy man is a man who grins"? That was me. And then it hit me.

With us, as always, was our ever-present Yosemite park ranger. With HIM was his pickup truck. In seconds I had anxiously formulated that eight average-sized crewmen and their equipment could *possibly* squeeze into the truck and flatbed, and with that I began asking, quite politely, if my co-workers might be willing to tough it out in the no-frills section. Grimacing, but knowing that there was no other way out that might still allow us enough daylight to film our scheduled scenes, they all ultimately said yes. Ten minutes later, crammed like sardines into the back of a beat-up Parks Services pickup, we were making good time along the thin desert roads, closing in upon our next location and making up for a bit of our lost time. That's when disaster number two set in.

We found the van that was supposed to pick us up. Great news? Hardly, because the van was now broken down with a busted axle, unpushable and blocking our pickup's path in the middle of the only road that would take us where we needed to go. "Hey guys," I ask only half-kiddingly, "you willing to jog the rest of the way?"

Surprisingly, that idea was not met with total disdain, and before long we'd actually begun moving toward our location, lined up and looking for all the world like French Foreign Legionnaires lost in the desert halfway through some terrible old war movie. At that point I heard a rumbling in the distance, and found . . . our park ranger. Resourceful and smart, he had backtracked through the desert and found a way around the van. Roaring up behind us now, like the cavalry to the rescue, he skidded to a stop, stuck his head out the passenger-side window and shouted, "You guys want a lift?" Immediately scrambling back into the relative luxury of the grimy flatbed, we arrived at our location within three minutes, only to find the sun dipping dangerously close to the horizon.

At that point, we faced two possibilities: One, make the best of what we had and hope for the best, or two, hold everybody over and come back tomorrow, a move that would indeed set this film at least a quarter of a million dollars over budget. At that point, it was amazing how quickly Harve and Ralph performed one-eighties around their own exhortations to be more laid-back. "We've gotta take a shot at this," they wailed, and by now, more comfortable with the unavoidable, unbelievable problems that seemed to pop up every day on our sets, I simply smiled and said, "Sure, why not?"

I quickly huddled with Andy Laszlo, asking him what he thought might be our best shot at getting this thing on film, and he suggested shooting with a minimum of lights, thus allowing our thundering hordelet to appear heavily backlit, and ultimately as silhouettes on screen. With no better alternative, I agreed almost immediately and got back to work.

Here in the desert, where they'd been waiting for over two hours now, stood a large crowd of sweat-soaked, partially dehydrated extras, all of them covered in burlap so as to appear like ravaging Hunlike marauders.

However, with them wilting rather noticeably in the late-afternoon sun, I made a concerted effort to revive the lethargic Visigoths by manning the nearest megaphone and making like a cheerleader. Forcing a smile and spewing bad jokes as best I could, I broke the big group into several smaller, more manageable herds, with each group ultimately given its own cue to come storming toward the camera at a half-running, half-jogging pace we later nicknamed "the Sybok shuffle." Half-assed, maybe, but it was ultimately rather impressive on film.

The logistics problems surrounding these scenes were phenomenal. However, I really learned something that day. Standing there in the desert, exhausted, dirt-encrusted, and less than thrilled with the proceedings, I simply refused to give in to the chaos around me, and we were able to concoct the proverbial silk purse from a sow's ear, yanking a solid, striking action sequence from the jaws of defeat. That small victory really helped me maintain my confidence and sanity throughout the rest of the picture, as well as that night's dinner.

Over the course of the next three weeks we filmed the rest of our on-location desert footage, spending another week under the bright sun and the following fourteen nights under the moon, routinely breaking for lunch at midnight, shooting until dawn, and then stumbling back to our hotel rooms, exhausted, where we'd sleep the day away, rising like vampires as dusk began approaching. From there, we'd head out into the desert, making our movie while simultaneously scaring the hell out of the local coyotes.

Throughout these evening shoots, juggling horses and actors (two of the most difficult species on the planet), we ultimately fared pretty well. In fact, with me growing progressively more relaxed behind the camera

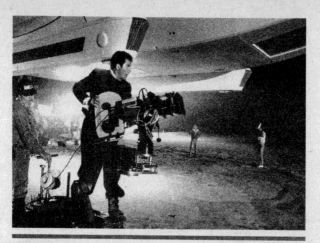

OUR FINAL SHOT IN THE DESERT, JUST BEFORE SUNRISE

and our cast and crew growing more comfortable all around, the mix-ups that had plagued us early on now ceased almost entirely. And despite the fact that we were constantly battling time and fighting the light (this time scrambling to finish before sunUP), there was a growing sense of exuberance amid the dust, of people banding together in the face of a dreadful situation for one common goal, and despite the chaos, we continued getting some absolutely beautiful results. As dailies came in, we couldn't help but feel really good about our work, and that in turn fed the mood of our set. Our only real problem was the Rockman.

Testing out my one Rockman the night before we were to shoot him, we were all stunned to find that he actually looked quite horrifying and believable in the nighttime lighting. Breathing fire from his mouth with a ferocity that would've put Godzilla to shame, this Rockman was undeniably menacing. In addition, he smoked beautifully on command, with the smoke obscuring most of his hard, rubbery edges and allowing the creature to appear even more realistic.

Actually, to load up the Rockman for smoking, four effects guys had to spend the night sucking on cigarettes, then blowing smoke into the specialized tubing of the suit. After three or four blows per man, the suit was full and ready to go. With that, the effects guy *inside* the dreadfully hot rubber suit would simply don his head, roar to the best of his ability, and look frightening. In practice, he smoked, blew fire and roared beautifully. Not so on film.

Less than twenty-four hours later, during our last night on location and standing on the same spot, the Rockman no longer did much of anything. He stopped breathing fire; he smoked less impressively; and within minutes, I was horrified. Suddenly, one of the most important elements of the ending of my film was falling apart. However, with no other alternative, we got ready to shoot.

Filming (of course) on top of a remote mountain peak, our camera crew, sound guys, lighting guys and effects crew roped themselves together and started climbing through the darkness. If all went well, we'd be ready to shoot by 10:00 P.M., allowing us two full hours to get some adequately horrifying footage of our affordable monster before union rules would force us to break for yet another midnight lunch. We'd certainly be able to kickstart the suit by then.

Over Andy Laszlo's admonitions that "This is madness," we headed up the hill and ten minutes later, winded but not permanently damaged, made it to the top. At that point, half-exhausted from the climb, we set up. The lighting guys cast a reddish hue over the proceedings, the effects guys began risking lung cancer with a vengeance, and before long they'd stuffed the

Rockman's big rubber lungs with enough carcinogens to choke a cow. And while our Rockman never did regain his ability to breathe fire, he was blowing smoke again within minutes. "Good enough," I declared, "let's get ready to shoot." And then the wind shifted away from us.

While that would seem to be no big deal, with the wind blowing out, so did the Rockman's smoke, and without any smoke, our guy in the silly rubber suit ultimately just looked like . . . well, a guy in a silly rubber suit. There was just no way, even to the naked eye, that we could've gotten away without some sort of foggy camouflage. We gave it our best shot, but ultimately, even as midnight approached, we hadn't gotten lucky. With the wind's continued lack of cooperation and the Rockman's suit looking stiffer and phonier with every turn, it soon became obvious that this shot was *never* gonna work. We weren't gonna get it, and for the first time since we started the film, the elements and fate were going to beat us.

Finally, with absolutely no time left to squeeze in a return visit to this location, we knocked off several wide shots, hoping that somehow we might be able to approximate the Rockman location back in the studio at a later date. At that point, my hard-won recent smile disappeared, and I realized that the already compromised ending of my movie was now in serious trouble. As we broke for lunch, I was decidedly less than hungry.

And now I was facing yet another dilemma. With just about four hours left between us and daylight, we still had to capture several more shots at another location down the hill. Time was gonna be really tight, and with that in mind, I launched into a speech.

While most of the crew was devouring their dessert, I was wracking my brain trying desperately, and in vain, to come up with the words to that speech from *Henry V*

ABOVE: SAFELY BACK ON THE AIR-CONDITIONED BRIDGE
BELOW: STILL TRYING TO REASON WITH A KLINGON

that reads, "Once more unto the breach, dear friends," but ultimately, amid the heat and the chaos and the heartburn, I just couldn't come up with the words, so I paraphrased, asking the crew for their attention from atop my plastic folding chair. "Listen, you guys," I started out, "you've been knocking yourselves out, killing yourselves, running around the desert with me throughout this entire shoot. You've risen far above and beyond the call of duty, and while I can't thank you enough for that, I have to ask you to rise to the occasion and run even faster, just one more time. Because if you don't, there's just no way we're gonna finish this thing before sunrise."

With that, these guys who'd toughed it out to the point of exhaustion unanimously and quite literally ran down that mountainside toward our final location, the Enterprise shuttlecraft. Working at an absolutely ridiculous pace, we managed to finish our night's shooting just as the first sliver of sunshine began popping out over the horizon. To this day I've never seen any crew work so selflessly and tirelessly for the good of any picture. I was really touched.

After a few hours of daylight sleep back at the hotel, I ran downstairs to watch dailies, only to find that as expected, our rubbery Rockman looked absolutely terrible on-screen. Stiff, phony and decidedly less than threatening, this thing looked more like a walking rubber boot than it did a monster. With that in mind, reshooting our Rockman went out the window, and we knew we'd have to conjure something up either back in the studio or with optical effects. Still, at that point in time, we were all just too fried to even *begin* thinking in terms of solutions. It was all we could do to get on the plane and head home. Never before has an airline seat felt so comfortable, never before has an air-conditioned seventy-two degrees met with so much appreciation. Never before has a nap felt so good.

However, all too soon the enforced relaxation of the twin-engine transportation came bumping back down onto the tarmac at LAX, and the cycle started all over again. Immediately driving over to the Paramount lot, I spent the better part of that afternoon checking out the sets that had gone up during our absence. The *Enterprise* bridge, the forest location that would house our campfire scene, the interior of the bar in Paradise City, the interior of a Klingon bird of prey, all of these things had existed merely as sketches when we left for the desert, and as I took a quick walk around, I found myself distressed by the demise of the Rockman, but nonetheless happy with the results of our time spent in the netherworld. If all went well, I mused, the rest of our shoot should be a comparative breeze.

I was *almost* right. Despite problems with shooting the shuttlecraft interiors, despite technical problems with Bran Ferren's rear-projected special effects, despite one particular film magazine that twice scratched up an entire day's work, we ultimately got through our setbound shooting amid minimum madness. In fact, as things progressed, with our crew now a well-oiled, well-fed, well-rested machine, we moved along rather well, shooting our cast of accomplished and highly professional actors with an efficiency that actually found us flirting with the idea of getting ahead of schedule. During these in-studio days, we got in and out of the *Enterprise*, had our gang fight in the Paradise City bar, and shot our climactic dialogue upon a replica god planet extremely smoothly. And then I spent the better part of a week being hung over the set.

First, we hit the *Enterprise* "turbo shaft" for a scene in which Spock grabs me in one arm, Bones in the other, and uses his jet boots to whoosh us straight out of harm's way. Rigged up much like Leonard was at our phony El Capitan, De and I now got to join Leonard in experiencing the . . . uh . . . rather unique sensations attached to spending the entire day with your torso encased in a fiberglass body suit. Let's just say it wasn't pleasant, and that when you stop and consider that the three of us ultimately spent some six hours being yanked up and down this prefab shaft, you'll readily understand how this particular set quickly became known as the House of Pain.

We even got extremely lucky with a scene we were never quite sure would work at all. In an effort to make Spock's catch of the plummeting Kirk seem a bit more realistic, our effects guys concocted an entire set that looked like somebody had simply flipped the floor of Yosemite a full ninety degrees. Trees grew sideways from the turned-over forest floor. Giant boulders hung sideways from the dirt, and the jutting face of our faux El Capitan actually served as the floor of our gigantic optical illusion. Hovering above all of this, dangling like marionettes over the scenic wizardry, were Leonard and I. Hanging like slabs of beef, we slowly and clumsily maneuvered ourselves into position, then spent the morning mastering about ten seconds' worth of film from the point where Spock catches Kirk through Kirk's line "Hi, Bones, mind if we drop in for dinner?" In the end, sore and disoriented, we both got unhooked and waddled over to the commissary for lunch.

At about this time, in a new round of meetings with Bran Ferren, we developed an idea as to how we might impressively replace, perhaps even improve upon, our Rockman. Basically, we had come up with an idea that would have found an amorphous luminescent blob of light and energy rising up out of the defeated pretender to the throne of God, which would then come after Kirk, shape-shifting and ultimately taking on menacing serpentine qualities. With handshakes and smiles all around, we agreed to give it a go. Weeks would pass before the results would arrive.

Finally, on our last day of shooting, I'd saved for us the campfire scene. Sitting on a Paramount soundstage made up to look like the forest basin at Yosemite, Leonard, DeForest and I spent our last ten hours together laughing, singing and making fun of each other, both in and out of the script. With nothing ahead of us, we could really relax and enjoy the scene, playing it out at our leisure with plenty of time to experiment. It was great fun, with Leonard loudly humming "Home on the Range" between takes while pitifully trying to cover the song on Spock's lute.

Later, when De Kelley finally opened his mouth, spewing forth one of the most vile "Row Row Row Your Boat's" ever emitted by a human being, we couldn't help getting hysterical. Not only was this guy tone-deaf, he was thoroughly arrhythmic as well, and getting him to jump in as the third leg of our ear-splitting round was all but impossible. Finally, after spending the day with two men whom I admire as much as any in the world, amid smiles, warm feelings and genuine camaraderie that we'd built up over the years, we cut and printed our last take. With that, after a quick glass of champagne, a piece of cake, and a long group hug, they were gone, and although I'd see them again at our official wrap party later in the week, I couldn't help but feel a real loss.

However, I had no time to reminisce or get maudlin; I had a movie to edit. The Yosemite footage, although it nearly killed us, looked terrific, as did the stuff we shot back at Paramount, and as expected, our recurring actors had once again performed well, as had Laurence Luckinbill and the rest of our cast. Finally, when we'd cut and pasted our story into place, although we were still missing our special effects, I screened the film for the studio suits.

RIGHT: Shafted!
BELOW: "Hi
Bones, mind if
we drop in?"

SINGING (BADLY) 'ROUND THE CAMPFIRE

Biting my nails at the back of the screening room, I listened intently for any reaction that the suits might blurt out, and I was almost immediately comforted by the fact that one of them gasped at Kirk's fall from the mountain, and shortly thereafter, they all chuckled through the campfire scene, laughing where they were supposed to, and smiling through the juxtaposition of futuristic outer-space heroes and primitive no-frills landscape. At the film's end, I got the official word, and was told that while they felt a couple of scenes might need a quick trim or two here and there, they really liked the film overall. Additionally, they felt that once the special effects arrived, my now choppy ending would come together nicely as well. I left that screening room on cloud nine, reveling in my momentary victory until the following morning, when disaster struck once more.

My special effects had come in, and I ran with them down to the nearest screening room. Once inside, I arm-twisted the projectionist into an unscheduled viewing, and at that point, I sat there, dumbfounded, staring at a series of effects that were decidedly less than special. In particular, my God effect looked cheesy, and the hastily concocted amorphous light blob, designed to replace our disastrous Rockman, was just plain terrible. The end of my film was once again in serious trouble, and at this stage of the game, with mere weeks before we'd have to call the work complete, there wasn't much I could do about it. Harve and I tried to scrape up the funds to reshoot an ending, but found the studio purse strings knotted tightly. No matter how you looked at it, I was now officially screwed.

From there, feeling less euphoric about my seventy-millimeter baby, we went back into the editing room in an effort to minimize the damage. With that in mind, we reduced God's screen time and cut the amorphous Kirk-chasing blob altogether, opting instead to reuse one of Ferren's close-up images of the false God's face, intercutting it with a lot of blue smoke and phony lightning in an attempt to make it seem like the God pretender himself was now chasing after me. In the end, once again trying to accentuate the positive, I came away feeling like we'd pulled a rabbit out of the hat, and that our last-minute improvising had successfully allowed us to dance around the inferiority of our effects while supplying the film with an acceptable, if not entirely satisfying, ending. Wanting desperately for this film to succeed, I simply did not perceive its final ten minutes to be bad. Only much later, well after the film had come and gone from theaters, was I clearheaded enough to realize that they were horrendous. Y'know, we ultimately spent our first one hundred minutes seeking God, and then, when we'd finally found him, he looked not unlike a big one-hundred-watt floodlight with a face. That really hurt us, and to simultaneously muddle through a hastily thrown together ending left us dead in the water. It was the ruination of that film.

By the time I'd finished my cut of the picture, its running time stood at just over two hours, which the studio decided was just too long. Their ultimate goal would've put *Star Trek V* at about one hour and forty-five minutes, a length that optimally guarantees that theaters all across the country will run the film twice per night, with both screenings beginning fairly early in the evening. My only problem was that even at slightly over two hours, I had no idea as to where we might cut this thing. I really felt like we'd gone down to the bone already. That's where Harve came in.

Since I had completed my "director's cut," the film was now officially in the hands of Harve Bennett, and as producer, he had the right to recut the film. He had the final say, and while that sounds odd, it is standard operating procedure throughout Hollywood. At any rate, Harve went into the editing room, and with a more objective eye (i.e., a less personal commitment to each

SYBOK PUTS THE SQUEEZE ON KIRK

and every shot in my film), he began chopping. Throughout the next week he'd call me in my office, proudly proclaiming, "I've got it down to 1:53," or "It's down to 1:51:25," constantly updating me as to his "progress" and making me more and more nervous about what he might have cut.

Finally, after what seemed like months, Harve called me up and invited me into a screening room to see his new, leaner, meaner Star Trek V. Prepping me before he ran the film, Harve went through a whole song and dance about how every director who shoots film ultimately falls in love with every single frame of his final product, and how he, as producer, coming in with an objective opinion, could really dig in and mercilessly make any cut that might bog down the film, or fail to advance the narrative of the story. "Oh sure," I replied, "I can't wait to see it."

Of course I was lying, positive that Harve had simply butchered my baby to bits, but as the lights dimmed and this thing unreeled, I wasn't entirely horrified. He had tightened up some of the action sequences in the desert, trimming some of the stunts and fisticuff footage from the film in an effort to move from the desert into Paradise City as quickly as possible. That was fine, as were most of his other cuts. He trimmed some dialogue, tightened up some of our loving shots of the local scenery, and I was okay, although not overjoyed, with most of that. My most vehement objections arose over Harve's amputation of two specific shots. One was a broad sweeping desert panorama, focusing upon Sybok's initial ride into the desert, and the other was a gorgeous establishing shot taken at sunrise over one of the local landscape's tallest peaks.

When the lights came up, we haggled, Harve gave, I took, I gave, Harve took, and in the end, while neither one of us was *absolutely* content with the final cut, we could both, at least, live with it. And then the previews began.

In a pair of preliminary screenings we did reasonably well, with the fans' biggest questions understandably rising out of the film's hastily patched together ending. From there, Harve got the scissors back out and clipped yet another five minutes out of the film. Finally, with less than forty-eight hours before we had to call it quits to make prints in time, we held one last preview, which went surprisingly well. At that point we sat back, waited, rubbed our rabbits' feet and got progressively more nervous about our premiere.

Finally, in midsummer, we hit the multiplexes, and on the morning after our official opening night, I was awakened *extremely* early by a telephone call. Stumbling to the receiver, I grunted out a "Hullo" only to be immediately greeted by the unusually cheery voice of Leonard Nimoy. "Did I wake you?" he asked.

"Yes."

"Good."

"Why good?"

"That means I'll be the first to give you the news. They LOVE your movie!"

"What do you mean?"

"You got a great review in the L.A. *Times*," he told me, at which point he proceeded to spend the next five minutes reading it to me over the phone. I started to cry. I was touched by Leonard's call, as well as stunned by the realization that one of my fondest dreams had come true. Later that same day, one of the local TV news reviewers gave me a ten plus, and I began sensing a trend. I sensed wrong.

Shortly thereafter, *Variety*, perhaps the most influential of the show business papers, slammed the film rather unmercifully, and from there on, the reviews that came in were decidedly mixed. At the same time, the film's box office receipts, while ultimately topping the fifty-million-dollar mark, were nonetheless viewed as disappointing in the wake of Star Trek IV's megasuccess. Harve Bennett, however, has his own theories about our relative success:

I want to reflect for the record that no matter what the picture was or wasn't, no one has ever accounted for two things. One, "The Summer of Discontent," and by that I mean, from a standpoint of blockbuster movies, 1989 was the summer in which more blockbuster movies were squeezed into theaters than ever before—Batman, Indiana Jones and the Last Crusade, Lethal Weapon 2, Rain Man, Back to the Future Part II, Look Who's Talking, Honey, I Shrunk the Kids—all of these things came out one week after another, piled on top of each other, and there is very little way that we could have done any better at the box office— in fact, in the face of all that competition, we shouldn't have done as well as we did. We should have been lost in the shuffle. We did very well.

Two, throughout Star Trek's first four movies, we were playing to a starved group of fans who had grown tired of the reruns of their beloved show in the seventies and wanted a fresh Thanksgiving dinner of Star Trek. Every two years they got it.

Every time a new Trek movie came out, it was Thanksgiving Day among the Star Trek cult and they had turkey and stuffing and they came out and the family gathered around the table and they ate five times too much and went to five times too many screenings and they couldn't get enough. The appetite for the franchise was intense. And then between pictures they would return to the old sandwiches and the turkey soup of the original episodes, which they had already seen a hundred times each.

However, by the time *Star Trek V* came out, the appetite had been diffused. The fans were less hungry. *Star Trek: The Next Generation* was into its second successful year, airing in most markets on Saturday or Sunday nights, seven or eight P.M., and instead of having to go out to the theaters, the fans were getting served warm turkey without ever having to get off the couch. No one has ever factored that into our performance, and I've been told by the more casual fans, "Oh well, we wanted to see *Star Trek V*, but we didn't wanna miss an episode of the new show, and by the time we got around to seeing the new feature, it was already gone from the theaters."

All of the previous *Trek* films had a theatrical run of about sixteen or seventeen weeks. Well, *V* didn't run nearly that long, because faced with that competition of the seven other blockbusters, the theater people began getting antsy. You know, "Listen, get this thing out so I can get *Batman* in here." We ultimately had the shortest theatrical release of all the *Star Trek* films. I think it ran ten weeks.

At any rate, despite the lukewarm reviews, the unspectacular box office and Harve's positive spin, I see *Star Trek V* as a failed but glorious attempt to make a picture full of character growth and a deep philosophical base, delving into man's universal desire to believe. I really wanted to use *Star Trek* as a means to tell a story that would've taken these beloved characters into waters they'd never before tested, simultaneously making them question their own beliefs and ultimately their faith in one another. Obviously, it didn't come out as I'd hoped.

And while I didn't by any stretch of the imagination consider *Star Trek V* a bad film, and indeed I was tremendously pleased with much of what we'd accomplished, I ultimately came away feeling like the big brass ring had somehow eluded my grasp. I was truly convinced that this was going to be a terrific film, but by the time it all came together, it was not. We'd come close, but since we were dealing with neither horseshoes nor hand grenades, close simply didn't cut it, and I was sure it had marked the end of the *Star Trek* films once and for all.

But that all changed as we approached the original series' twenty-fifth anniversary.

STAR TREK VI:
DISCOVERED COUNTRY

You all know that *Star Trek VI: The Undiscovered Country* hit the multiplexes in December 1991, billed as the "final voyage" of the Starship *Enterprise* and acting as the grand finale of *Star Trek*'s yearlong twenty-fifth-anniversary celebration. However, what you probably *don't* know is that as originally conceived, I wouldn't have been in the picture, nor would Leonard, De, George, Nichelle, Walter or Jimmy. Instead, Harve Bennett had cooked up a tale that would've taken the franchise in an entirely new direction. It happened like this.

Star Trek V: The Final Frontier, my baby, though mired amid the biggest traffic jam of summertime megahits ever seen and received rather poorly by most critics, still managed to rack up its share of box office bucks. Though never even approaching the bona fide cash cow status of *The Voyage Home*, *Star Trek V* still vacuumed up more than fifty-two million dollars during its ten-week domestic run. In a business where bankability generally counts for much more than creative success, that meant just one thing. The *Star Trek* franchise, no matter the obstacles, was indestructibly profitable. With that in mind, the studio wisely decided to try and cash in on our rapidly approaching twenty-fifth anniversary, and a sixth film quickly became a distinct possibility. However, there was one fly in the Romulan ale.

Although *The Final Frontier* had indeed brought in a beefy fifty-two million, it also came with an extraordinarily large price tag of slightly over thirty million dollars. With seven main characters fattening the payroll, unavoidably huge special effects bills, planets to build, starships to construct and whole alien races to conjure up, Paramount was faced with the unavoidable reality that all subsequent *Trek* films would have to cost even more. You simply couldn't do a *Star Trek* film cheaply, and there seemed absolutely no way to cut corners until Harve Bennett pulled a rabbit out of his hat.

Somewhere in the middle of producing *Star Trek IV*, Harve had begun toying with an idea that would've allowed Paramount to forget about continued sequels entirely, opting instead to travel backward in time with a *prequel*, which would have introduced audiences to handsome young Starfleet cadets Kirk, Spock and McCoy, as well as their gifted young professor of engineering, Montgomery Scott.

Poking around on the PC, Harve had come up with a rough story idea that would've introduced us to young Kirk, still anxiously awaiting acceptance at the Academy, while residing, a bit rebelliously, back home on the Iowa farm, copping feels off the local females and buzzing airplanes through haystacks in an effort to vent some of his restless energy. Spock, having recently left Vulcan against his father's wishes, and Bones, who had spent his young adulthood looking after his terminally ill father, would have ultimately met up with Kirk once he had been officially invited into the hallowed halls of the Starfleet Academy. Harve Bennett continues:

Spock and Kirk would've spent the first half of the film as rivals, only to be drawn together when Kirk becomes the only cadet who'll stand up for Spock in the face of some ugly racial prejudice. That ostracizes Kirk among a certain cadre of people at the Academy, people whom we learn later in the story are being manipulated by an uber-heavy, a racist organizer, somewhere out there in space.

Anyway, as the events of the story moved forward, we'd have built to a climax where Kirk, Spock and a handful of other cadets would've been thrown into their very first "against all odds–style" mission, being told, "Only you cadets can save us. You've never flown a spaceship, but you have the training and now we need you. You're our only hope." So these cadets go to the rescue, and there is a frightening battle and great heroism by these young people and a death of great sadness.

And at the end of the story Spock and Kirk are parting, presuming never to meet again. And it was very poignant. They're each the better for having known each other and they go off to be midshipmen. There was also a genuine love affair for Kirk, with one of the academy's pioneer female cadets. And it is true love. It is the love of his life. I thought it was terrific, just a really good story.

Harve took that idea to the then-head of Paramount's Motion Picture Group, Ned Tanen, who absolutely loved the idea, for several obvious reasons.

First, and most obviously, by eliminating the bulky salaries of seven established cast members, this *Star Trek* film would prove far cheaper to produce than any of its predecessors. Second, in a best-case scenario, should this film become a whopping box office hit, any number of sequels could follow, each of them unencumbered by an aging and expensive (albeit talented) cast. By focusing upon newer, younger and, if you'll pardon the expression, "hunkier" versions of their already beloved characters, Paramount could, in effect, breathe new life into a franchise fast approaching senior citizenry.

Finally, even in a worst-case scenario, even if their Starfleet Academy film was laughed out of theaters, we of the original crew could've come back at any time, ready to save the universe once more while wringing one more probable moneymaker out of *Star Trek* franchise. Basically, no matter how you looked at it, this film offered the studio a no-lose opportunity. However, a series of events soon began clouding the future of this seemingly surefire project. Harve continues:

I bring David Loughery back to script this thing, and just as we start writing, there's an administrative change. Ned Tanen's out, and Sid Ganis takes his place. Now, Sid is kind of like Francisco Madeira in *Viva Zapata!* Y'know, he says, "Well, we could do *this*, but on the other hand we could do *that*, or maybe we could even try that *other* thing, and . . ."

Anyway, after Sid comes in, David and I start rewriting, and after a while it becomes clear that we're now doing drafts just to be doing drafts. We're not moving forward. I asked Sid about it and he said, "No, no, no, we're solidly behind you," and at that point, there were some investments made which made the two of us feel a little better. We did some location scouting at Washington and Lee, a gorgeous university in the Cumberland country of Virginia. And we'd gotten an okay to add a modern building there, where the film's cadets would've done their flight-simulator training and learned how to be space guys.

And finally, after almost two years playing around with this thing, and after we've spent maybe a hundred thousand dollars in prep money, we have a summit meeting. Frank Mancuso comes down as Sid's emissary, and he says, "We love your movie, we think it's a terrific yarn, but can't we use Bill and Leonard?" I said, "Not a chance. Not in this story. I mean, there's just no way these guys can play seventeen. That's going to be a hell of a stretch." Anyway, we talked about that for a while, and I finally decided not to say no. Instead, I said, "Lemme think about it." Because I figured anybody who can move the death of Spock to his betterment should be able to figure *something* out here, too. So I went home, thought about the whole thing and came up with a solution which to this day I consider my finest piece of thinking.

The next morning I called Mancuso and said, "I've got it and I'll write it for you." And I did. And what I wrote was a lot like Twelve O'Clock High in structure. Kirk, you, Bill, have returned to the academy, in awe and wonder, to the place of your youth to address the graduating class. But of course now you are Admiral Kirk, a legend. And the cadets are impressing you with, "Sir, yes sir!" And they want to hear what you're really like and what Spock is really like. And you, in effect, say, "Well, it's a very interesting story," and you start to tell the story. And then the story shifts backward in time and unfolds itself.

Much later, at the end of the story, we find Kirk at a grave where his one great love has been buried, and it's obvious that he's still, after all these years, grieving for her. At that point, he looks up and there's Spock, who says, "We were wondering if you were ever coming back to us." And you reply, "Yes, I'm sorry, I have very deep feelings, you wouldn't understand." And Spock says something like, "Captain, I may not have feelings but I have memories." And you relate to each other and have a couple of very lovely little poetic lines. Then you rise and you guys embrace and Spock says, "Beam us up, Scotty." And the last shot of the picture is of the *Enterprise* going out again on another mission.

Why was this so brilliant? Because one, it had reinvolved you and Leonard as a framework, and two, it clearly said to the audience, "Don't worry, we're not killing the franchise, we're simply stopping to remember. We're paying homage and telling you why Kirk found it necessary never again to have a long-term permanent relationship, why Spock and Kirk are joined so irrevocably at the hip, why Bones is tied into them as the guy who's always saying 'No, no!' all the time." We're saying that the ship is still there, but if you love these young people, we can do movies with these midshipmen *and* the classic guys. Every conceivable opportunity was available to us, and at the same time, this picture clearly had as much breakthrough box office potential as *IV*. It would've been a must-see picture for *Star Trek* fans, and if all went well, we could've milked it forever.

I submitted that idea, and then Frank Mancuso, who was the head of the studio at that time, calls me and says, "This is a great script. We're going to make this movie." I said, "Thank you God, I've finally reached the point of decision." Mancuso then says, "But first we want you to make a conventional *Star Trek* movie with the original cast. We'll make your movie after that one, and we'll make you a pay-or-play deal." I said, "Wait a second, when do you want this classic *Trek* film done?" He said, "Well, by June of '91." That would've given me eleven months, less than half the time we had on our quickest movie, which was *Star Trek III*. That took us twenty-four months from blank page to finished picture. There was just no way that was gonna happen.

So now, even though Mancuso was waving money at me, large money, spread out over the next four years, I said, "Frank, it is my honest opinion that if we try to make your film first and *then* the Academy thing, you will not make the Academy thing. You will pay me, because you'll have to, but you won't make my picture because we'll have killed the franchise. If we do a rushed, eleven-month job on a classic *Star Trek* movie with the original cast, I can't conceive of the end result being any good. It'll be a bad movie, it will kill the franchise, and when that happens, no one will care about seeing the prequel. Your smartest move at that point would be to make the *Next Generation* movie."

He said, "C'mon, just do it. Just do it. I'm sure

it'll work out." And I said, "I'd really have to think about that," and I called him back the next day and I said, "I just can't do it." He said, "You mean you don't wanna do it." I said, "No, I can't. Spiritually and physically I can'bring nothing to the table. I can't think of a story, and making a film like this in less than a year is something that's almost abhorrent to me."

So he said, "Please reconsider." But I couldn't, so I left the studio. My contract was just about up, and they didn't renew. Actually, they asked me to stay but said, "Oh well, if you want to stay and *not* do our *Star Trek* film, we'll give you one-eighth of what you're getting now." I mean, it was a slap in the face and it would've been silly for me to stay.

Only much later did I find out the reasoning behind their mad rush to make a new *Star Trek* film, and when I did, it came down to this one simple fact. No one, in two years of development, had ever told Martin Davis, the chief executive officer of Paramount's parent company, Gulf + Western, that his next *Star Trek* movie was about teenage kids instead of the usual suspects. Finally, when someone told him that the green light was ready to be given, he apparently asked, "Oh good, are Bill and Leonard happy with the script?"

"Well, they do a kind of a cameo," he's told. "Cameo?!!!" That's when Davis hit the roof, demanding a full-blown classic-cast adventure, and that's where the buck stopped. That's when the initial enthusiasm for my script turned into "No, no, no, we'll do that later." I was stunned, feeling as low as I ever had. It was the bottom of despair. I also felt a strong sense of betrayal.

Y'know, we all have a false sense in our worlds, no matter what they are, that by doing the things we are asked to do, by making successes, by making other people money, by having three or four winning seasons in a row, that we are, in effect, going to be a permanent party in the world we live in. That didn't happen for me, and I encountered the crushing recognition that I had been jobbed. I was very angry, and that anger ultimately took on a rather unflattering form. I drank.

For the first time in my life I drank excessively. I don't mind saying that I drank a lot. That's the truth, and thank God I got over that. I got a life back, but I was terribly hurt.

At this point, I should also mention that while Martin Davis was officially stamping out Harve's Starfleet Academy idea, Gene Roddenberry was simultaneously lobbying against this film at every turn. Nearing the end of his life, with his health now rapidly deteriorating after decades of abuse and excess, Gene nonetheless summoned up every bit of his remaining energies to fight Harve's proposed storyline. Although he had no real pull anymore, his comments more often ignored than revered, Gene wouldn't give up. He was genuinely horrified that this film would reduce his most beloved characters down to thinly veiled teen idol status while they pranced about the screen in a shallow buffet of cheap gags and beefcake. Going so far as to publicly describe Harve's proposed storyline as a cheap knockoff of the cretinous *Police Academy* movies, Gene became increasingly vehement and vocal in his protestations. Richard Arnold recalls:

I'll never forget being in Gene's office one day and overhearing a phone conversation I should never have overheard. It was between Gene and Sid Ganis, and Gene was saying that for Harve to assume that the casting of the original seven actors in those seven roles had nothing to do with the success of *Star Trek* was the very height of arrogance. He just wouldn't listen to any further discussion of *Star Trek VI* with a new cast.

Gene said, "Sid, you think you've got me on my back, and now you're trying to get me to spread my legs. Fuck you." Bam. He was really angry, and as a result his relationship with Sid was not very good toward the end.

At any rate, with Harve's departure, and the studio bigwigs now being pummeled by their commander-in-chief, while simultaneously being driven to distraction by the rampaging Roddenberry, Mancuso and company rapidly began scrambling to get the Davis-mandated twenty-fifth-anniversary classic *Trek* film on-screen as quickly as possible. That soon translated into promoting the tried-and-true Ralph Winter to producer of the new film (surprisingly, as illogical as it sounds, a film's producer indeed outranks its executive producer), and immediately thereafter, Paramount asked the most qualified man they could find if he might be willing to step into the role of executive producer. That man was Leonard Nimoy. He explains:

By the time Frank Mancuso called me and said, "Let's have lunch," my agent had already informed me that he was going to ask me to make *Star Trek VI*. However, when we started talking about that idea, I was still surprised in that he offered to let me direct, executive-produce, whatever I wanted to do. His exact words were, "Be my partner. Help me get a *Star Trek* movie into the theaters in time for the twenty-fifth anniversary."

So of course my first question was, "What about Harve Bennett?" I knew that he'd been pitching an idea of his own, and I didn't want to step on his toes, and I didn't want to be used by the studio as just some convenient means of excluding Harve from the picture. At that point Mancuso said to me, flat out, "Harve Bennett is gone," and there was a real touch of anger in his voice. I was surprised, because I'd never heard that before and Frank is a very gentle gentleman.

Once I'd heard that, I said, "Well, let me think about it, and see if I can come up with an idea that might seem worthwhile." Three days later, I had it. I came back to Mancuso and said, "Okay, here's my idea. The Klingons have this terrible problem. Their economy is screwed up just like the Russians. We've always used the Klingons as our analogy for the Communist Bloc, and now, for the first time, they'll have to reach out for help and admit they have a problem. The crew of the *Enterprise* will try to help them."

Mancuso says, "Will there be a Gorbachev?" This was right around perestroika time, and I said, "Absolutely." He said, "Great! Do it! Will you direct it?" And I replied, "I can't say, as I sit here today, that I will direct it, because I definitely want Nick Meyer to write it, and we may have to offer him the director's chair in order for that to happen. If he wants that, we should jump at it, because this picture's gonna have to come together in just about fourteen months." It was now the summer of 1990 and we now wanted to open the picture in September of '91. At that point, I asked Mancuso if it'd be okay for me to approach Nick Meyer about this myself, and he said, "Sure." So I immediately put in a call to Nick, and we made plans to meet ten days later, on Cape Cod.

With Leonard now officially ordained as *Star Trek*'s "keeper of the flame" and Nick Meyer rapidly being lured back into battle, you'd have to assume that *Star Trek VI* was now primed and ready to come together smoothly, rapidly, with a great deal of creative satisfaction and minimum migraines. However, as you must realize by now, the universe that houses *Star Trek* is a strange and highly illogical place. As you've seen over and over again throughout the preceding pages, these things almost NEVER progress smoothly. This go-round proved no exception, and before long the creative works were once again gummed up rather magnificently. Leonard continues:

Before I'd even met with Nick, I got a call from a Paramount executive named Teddy Zee who said, "I think it's great that you're producing the new *Star Trek* picture, and I have a couple of writers that I'd like you to meet." I said, "Not necessary, because I know precisely how this thing has got to work. If it's going to work at all, it's got to come together very fast, very clean, and it has to be done by somebody who's done it before. There's no room for error here, we just don't have the time."

"But these guys are great!" he tells me. "They're big *Star Trek* fans. What have you got to lose? See them." What did I have to lose? A lot, as it turned out.

Anyway, at that point I thought, *Even though I'm not gonna need these guys, to refuse to even meet with them would be rude.* So later that day, in come these two guys, Konner and Rosenthal, with Teddy Zee, and Zee starts holding court about how this story should be about Romulans, and I really didn't need to hear that, so I said, "Wait, let's get focused here. This is not just another *Star Trek*, this is the close of our hostile relationship with the Klingons at the end of twenty-five years. That's the story we're telling, so please, let's not start exploring a whole lot of other ideas." At that point I skimmed through my basic storyline.

And these guys just sat there and said, "That's great!" so we started to bat around a few ideas. We played with some variations on the main theme, ways in which we might flesh out the plot, and then they went away to play with some ideas. Three or four days later, I get back maybe three pages of notes from these guys, and as I read them, it seemed to me that these notes were totally useless.

Their typed notes were just a rehashed collection of everything we'd discussed in our meeting. There was no progress, no breakthroughs, no new story ideas, and when we met again, I told them that. I said, "You haven't given me anything. You need an event. Something has to happen. Kirk and Spock have to get in trouble. Where's the story?" They go back to their office and take another stab.

GRACE LEE WHITNEY CAN COAX
A SMILE EVEN OUT OF A VULCAN

Three days later, I get back notes of the meeting again. Pages and pages of them. Almost every word that's been spoken between us, they've managed to type up and regurgitate as their own. I had no idea what was going on, but as it turned out, these guys were very wise, very clever.

Here's the game. Teddy Zee, as an executive on the lot, was the guy who'd apparently advocated giving these guys an overall contract. Now, as a studio executive, he's paying for these guys out of his own budget line, and as time passes, he's got to prove those expenses worthwhile, by having these guys get their work on-screen. Y'know, if the guys he's brought into the studio ultimately end up writing the next *Star Trek* screenplay, that makes him look like a hero. That's why he was pushing them in the first place, and now that he had his foot in the door, he wasn't gonna give up.

But after the second go-round with these guys, I told Teddy, "I don't want to meet with these guys anymore. It's over. I'm going to meet with Nick Meyer. I'm going to ask him to write this thing, and if he says yes, he'll most likely direct it, too. Period." Now I go.

Assuming that was the last he'd ever hear from those guys, Leonard got on a plane, flew East, and shortly thereafter had his meeting with Nick Meyer. Nick picks up the story from there:

first heard about this film months earlier, when Frank Mancuso and Martin Davis were in London looking to buy some theaters or something. I was living there at the time, so they called me, took me to lunch at Claridge's, and Frank Mancuso said, "We want to do a *Star Trek VI*, and we want to do it for around thirty million dollars." So I said, "That sounds possible, I don't know what the subject could be, but the budget's just about right." I think they came to me because they'd already begun talking with Leonard and he mentioned that it'd be good to get me aboard, too.

In the summer of 1990, I was on Cape Cod with my family. I had just finished another movie and I was cooling out when I got a phone call from Leonard saying, "Can I come out and chat with you?" I say, "Of course," so Leonard comes out and we had a terrific day. He tells me Paramount wants to do a *Star Trek VI* and he's got an idea for it. At that point, I said, "Great. Let's go for a walk," and we ended up walking along the coast, talking about his life, my life, how things were going and when we finally got down to business, he said, "I want to do a movie about the wall coming down in outer space." That was the line. That's what got me.

I heard that sentence and said, "Oh, that's good! I know how to do that." I mean, it was perfect, because everybody was still preoccupied with the events of 1989, and then Leonard asked me, "What would happen if some terrible thing happened to the Klingons and they tried to make peace?" We talked about that for a long time, and we fleshed out the character who would be like Gorbachev, and we ultimately walked up and down for, I don't know, hours and hours. By the time Leonard went home, we pretty much knew what this movie was gonna be about. And as Leonard finally said good-bye, I told him, "I want you to know I'm in. I'll do this movie." He said, "You know, we'd like you to write it *and* direct it." So I said, "Well let me write it first. If I like it, I'll direct it."

From here, this story should proceed in a straight line toward a highly probable happy ending. But again, this being *Star Trek*, nothing was as it seemed. In fact, despite the ironclad, surefire creative pairing of Nimoy and Meyer, this film was about to take a left turn that was abrupt, unexpected and just plain weird. Nimoy continues:

I meet with Nick, and we ultimately spend five or six hours together. Ideas are flowing, we're plotting, and by the end of the day, we had a pretty good sense of what this picture was going to be. The assassination, the frame-up, Kirk's court-martial, all of that stuff was coming together beautifully. At the end of the day, we shook hands, I came home, and contacted the studio immediately. I said, "I just met with Nick Meyer."

"He's wonderful," Leonard continued, "he's ready. He needs it. He wants it. He's up for it. He can do it fast. He can do it well. He's our guy. Please make the deal." A week then goes by during which Leonard hears nothing from the studio or Nick. Finally, unable to suppress his curiosity any longer, Leonard calls Nick himself. "What's taking so long?" he asks. "How come these guys haven't contacted you?" At which point Nick replies, "Didn't you know? I'm coming to L.A. tomorrow for a meeting with Sid Ganis. I asked Sid if it was going to be about *Star Trek*, and he said, 'Yes, among other things.' I assumed you knew all about it." Leonard continues:

So there was already subterfuge going on. Suddenly the studio is calling Nick Meyer and not telling me, their executive producer, anything about it. There were a lot of games going on, and when Nick then flew in, the games escalated, and his meeting turned out to be a very bizarre event. They met at Gary Lucchesi's house for dinner, and Sid Ganis was there. They ate, and after dinner somebody apparently suggested, "Let's get into the spa." They get into the tub and after a few minutes, Sid says, "You know what? I've got to leave. It was great seeing you." That was it. He didn't say word one about *Star Trek*.

It made no sense, and the only theory I could come up with was that somewhere in between their call to Nick and the actual meeting, somebody, with Teddy Zee's campaigning, got to Sid and said, "Look, we're already paying these writers who insist they can do this, so why would we pay Nick to do the same thing? Since we have to pay Konner and Rosenthal anyway, why not have them give it their best shot? If we get a Star Trek script from them, what's wrong with that? Y'know, if it turns out to be no good, Nick will just rewrite it." I think it's entirely possible that by the time Nick arrived at that meeting, they'd already decided to move ahead with the other guys. I knew nothing about it, Nick knew nothing about it, and a couple of days later, when I found out that Konner and Rosenthal had been officially hired, I went up the wall.

And then it got even more bizarre. These guys turned in some pages, or a rough draft, or an outline or something, and it just wasn't working. At that point, again without consulting me, the studio called Nick, in London, and said, "This script's not turning out very well. Will you help us out? Will you meet with these guys?" And Nick, being the obedient servant of Paramount, says, "Sure. Fine, send them over."

Nick Meyer picks up the story from there:

This whole thing was very weird. Leonard called me and said, "Something very odd is going on here." He said, "They've just hired two guys to write our movie," and I said, "Oh no, not again," because back on *IV*, Harve and I had lost a battle over the credits, in which the Writers Guild got called in, and we ended up going to arbitration with the guys who'd written the first draft of the script, and we lost. I ended up as the fourth name on the screenplay credit where I really felt I should have been in first or second position with Harve Bennett and nobody else. So with those unpleasant memories nagging at me, I backed away. I actually dropped out of the whole thing for a while.

But then I got a call from Teddy Zee, who said, "My guys are having problems getting started, is there anything you can do to help them get going?" Remember, at this point I had nothing to do with the project. I wasn't the writer, I wasn't yet the director, I was just Nick Meyer living in London. So I said, trying to be helpful to Paramount Pictures where I had an overall deal, "Okay, send them to London and I will walk them through the story that Leonard and I have come up with and I've since been embellishing." At that point, one of them came to London and spent three days with me in my living room. He had a legal pad with him and a tape recorder and during those three days, I talked him through the whole thing, I gave him every bit of the story that we'd previously come up with. Scene by scene, we went through this thing, and I gave him whatever was developed up to that point. I had nothing down on paper. When we'd finished, this guy took all of his notes and went back to Los Angeles.

As you'll see in the ensuing pages, Nick's creative assistance would shortly prove that old proverb about no good deed going unpunished true beyond a shadow of a doubt. For now, though, he was facing a bigger and more immediate problem. Leonard Nimoy had gotten wind of his screenwriting tutorial and to put it mildly, he was less than thrilled. Leonard explains:

I said to Nick, "How dare you do that when it was my story? Did you ever think to call me and ask, 'Leonard, did you know this is happening? Is it okay with you?'" I wanted to kill the son of a bitch. It was outrageous. Ultimately, those guys went away, wrote their screenplay, turned it in, and I heard it was useless. I never even read it. They never asked me to read it.

At that point, things proceed to get curiouser and curiouser, thanks to a sudden shake-up among the studio suits. Suddenly, after a series of expensive feature film failures, Sid Ganis is gone, replaced by the bottom-line-loving David Kirkpatrick in an attempt to stop the bleeding. Pennies are pinched, beans are lovingly counted, and before long, the studio begins running with a decidedly hard-nosed, businesslike philosophy.

Meanwhile, with the clock ticking loudly, *Star Trek VI* stumbling along without a screenplay, and the relationship becoming a bit strained between Nimoy and Meyer, the unexpected happened once more, and this runaway train actually got back on track. However, that doesn't mean the ride got any smoother. Nick Meyer explains:

I knew Konner and Rosenthal had encountered a lot of trouble getting going, and weeks later I heard rumors that they were still having problems. It was only a matter of time before I'd be drafted back into service. At about the same time,

I got a call from Denny Martin Flynn, my assistant who is also a screenwriter and a novelist, and he told me that he was ill. He had a malignancy and he was going to have to enter the hospital and have this malignancy removed. It was scary. I immediately got on a plane to come see him.

While I was on the plane I began thinking about what I might be able to do to help this guy through this thing, and I said to myself, "What we need is something for Denny to do that's going to get him excited and keep him interested, something to take his mind off the radiation and all that shit." That's when it hit me. I thought, "I've got it, I'll call David Kirkpatrick and tell him that Denny and I will write this *Star Trek* movie together."

When I got to the hospital, I asked Denny if he'd be interested in doing that, and he said, "Absolutely." At that point I called David Kirkpatrick about the idea. And by that point, I guess things looked pretty grim in terms of the other script. I don't know for sure, because I wasn't privy to it. All I knew was that when I spoke to David Kirkpatrick he told me something to the effect of "We're just waiting until they turn in their draft and then we're gonna be back to you."

That's what happened. So then these guys turned in their script, the studio didn't like it, and at that point it was turned over to me and Denny. I never even read that first draft. I never read the Meerson/Krikes draft of *IV* and I never read the Konner/Rosenthal material on *VI*. I didn't want to see it because I think once that stuff is in your head it's just gonna confuse you.

Anyway, the end result was that Denny got out of the hospital and through computer connection between Los Angeles and London we then wrote the first draft of *Star Trek VI*. When we finished, we showed it to Leonard, and Leonard had suggestions and problems.

Actually, on Leonard's end, as he explains below, things weren't quite that simple:

Weeks had now gone by, and then they put Nick on the screenplay. He goes off with Denny and BAM! Here's your screenplay. Now I get a call one night from David Kirkpatrick, who's now running the company. Kirkpatrick and Lucchesi are on the speaker phone in Kirkpatrick's office, and Kirkpatrick says, "Leonard, how are ya?"

"Great, David." He says, "I know there's a spin going on here, but I can't quite figure out what it is. We now have a script from Nick, and we thought you might like to take a look at it." They don't say a word about the useless first version they bought, or about the two months it cost us. They then say, "We'd like you to read it and tell us what YOU think." So I read it.

Having given Nick's work a quick once-over, Leonard got back on the phone with Kirkpatrick and spent a couple of moments hashing through his immediate creative thoughts and concerns. When he'd finished, Kirkpatrick, speaking for the studio, replied, "We feel exactly the same way, and we'd sure appreciate it if you'd give those same notes to Nick. Will you call him and give him your notes so that he can start working on the next pass? We have responded to him already." That last sentence struck Leonard as a bit unusual, but at the time he didn't know what to make of it. However, he'd soon get a much sharper perspective. Leonard continues:

So I called Nick, and while I'm giving him my thoughts he says, "Whoa, wait a minute. Before you go any further I think you should know that I have a memo from Paramount. They're over the moon about this script." At that point, I realized that I'd been had. I'd been sent into the barrel by executives who'd screwed the situation up very badly. They had lost control of Nick Meyer and what they were really doing in asking me to call him was saying, "Would you please help us corral this guy?"

So I said to Nick, "'Over the moon,' huh? That's interesting because they didn't tell ME that." So Nick says, "I'd be happy to fax you their memo." I said, "Please do," and he faxes me a paragraph which says something to the effect of "This is a great *Star Trek* script. You have captured the blah blah of the blah blah blah. You have accomplished the blah blah blah and the only problem is that the Trekkies will be cheering and screaming for another *Star Trek* picture when this thing is over."

Nick was now using whatever weaponry he could find to try and beat the crap out of me.

Actually, in all fairness to the studio, and shame on Nick, there was a lot more in that memo than just the excerpt that he sent me. It went on to say, "We'd like you to address these specific issues," and that was followed by pages and pages of story-specific notes. Nick never faxed those to me. He only let me see the one paragraph that best served his purposes. When

Paramount ultimately sent me the rest of their memo, I thought, *You son of a bitch.*

At that point I started chipping away at Nick, and it went on and on. There were some gaps in the story that had to be dealt with, and there were some flaws, and a few scenes that needed adjustment, and after a lot of back and forth, it started to fall together rather well. My only regret grew out of a line which I had given to Nick that said, "Only Nixon can go to China." To me, that's what this film was all about. Kirk is the perfect person to make the first overtures toward peace with the Klingons because he has always been their greatest archenemy. Politically, the job had to fall into his hands, but at the same time, I said, "Kirk has to get some insight into the Klingons that changes his life. He's got to learn something once he goes behind the curtain. He's got to come away thinking, *Now I understand why these people have always been so angry, such nasty, vicious murderers. I don't like it, but I've learned something very important.* I wanted that knowledge to change Kirk, and the rest of us as well. But Nick was never comfortable with that idea, and no matter how we tried to make it work, it just never came to be.

Still, as the picture began taking shape, Meyer, Flynn, Nimoy and the studio all found themselves fairly happy with its progress. However, with time continuing to be a factor, these guys knew that the luxury of extensive rewriting time was simply beyond their grasp. With that in mind, they had to rely on their combined experience, familiarity with the characters, and gut feelings in constructing their story with minimum delay. Meyer explains their working relationship:

Leonard had some changes that he wanted me to make, and after I'd worked on them, I showed the script to you. You had a lot of notes, and we just continued the process of revision and alteration and this and that until incrementally the thing acquires layers and textures and ultimately gets a lot better. Denny and I kept on writing right up through production. You know, we just kept at it, trying our best to make this thing perfect, which of course is impossible.

I should also add that Leonard really pushed hard. He just kept saying, "There are ways to make this better," and I remember he ultimately made me very angry, but the truth is that he was right. For example, look at that great confrontation between Spock and Valeris in the sickbay. Leonard came up with that, and it was not in the script that Paramount bought, and it was not in the script that you saw. Later, I remember you called me up and said, "You should be very proud of that scene," and I just said, "Thank you."

What was very clear about the screenplay that I had written with Denny was that Kirk had all kinds of stuff to do. He was all over the place. Spock, however, was more problematic. What did he have to do except figure out the locked-room mystery? Leonard was looking for some emotional payoff, and what he kept pushing for was a scene that would enhance and explore the relationship between Spock and Valeris. I said that's impossible, there's no way. He said yeah there is, if we just keep looking for it, you'll find it. And damn, after he made me sufficiently crazy, we found it. And bless him for that.

From there, with cast and creatives feeling pretty good about the script, there was nevertheless one rather formidable naysayer. He was Gene Roddenberry. Richard Arnold explains:

Gene was really bothered by the Klingons in *VI*. He wasn't bothered by the Klingons in *III* or in *V*. Those Klingons were Klingons, but the Klingons in *VI* were, in his words, "too civilized, too decent, too much of the good guys in the story." He felt that in *VI* things were set up backward, that the shoe was suddenly on the other foot, that the Federation was wearing the black hat. The good guys had suddenly become the bad guys. The Federation was now causing the problems.

Y'know, the Klingons had come to the Federation, hat in hand, saying, "Let's have peace," only to meet with resistance on the Starfleet end. They were the ones who weren't prepared for it, which was not the way Gene would have handled it. He would have reversed it, he would have had the Klingons being the ones who couldn't handle the idea of peace, with the Federation saying, "Come on, let's try and work this out."

Like Gene, I too was bothered by some of the attitudes and comments expressed throughout the script by Federation types. Scotty has a line about how "that Klingon bitch never even shed a tear," and Uhura as originally scripted would've made reference to the kinder, gentler Klingons by saying something to the effect of "Yeah, but would you want your daughter to marry one?" That line was removed when Nichelle flatly refused to read it.

Kirk too was not immune to the unexpected prejudice. Confronted by Spock with the fact that unless a peace agreement is achieved with the Klingons, their entire race will most certainly perish, Kirk's scripted response was a very bitter "Then let them die!"

When I initially read that line, I requested that Nick change it. I just couldn't imagine Kirk, even after the death of his son, being *that* rigid, *that* cold, *that* unfeeling. At the same time, you couldn't doubt for an instant the dramatic strength of Nick's scripted moment, and while I failed in my attempts to come up with an alternate line of equal strength, I nevertheless came up with a compromise that would've made me feel a lot better. Kirk would indeed say, "Let them die," but almost immediately, his face and hand movements would have made it clear that while those words had exploded out of his mouth, he didn't really mean them. "Oh shit, I'm sorry I said that," he'd imply visually, and with that addendum, I found myself much more comfortable playing the scene. I told Nick about it, he liked the idea, we shot it, and months later, when I'd come in to rerecord Kirk's lines for a couple of scenes, I couldn't help but notice that Kirk's facial reaction to that particular line had been cut. I cornered Nick about it, and he immediately told me, "Okay, sure, we'll put it back in." I'm still waiting.

I wasn't the only one questioning the attitudes of the crew of the *Enterprise* . Gene Roddenberry, the dyed-in-the-wool utopian, went through the roof one more time, and he too would ultimately confront Nick Meyer with his objections. As it turns out, he too would be sandbagged. Again, Richard Arnold explains:

Gene didn't like Kirk's "Let them die" line at all, and he felt that the captain's bigotry and indeed the narrow-mindedness among all of the characters really came out of nowhere. Suddenly these people who were in "Let That Be Your Last Battlefield" were guilty of the same sort of backward, ignorant thinking that they'd fought against throughout the entire run of the old series. *Star Trek VI* seemed to be much darker and more military, darker than ever before.

That really bothered Gene, but the harder he fought in trying to get Nick to cooperate, the worse it got between them. At one point Nick walked out of a meeting with Gene, just up and walked out, less than five minutes into it. That got Gene really pissed and he forced Leonard to drag Nick back into the office. He wasn't looking for an apology, he just wanted Nick to listen.

When he finally got there, they went through the script together, and as Gene was pointing out specific problems, Nick was saying, "You don't like this? Okay, fine, it's out. We'll change this. Whatever . . ." And then he went away, never came back, and didn't do any of it. Didn't change a thing, did it his way instead. And that really hurt Gene. Nick had an attitude of, "What do you know about this?" I think Nick had been guaranteed a certain amount of control, either by Leonard or by the front office, and he just couldn't stomach the idea of Gene's interference. Which unfortunately was also the way the studio treated Gene toward the end: "We're happy to use your name and your creation, but don't call us, we'll call you."

Still, despite the occasional creative pothole, the overall script for *Star Trek VI* began falling together rapidly, shaping up over the next few weeks as a tight, well-crafted tale of action, mystery and political intrigue. Having now gone almost a full month without a catastrophe, we were well overdue. Nick Meyer explains how our luck ran out:

It seems like whenever you make a movie, there's always one aspect that's horrible. If it's not the scripting, it's the production, or the preproduction, or the postproduction, whatever. However, all of those things ran pretty well on *Star Trek VI*. Our problems came out of the budget and caused the worst battle since World War II.

By New Year's Day 1991, Nick had already taken a six-month lease on a house in L.A. and moved here from London, with his wife and children in tow. Three days later, he attended a strange meeting in David Kirkpatrick's office. "I remember," says Meyer, "that I went out of my way to tell Kirkpatrick how excited I was to be working on the film, and that he replied by saying, 'Well, of course you're excited, this is a twenty-five-million-dollar film.'" Now, Meyer had assumed all along, ever since his London lunch with Mancuso and Davis, that this picture was to be budgeted at thirty million, and he was not about to let himself be mugged for five million bucks.

"Wait a minute!" he said. "Wait a minute. Hold it. No, no. Martin Davis, Frank Mancuso, London, Claridge's, thirty million, remember?!?!" He then continued, explaining that there was fourteen million dollars "above the line" in this movie. That means actors, directors, stars—everything all of these people make is considered "above the line." "It's an enormous amount," he explained, "but you've got twenty-five years' worth of baggage there, and that's where it stands . . . fourteen million. Next, you have four million dollars in special effects, and that's just to match the special effects budget of *Star Trek IV*, which was made three years ago. That figure stinks, but I can live with it. That's eighteen million. Add in a minimum of two and a half million for postproduction, and while I'm not a rocket scientist, even I can add that up to twenty and a half million dollars. Now where's the movie gonna be if I have to make it out of the four and a half million bucks we've got left? Now, and I kid you not, Kirkpatrick says, 'Will you excuse us for a minute?,' and this whole group of suits goes into another room."

At the time, Paramount's feature film division was basically drowning in red ink, having lost upwards of four hundred million dollars in the previous three years. How is it possible to lose that much money in that period of time? Simple—just make a long string of very expensive films that nobody goes to see, films like *Another 48 HRS*, *The Godfather Part III* and, most notably, *Days of Thunder*. So now, as things were beginning to get really hairy for Paramount, and as executives were beginning to be thrown overboard based on the studio's losses, Kirkpatrick and company have suddenly implemented a whole new program of austerity, and Nick's thirty million had mysteriously dwindled to twenty-five.

However, Nick had done his homework, and he was not about to roll over. "Let me give you some statistics," he began:

Every Star Trek movie from three through five has cost an average of forty-one percent more than its predecessor. Star Trek I cost forty-five million dollars in 1979, and that was, you know, craziness. Star Trek II cost eleven-point-two, Star Trek III cost seventeen, Star Trek IV cost twenty-five million, and Star Trek V cost thirty. There's only two Star Trek movies that don't conform to this forty-one percent figure. One is Star Trek II, and the other will be Star Trek VI, which should cost just about the same as Star Trek V. They both happen to be mine, but don't ask for the impossible. Don't strangle this thing in the cradle." And one of the studio executives then launched into a sermon about how "we're in the nineties now, and we're in a period of retrenchment, and blah blah blah, and we've been in a drought." At which point I said, "Fine, let's make a nineties movie about two guys on a park bench. But don't quote me a franchise from the eighties, which is Star Trek, and tell me I have to make it by nineties' terms, because you won't end up with much of a movie."

Somewhere in the middle of all this, the suits come back with a counteroffer of twenty-seven five, which I rejected, recalling that—this is me at my worst—I said, "Guys, you're not listening. This is not a negotiation, it's not about me." To which they replied, "You're not being professional. You're not being cooperative. You're being obstructive, and this and this and this." And this kind of stuff went on around the clock for three weeks, until it finally got so bad, they actually reduced me to tears. I ended up sitting on the floor in Gary Lucchesi's office, crying, and he came over to me and said, "It's a tough business. If you want love, go home." This kinda stuff went back and forth over the course of the next several days, until finally Star Trek VI . . . was canceled.

It's true. With the producers and the studio unable and/or unwilling to compromise, Star Trek VI was officially dead. And then, as you've probably noticed seems to happen throughout the lifespan of Star Trek, just when you think we're dead in the water, an incredibly unlikely series of events somehow conspires to revive the "ongoing mission" one more time. This time around proved no exception.

This time, from out of nowhere, and without warning, Frank Mancuso leaves Paramount after thirty-one years, and his replacement, Stanley Jaffe, is not only the father of one of our producers, Steven-Charles Jaffe, he's also a man who's worked well with Nick Meyer in the past, having hired him to rewrite the ending of Fatal Attraction. Meyer calls Jaffe. Jaffe says, "I hear you're having some problems on Star Trek VI." Meyer says, "Yeah, I need two and a half million dollars more or I can't make this picture." At which point Jaffe just says, "Okay, you've got it." Simple. That's how this movie ultimately got made.

With the official thumbs-up finally given, Nick and Leonard now had to get their script on its feet and shooting as quickly as possible. They got down to business immediately, hunting around Hollywood while tending to Nick's desire to have this film populated with the finest guest cast possible. Almost immediately, they bagged a prize trophy. Determined to cast the villainous role of General Chang with an actor strong enough and articulate enough to project and emote even beneath the required gobs of Klingon latex, Meyer was thrilled to land a well-respected, larger-than-life actor with a range and power that would've blown through solid rock. Of course, his name was Christopher Plummer.

You know the résumé, long and impressive, topped as everyone knows by acting in such classic films as *The Man Who Would Be King*, *Murder by Decree*, and Edelweissing his way through *The Sound of Music*. Plummer would go on to make an absolutely fantastic villain, chewing our scenery to bits while spitting out Shakespearean snippets with an evil leer and a villainous smile. He was an absolute joy to work with, and the only problem we encountered was that I generally spent the better part of my time on the set with him blowing take after take as his jokes reduced me to a quivering, smiling, guffawing and thoroughly useless mass of putty.

At the same time, lesser-known but no less gifted actors began rounding out our supporting cast, populating the film with an unusually talented cast of characters. Perhaps most significant, Kim Cattrall, who'd been Nick Meyer's original choice to play Saavik almost a decade earlier on *The Wrath of Khan*, finally climbed aboard the *Enterprise*, creating the role of the brilliant and unscrupulously ambitious Vulcan traitor, Valeris. This came about thanks to four fortunate twists of fate.

First, as the script was originally written, Valeris did not exist, and in her place, Saavik herself would've ultimately been exposed as the manipulator of Kirk's and Bones's frame-up. However, when Leonard contacted Kirstie Alley, now hugely successful playing Rebecca Howe on the sitcom *Cheers*, it quickly became obvious that in the decade since her last joyride aboard the Starship *Enterprise*, her pricetag had skyrocketed to the point where it simply would have been budgetary suicide to bring her back.

Second, upon Alley's rejection, Leonard and Nick began waffling over whether to recast the role once more or move forward in conjuring up a whole new character. And that brings me to twist of fate number three, which found Gene Roddenberry once more smoking from the ears while vehemently protesting yet another aspect of *Star Trek VI*. Saavik, he decried, should never be exposed as a traitor. He felt that she had now formally achieved "beloved character" status, and that to expose her as the devious saboteur of the Federation's peace negotiations with the Klingons amounted to little more than a cheap theatrical gimmick. With that, the memos flew once more. Leonard

ONLY RARELY DO KLINGON GENERALS AND STARSHIP CAPTAINS GIGGLE TOGETHER

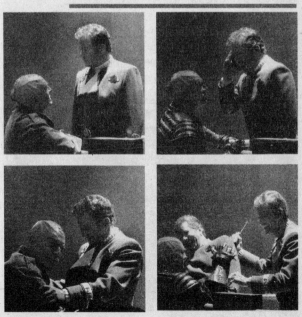

winced, and Nick slapped his forehead and this time even went so far as to publicly belittle Roddenberry's position with a rather curt "I created the character of Saavik in *Star Trek II*. She was not Gene's. If he doesn't like what I plan on doing with her, maybe he should give back the money he's made off my films. Maybe then I'll care what he has to say."

Fourth and finally, with Roddenberry railing and no real workable alternative, Nick and Leonard decided to jettison Saavik once and for all, opting instead to try and create someone new. They immediately began seeing actresses who might fit the part, and first on Nick's list was Kim Cattrall. He called her in, she arrived, and promptly refused the role, mistakenly assuming that she was being asked to resuscitate Saavik. Only when Nick assured her that she'd be creating her own character, entirely from scratch, did she reverse her initial decision and agree to appear. Once aboard, however, Kim jumped into her role headfirst, designing the character's hairstyle and then shaving off her own sideburns

SPOCK SUCKS SECRETS OUT OF VALERIS

in an effort to make Valeris's Vulcan ears all the more prominent.

Next in line came Jack Palance . . . almost. Meyer desperately wanted the one-armed pushup champ to play our Klingon Chancellor Gorkon, but when Palance proved highly expensive as well as mildly ambivalent, the role was offered to David Warner, who'd played Jack the Ripper in Meyer's *Time After Time*, as well as Federation diplomat St. John Talbot in *Star Trek V*.

At the same time, Christian Slater shocked everybody by confirming his Trekkie status and officially requesting a cameo in the film. Naturally, Leonard and Nick shoved him in there immediately. At the same time, Mark Lenard agreed to return as Sarek, while John Schuck and Brock Peters both signed to reprise their *Star Trek IV* roles as a ruthless Klingon ambassador and Starfleet admiral, respectively. Shortly thereafter, Kurtwood Smith, who'd recently stolen *Robocop* as supervillain Clarence Boddicker, now found himself in the much more respectable role of the Federation president.

Additionally, the very talented Rosanna DeSoto came in to play Chancellor Gorkon's daughter Azetbur, and Rene Auberjonois (ultimately cut from the theatrical release of the film, though now shape-shifting his way through *Deep Space Nine* as Odo), and supermodel Iman, if you'll pardon the obvious pun, rounded out our cast quite effectively. Finally, in one piece of carefully crafted instant trivia, Nick Meyer came up with an idea that found him rewriting his generically written role of "Klingon defense attorney" and customizing it to suit the talents of Michael Dorn, who, as every one of you knows, was already on the Paramount lot playing . . . *The Next Generation*'s Worf. When he'd completed his revision, Nick wandered across the lot and cornered Dorn, who then publicly recounted the simplicity of his acceptance. "Nick came over to me and said, 'Michael?' I said, 'Yes,' and he said, 'Hi, I'm Nick Meyer, and I've just written a part for you.' I said, 'Oh really, in what?' and he answered, 'Star Trek VI.' I said, 'Great.' He smiled, I smiled, and that was it. I wish all my roles were so easy to come by."

At that point, with our script written and cast in place, you'd think it'd be time to start shooting. You'd think wrong. Once again, as on Star Trek V, the studio accountants were sweating, feeling like there was no way in the world Nick's movie was ever gonna come in on time or on budget. With that in mind, they lowered the boom and Nick, Leonard and Ralph began slicing. Immediately, they lopped half of their special effects opticals right out of the film, shrunk our shooting schedule down to a very tight ten weeks, and decided to forgo building a lot of brand-new sets in favor of shooting as often as possible on redressed sets from Star Trek: The Next Generation. Further, when the Enterprise bridge set from Star Trek V was hauled out of mothballs and categorized as salvageable, they immediately declared that this time around, Captain Kirk would be driving a used vehicle.

Finally, and perhaps most significantly in terms of the final film, a scripted prologue to the proceedings, one that would've fleshed out what each crew member was doing now that they'd been effectively put out to pasture, was beheaded without ever seeing the light of day. About ten minutes long, it would've followed Kirk's rounding up of the old crew, recruiting them for this one final mission.

As originally scripted, the film would've opened upon the U.S.S. Excelsior, under the command of Captain Sulu. From there, we would've found Kirk in bed, making love to yet another conquest. Not all that unusual, except for the fact that this woman is Carol Marcus, and as this thing moves forward, you'd have gotten the distinct impression that these two had not only reconciled, but were now well on their way toward spending their autumnal years together while making like newlyweds at every opportunity.

However, when a knock on the door brings the news that the old crew of the Enterprise has been ordered to reassemble once more, Kirk risks his relationship and leaves Carol's embrace, finding even greater seduction in the opportunity for one last adventure. With that in mind, he sets out to round up the rest of his crew. Though Starfleet describes Spock's whereabouts as "highly confidential," Kirk would nonetheless locate the rest of the crew rather easily.

He'd have found Scotty bored out of his mind to the point where he's now spending his days taking apart the Klingon bird of prey last seen in Star Trek IV in a futile attempt to at last uncover the secrets of her cloaking device. Uhura is next, equally bored, working for a Federation radio station as the host of a call-in advice program. Chekov too is uneasy, yawning his days away at a chess club while repeatedly trying in vain to defeat higher life forms with special Russian strategies. Finally, Kirk finds McCoy most unhappy of all. Hailed as a conquering hero, Bones is nonetheless drunk and disorderly at a high-society medical dinner in his honor. Disgusted by the money-hungry healers he's forced to endure in the civilian world, even the dependably cantankerous Bones jumps at the chance to once again become useful aboard the Enterprise.

Once assembled, the crew would have traveled together to Starfleet Command, where Spock would've made his entrance, informing the crew that their mission will be to safely transport Klingon General Gorkon to his politically volatile peace conference.

I was sad to see all that get tossed out the window, but as interesting (and unusual) as it would've been to flesh out the entire *Enterprise* crew as people, there was no denying that when push came to shove, those scenes provided an obvious target for the budgetary red pen, in that our basic storyline held up just fine even without all of their opening color and backstory. With that in mind, rather than risk watering down our entire picture with an extensive series of smaller cuts, Leonard and Nick bit the bullet and decided to keep most of the film intact by amputating our prologue.

Finally, on April 11, 1991, we began fifty-five days of thoroughly enjoyable shooting conditions, during which we all got on the roller coaster one last time and tried like hell to make the best of it. somehow, after a quarter-century of periodic collective employment, I think we were all well aware of the fact that this picture would most likely prove to be our last class reunion. With that in mind, I think we all kicked back a little bit more than usual, enjoying ourselves, celebrating and cherishing these last few weeks together. I for one had a great time.

Now unleashed from the unending responsibility and backbreaking workload of *The Final Frontier*, I was free to hang around the set with my castmates, and this time, really for the first time, I made a conscious effort to avoid the telephone, the makeup man, and the book in my trailer, opting instead to reach out and maybe finally get to know my costars a little bit better. As you

ABOVE: Iman gets even better-looking!
BELOW: One last kiss before I kill you

know, I hadn't won many popularity contests over the years, but these final days of production found me reminiscing about days gone by and stories untold. They were also the days that sparked the desire in me to pound all of this stuff into the nearest PC. At any rate, over the course of the next fifty-five days' shooting, we all had a ball, enjoying our work and each other's company to an extent never before realized. At times it got downright silly.

For example, our first days of shooting took place amid the swingsets and sandboxes of L.A.'s Bronson Park. There, nestled just beneath that world-famous "Hollywood" sign, as we all risked overexposure in the southern California sun, we shot our scenes upon the "frozen prison ice planet" Rura Penthe. Under heavy faux-fur parkas and a daily deluge of plastic snow and Gatorade, De Kelley and I plodded through our paces, sweating heavily while trying our best to look as if we were freezing to death. By the end of day one, as you might imagine, we were both thoroughly exhausted.

The following morning, with the sun rising even more ominously over the horizon, De and I met up under the biggest shade tree we could find and had breakfast together. Laid out in front of us, spread from end to end of a huge craft services table, was every possible breakfast food you can imagine. I immediately grabbed a yogurt and some juice, then sat down in my designated director's chair waiting for De. Ten minutes later, he was still standing at that same table going "Hmmm . . ."

"Just pick something, will ya?" I yelled over, at which point De grumbled and mumbled something that most likely cast aspersions upon my character. Finally, by the time I'd almost finished, he arrived, bearing just a raisin English muffin. "That's IT?" I yelled at him. "It took you fifteen minutes to pick up one lousy English muffin?"

"Well," he said, "I had to toast it."

After I'd made sufficient fun of my friend, we sat there together in the shade, talking about how exhausted we both were after the previous day's shooting, about how today's shooting looked to be even tougher, and about how perhaps we really *were* getting too old to be doing this kind of stuff anymore. We commiserated about the various cracks, pops, aches and pains that had begun advancing upon us with the passage of time, and agreed that even worse than our physical ailments were the traces of forgetfulness that had snuck into both of our lives.

Actually, though De's memory is really very good . . . for a man his age . . . he expressed a real annoyance at even the slightest memory lapse. I replied that of course, my memory is a steel trap, and that I forget absolutely nothing, except maybe for the little things like my address, my phone number, what I had for dinner last night, that kind of stuff. Before we'd gotten much further, we were called away to once again begin perspiring amid the plastic icicles of Rura Penthe.

Over the course of the next few mornings, while De and I continued playing snowmen, I couldn't help but be astounded that every single morning, De went through the same breakfasttime routine. Ten minutes of "Hmmmmmm," five minutes of muffin toasting, two minutes of precise butter formations, and finally ten minutes of eating each muffin half with precise counterclockwise rotation. Never before had I seen a man so set in his ways, and that's when an evil, twisted plan hit me. I put it into motion the following morning.

Watching De's morning ritual once more, I sat patiently through the "Hmmmmms" and waited until the precise moment when De popped his raisin English muffin into the toaster. Then I leaped. Grabbing hold of the nearest makeup man, I asked him if he might distract De's attention. "Excuse me, De?" he then yelled out. "Could I just give you a quick touch-up?"

"Well, all right," grumbles De, ". . . but y'know, I have toast in there and . . ." By the time De's turning around to be powdered, I've run over to the buffet table, where I'm now carefully picking De's muffin halves out of the toaster. Before he's even turned around, I've got one in each side of my mouth and I'm wandering away, trying my best to look as innocent as possible.

Now the toaster pops and De, who's smiling broadly and chirping "Toast is ready," comes back, sees there's no muffin, and immediately assumes he'd forgotten to load up the toaster in the first place. A look of consternation comes over his face, matched by the annoyance that he feels in having succumbed to such a blatant memory lapse. He now sighs, slices once more, and just a tad more deliberately places a new muffin into the toaster. I couldn't resist.

Once again I flag the makeup man and once again he acts as my beard. Yanking De's muffin as quickly as possible, and burning my fingers in the process, I now shove my second muffin of the morning into my mouth and begin chewing, trying desperately not to laugh as I watch De turn around to find his phantom muffin missing once more. His eyes go wide, he sighs heavily, and it's obvious that he simply can't believe he's made the same dumb mistake twice.

Shaking his head, and now mumbling louder than ever before, he yanks yet another breakfast treat out of

REHEARSING THE PRISON FIGHT SCENE WITH NICK AND FRIEND

its cellophane, slices it and shoves it into the toaster with profound aggression. This was just too good to pass up. I now have the script girl corral De, asking him about whether or not he'd received the latest version of his lines, and while she's got him distracted, I once again steal his breakfast, shoving a third hot muffin into my face, just seconds before the toaster pops.

Now De turns, looks into the toaster, holds it upside down and shakes it, then begins furiously talking to himself. ")*(&''% %' # U (*&('*'," he says, casting doubts upon the chastity of the toaster's mother. He's pacing around now, furious with the strange turn of events, until he sees me, cheeks puffed to chipmunk proportions by the trio of muffin remnants that I haven't yet been able to squeeze down my gullet. His glare tells me that my goose is now officially cooked, and I start laughing uncontrollably. Not a good thing to do when one's mouth is full of dry toast.

"Shatne-e-e-er!" he yells, sounding like a cross between Robert Duvall in *Apocalypse Now* and Mr. Spacely in *The Jetsons*. "It was YOU!!!" Pointing a menacing finger, he ran toward me while I turned red, shouting, "You think that was funny?"

Actually, while I *did* think this was rather humorous, I was not turning red out of laughter. I had instead managed to get a big hunk of muffin lodged in my esophagus, and by the time anyone around us realized that I wasn't just guffawing myself silly, I was well on my way to death's door. "Call 911," I croaked, but luckily, one AD and one Heimlich maneuver later, I was fine, although for the rest of the day, De Kelley kept chiding me with, "Y'see what happens when you mess with *me*?"

By the time I was beginning to live that down, we'd finished our exterior shooting and moved inside Paramount's Stages 5, 8 and 9, where we'd be shooting the bulk of our movie. We were now joined by the rest of our regular castmates, whom De was kind enough to entertain over and over again with his humorous pantomime of my near-asphyxiation, and our "final" set was anything but funereal. We enjoyed our time together at every turn, this particular set was almost always brimming with laughter and genuine good feelings all around. We even had some fun with Nick Meyer.

That all began when we sat down to shoot the scene in which our *Enterprise* crewmen sit down to an uneasy dinner with a tableful of representatives from the Klingon Empire. With every one of our cast members seated around a large table all day, the set became very silly very fast, and throughout the day the mood never quite sobered up. In fact, even as we began shooting, some of us were performing some rather ill-advised stunts. Okay, maybe it was just me.

All over this formal dining table, our prop guys had laid out a four-star intergalactic dinner worthy of Zagat's highest rating. Romulan ale flowed from unusual decanters, strange chinaware and silver accented nicely, but standing at the table's dead center, and serving undeniably as our pièce de résistance, was a large platter filled with a weird-looking blue meaty substance.

"What the hell is that?" we all asked almost simultaneously. "It's squid," announced one prop guy, who proceeded to describe the dish as if it were his special of the day. "We wash it out in cold water, dye it blue, slice it into bite-sized chunks, cook it, then refrigerate it until needed."

"Does it come with a salad?" asked Leonard.

At that point, while staring at a heaping pile of big, cold, tough, disgusting squid, which was rapidly growing a bit whiffy under the hot lights, Nick speaks. "All right," he says, "we're gonna roll now and you guys really need to pretend that you're eating this stuff and . . . oh, hell . . . Twenty bucks to anybody who really clamps down and starts to eat that crap."

I needed no more, and on Take 1, I cut off a good hunk of that rubbery, tentacle-covered squid, chewed, swallowed, fought off the urge to retch, and called out "Where's my twenty?" immediately following Nick's cry of "Cut." At that point he grudgingly laid twenty bucks on my place setting.

Over the next forty-five minutes, we ended up doing maybe a dozen takes of the scene, and each time the cameras rolled, my gag-playing overruled my gag-*reflex*, and I ultimately grabbed a couple of hundred bucks out of Nick Meyer's wallet. Nobody else was touching this vile stuff, but I just kept digging in with great gusto, shoving it into my mouth, take after take, each time in exchange for a crisp new twenty. Ultimately, I was up like 240 bucks, and with my upbringing, getting ill for a couple hours is worth 240 bucks.

Over the course of the next several weeks, we all continued to enjoy our last ride. There was, however, one nagging, annoying, thoroughly disgusting irritant . . . Nick Meyer's cigar. All day long, all over the set, we'd find ourselves grimacing at the smell of Nick's vile, footlong stogies. One by one we'd made it a point to ask him, "Do you really need to smoke those things?" and one by one he'd answer with an annoyed "Yes, I need to smoke these things."

Finally, with a lung full of secondhand smoke and a costume that smelled like an ashtray, I confronted Nick once more. "C'mon, Nick, you can't tell me that you really need to smoke that cigar, can you?"

"Look, Bill," he replied, "I have to have three things in life. I have to have a cigar after breakfast, one after

lunch, and one before dinner. That's the way it's gotta be, and there's nothing you can do to change that."

I took that as a personal challenge, and by early next morning, I'd hatched a plan.

I went over to our prop guys and asked a favor. "Listen," I said, "can you make me up something that stinks worse than anything else on this planet?"

"Nope, sorry, don't have time," they told me, barely looking up from the five hundred last-minute disasters at hand.

"But you don't understand," I continued, "this might stop Nick from smoking those disgusting cigars on the set."

"Ohhhh," they cried out excitedly, "why didn't you tell us that in the first place?" With that, they dropped everything and cooked me up a stink bomb so vile it'd curl your grandmother's hair. It was truly putrid, and when they finished bottling this thing up for me, all I had to do to effectively clear any room within seconds was uncork the top. There simply aren't words disgusting enough to describe this smell, but if you think old sneakers meet kitty litter, meet stagnant water hole, meet burning rubber, that'll put you at about one-tenth the potency.

With this thing in my pocket, I practically raced into work the next day to find Nick halfway through his after-breakfast funk. "Oh, Ni-ick," I called almost musically, "could you come over here? I have to ask you something about a line."

He bit and ten seconds later, when he'd gotten within two feet of me, I uncorked and immediately stuffed my nose down inside my own uniform. "What line are you . . . oh my GOD!!! What the hell is that STINK?!!!" Nick pleaded, teary-eyed.

"The smell?" I replied. "Oh, that's my stink bomb. Isn't it great? Y'see, all I have to do is open this cap and . . ."

"Do you HAVE to do that?!!" he yelled.

"Well, yes," I replied, "I have to do it after breakfast, after lunch, and before dinner." Strange, I've never actually had a director punch me in the arm before.

At any rate, feeling better and smelling better throughout the rest of our shoot, things progressed extremely well. Nick's work was fantastic, and his last-minute script changes were almost always inspired. In fact, one of my favorite lines in the movie, a beautiful little grace note, was actually written by Nick late in the evening on the night before our last day of shooting. It comes at the very end of the film, as Kirk orders the crew to plot a new course for the Enterprise, targeting "the second star to the right and straight on 'til morning."

Could the crew of the Enterprise utter a more perfect good-bye? Somehow, I think this reference, borrowed from Peter Pan and now bestowed upon Captain James Tiberius Kirk and the crew of the Enterprise, really served to drive home the fact that the voyage was almost over. At that point, for the first time in weeks, the smiles left our faces, melancholy set in, and as our final day together wound down, our normally speedy production slowed to a crawl. Nick Meyer recalls:

The making of Star Trek VI was by and large a real pleasure, and everybody, for whatever reason, seemed to be having a really good time. The only day that I remember being really curious was our last day of shooting. Suddenly everybody slowed down, nobody could say their lines, and I thought, What's going on here? What's wrong with these people? But that was immediately followed by a thought of How dense can you be? We're at the last scene of twenty-five years' worth of scenes. These guys just don't want to say good-bye.

However, despite our sudden ineptitude, by midafternoon, we'd completed our filming, downed a glass or two of celebratory champagne, and said our good-byes. However, though the rest of us were now officially unemployed, Leonard and Nick still had work to do, and they ultimately spent the better part of the next four months in postproduction. During that time,

ABOVE: NICK STUFFING MY POCKET WITH HARD-EARNED TWENTIES

BELOW: NICK STINKS UP THE JOINT

an old mistake came back to haunt them. Leonard Nimoy explains:

Konner and Rosenthal dropped by the wayside until the very end of the whole thing. Then they reared their heads, claiming credit for the story and forcing Nick and me into arbitration over the credits, and the first sign that something curious was going on came when the WGA called, asking us to submit whatever materials we might have that gave us claim to the story. They wanted notes, memos, whatever we had written down. Basically, they wanted to see everything that we'd later use as evidence at our arbitration hearing.

And then we started fighting. The first claim these guys made was that since I'd been hired as an executive producer on this film, I was not eligible for a writing credit. And I met with the Guild about that, telling them about my initial meeting with Mancuso where I said, "Okay, here's my idea . . ." and he said, "Great! Do it!" and the Guild sided with me, stating that Mancuso's mandate authorized me to work as a writer on the picture. And that was that. See ya later, sweetheart.

Having won the battle, Leonard returned his attentions to *Star Trek VI*, but within a week, it became obvious that the war wasn't over just yet. The Writers Guild was calling once more, this time formally requesting Leonard's appearance at yet another hearing. No further details were given over the phone, but it was fairly obvious that Konner and Rosenthal weren't going down without a fight. When the hearing took place, Leonard, along with Denny Martin Flynn and Nick Meyer (who was hooked up from London via speakerphone), was confronted with a whole new arbitration committee, led by a man Leonard describes as "a very nasty, hostile guy, some embittered son of a bitch who hates producers and directors who claim they have something to do with the writing on their pictures." Within minutes, it became clear that they were once again questioning Leonard's notes, memos and ultimately the paternity of the script for *Star Trek VI*. At that point, Leonard spoke out.

Wait a minute," I said, "I thought all this was settled," and the nasty guy told me, "Well, sir, we do have the authority to ask you some more questions about this." Now, Nick is on the phone from London, but he's picked up the tone of the meeting and he wisely says, "Excuse me, are we being accused of something? Is this a trial?" Because the tone was like Star Chamber.

At that point the same guy comes out with this bullshit, asking, "What precisely did you have in mind for this story? What did you actually write? How do you call yourself a writer on the project?" I said, "Look, I gave you my notes, they're in front of you, and they lay out my original idea as to what this story would be."

He says, "You had a notion in search of a story. You had an idea in search of a plot." And I replied, "No, Nick Meyer and I plotted this thing out together. He's on the phone, why don't you ask him?" He says, "I don't know, I don't see it." I walked out of there wondering, "What is this?"

Y'know, after the first go-round, the Guild had decided that our credits should read "Story by Leonard Nimoy and Nicholas Meyer, Screenplay by Denny Martin Flynn." That's when these guys had filed this grievance, and this is where their voluminous printed notes, their regurgitation of everything we'd spoken about in those early meetings, came in handy. Every word I'd said to them had been documented, by them, on *their* typewriter. That's serious evidence, and they knew it. They had now turned all of that stuff over to the Guild.

The following morning, I got a call that the

ABOVE: NICK ALWAYS LISTENED CAREFULLY TO OUR SUGGESTIONS—THEN IGNORED THEM
BELOW: OUR EVER VIGILANT DIRECTOR

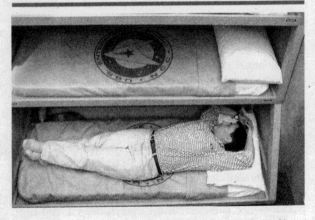

Writers Guild had now officially reversed itself, and the position they were taking now had our credits reading "Story by Konner and Rosenthal, Screenplay by Nicholas Meyer and Denny Martin Flynn." I'm out. I went through the roof. Suddenly all the rage that I had put aside with the studio's political games, with the meetings being conducted around me, with Konner and Rosenthal being hired after I'd specifically requested they be released, with Nick Meyer meeting with one of them in London and handing them the story that I'd come up with; all of that stuff came bubbling to the surface and I was royally pissed.

So I called my lawyer and said, "I will sue Paramount and the WGA on Monday morning if this isn't changed." I wasn't kidding, and it really would've hit the fan. Paramount heard that and got scared, as did the Guild, as did Nick, and over the next forty-eight hours, my poor lawyer went round and round between Nick's lawyer, Konner and Rosenthal's lawyer, and the head of the Writers Guild, working, negotiating, working, negotiating, until by Sunday afternoon he had worked out an agreement that was acceptable to everybody. It read "Story by Nimoy, Konner and Rosenthal, Screenplay by Nick Meyer and Denny Martin Flynn." Nobody involved wanted to face the prospect of a lawsuit, and they knew I was dead serious. I was absolutely furious, and I would've gone to the wall on it, but by Monday morning, it was all cleared up.

By early October, with the editing pretty much final, and music and opticals almost entirely locked into position, Leonard and Nick began screening the film for test audiences as well as VIPs, and it met with unrestrained enthusiasm on both fronts. In fact, as legend has it, Brandon Tartikoff, who just weeks earlier had replaced David Kirkpatrick as president of Paramount's Motion Picture Group and who'd apparently never seen a *Star Trek* film prior to screening *VI*, was heard loudly wondering throughout his private screening, "Why does this have to be the last one?"

Meanwhile, on the other side of the lot, Gene Roddenberry, having suffered two strokes and now confined to a wheelchair, was wheeled into a screening room to view the completed film. When it was over, giving thumbs-up all around, he went back to his office, called his lawyer and angrily demanded that a full quarter-hour of the film's more militaristic moments be edited from the picture. Sadly, however, by the time Gene's lawyer was able to relay Gene's demands, the "Great Bird of the Galaxy" was dead. He had fought for his vision of *Star Trek* literally to the end, passing away less than forty-eight hours after screening the film.

With Gene's death came the obligatory tributes: shallow TV news memorials, public accolades from his peers, mourning among the most hard-core Trekkers, and of course genuine sadness among our cast and crew. Gene, love him or not, was undeniably the creative spark behind *Star Trek*, and without him none of us would have been able to spend our lives in pursuit of such a joyful distraction. With that in mind, it was decided to dedicate *Star Trek VI* to his memory. However, even that didn't come off without a fight. Leonard Nimoy explains:

Very late in the game, I found out that Nick Meyer and Brandon Tartikoff, who'd just arrived at the studio, were meeting to decide how the dedication should read. I thought to myself, *Where do these people get off?* I think, maybe, Nick might have waved at Gene Roddenberry one day. I don't think the two ever had a real sit-down face-to-face meeting. And Brandon Tartikoff? He had nothing at all to do with the making of this picture. By the time he'd arrived at the studio, we already had our final cut in the can. So these were the people, of all people, who were deciding what the dedication to Gene Roddenberry should say. Again, nobody told me anything.

So when I found out about that, I called up John Goldwyn, who'd become our new studio executive on the picture, replacing Teddy Zee, and I vented on him. I said, "I think it's absolutely disgusting that these two kids are running around in a playpen they don't even own. It's not even their territory. Why aren't you people talking about this to somebody who's connected to the picture? Someone who's had a relationship with Gene? Why not have this thing put together by somebody who knows exactly who Gene was, and what he was? How dare you arbitrarily slap something onto the

ONE FINAL WRAP AND NICHELLE AND ME

top of the film as if it were some box office deci-sion? How dare you guys?" At that point, he sort of sighed into the phone and halfheartedly asked, "Well, how would you like it to read, Leonard?" After expressing myself on how badly I thought the situation had been handled, I hung up on him.

He rang me back for days, but I wouldn't take his calls. What fun to get angry. I handled it badly, but I'm too old and too rich. I'm at the point in my life where I can afford myself the lux-ury of saying, "I don't give a shit. If it kills my rela-tionship with you and the studio, so be it." That's the way it went down.

And ultimately, the argument over that dedica-tion was really over whether to keep it simple or make it more complex. Tartikoff wanted some-thing elaborate and flowery, but Nick thought that might be a little distasteful, a little flittery. Nick came up with the verbiage for the final dedication.

In the end, the film was released to enthusiastic criti-cal acclaim, and strong box office receipts of over sixty million dollars. However, despite the film's success, the standard rumors in regard to yet another sequel were nonexistent, replaced by rumors that a Next Generation movie would soon become a reality. Months passed, in fact more than a year, before those rumors would be proven true. At that point, however, with a younger, cheaper, and entirely new cast ready to run away with the franchise, I became convinced that this time I'd for-mally said good-bye to James T. Kirk once and for all.

As it turns out, my assumption was just a bit pre-mature.

STAR TREK VII:
REGENERATIONS

Star Trek VI: The Undiscovered Country rang in the holiday season of 1991 with a bit of a Christmas miracle. While providing good cheer to Trekkers everywhere, this movie was simultaneously wringing smiles out of even the most steadfastly Scroogian critics. The film was very solidly received, and a steady stream of enthusiastically positive reviews made it quite clear that despite our advancing ages and belt sizes, the crew of the Enterprise had managed to squeeze one last winner out of the franchise. Almost unanimously, our notices cited the film as fun, exciting and extremely well written, while one of my favorites even went so far as to glowingly refer to me and Christopher Plummer as "two old hamosauruses chewing up the scenery with obvious talent and delight." However, despite all the critical merrymaking, a postholiday letdown was already looming.

Perhaps due to the fact that people were distracted by the chaos of the holiday season, perhaps because multiplexes all over the country were once again snowed under by their annual Yuletide blockbuster glut, or perhaps simply because by the time we'd reached our sixth installment, the whole idea of a *Star Trek* movie just didn't seem all that special anymore, this critical sensation performed a bit underwhelmingly at the box office, at least by our standards.

All told, the film ultimately took in just about $60 million; and while that's an absolutely mind-boggling amount of money, almost twenty percent beefier than the returns on *The Final Frontier*, the spoils of both those victories were undeniably slim when compared to those of *Treks II, III* and *IV*, which blitzkrieged box offices in combining to rack up an absolutely staggering $265 million. With that, although *Star Trek* remained a reliably profitable moviemaking franchise, the perception began to circulate around Paramount's corner offices that clearly the glory days of Kirk, Spock and company were behind them. That notion, combined with the inescapable realities of an ever-more-expensive and ever-more-wrinkled crew, soon served to remove most of the remaining sheen from the formerly high-gloss hull of the Enterprise. Within a year, the studio confirmed everyone's suspicions by officially switching to Plan B.

By December 1992, Rick Berman, the producer of *Star Trek: The Next Generation*, was already wading through negotiations initiated by Paramount, and aimed at redirecting the *Star Trek* feature film franchise toward a *Next Generation* movie. As Rick Berman explains, this was by no means a spur-of-the-moment idea:

Brandon Tartikoff was really the man who brought this all about, and by the end of our fourth season, he had already initiated a plan to take *Star Trek: The Next Generation* off the air just after our seventh. A lot of the fans have been assuming that the studio decided only at the last minute to cancel this show, but in fact, it had been in the works for nearly three years. They decided to create and develop a whole new show that would run concurrently with *Next Generation* for a season and a half, at which point they'd take *Next Gen* off the air and the new show would inherit the throne. Obviously that new show was *Deep Space Nine*.

And I think they had three reasons for taking *The Next Generation* off the air. Reason number one was that the series was about to get a lot more expensive to produce, as television shows always do when they get into their sixth, seventh and eighth seasons. Y'know, the directors, the producers, the actors, all of these people start asking for a lot more money.

Two, they wanted to make a movie, and their feeling was, "You can't begin a movie franchise when people can still see these same actors in first-run television episodes for free." There'd be no incentive there for anyone to plunk down their $7.50.

And three, the financial and sales people in Paramount's domestic television area, who had very successfully sort of reinvented television syndication seven years ago when *The Next Generation* was born, were saying things like, "Give us a new show and we'll do even better. We'll make all those deals we made with all those stations for *Next Generation* seem archaic." Basically, they wanted to start anew in terms of their marketing and sales.

That's what started the ball rolling, but ironically, Brandon Tartikoff was gone less than six months later.

Tartikoff was replaced by Sherry Lansing. Despite the shakeup at the top, the studio pressed forward on a *Next Generation* movie. Now it was decided that this film would, in fact, be cross-pollinated by members of both the classic and *Next Generation* casts. The resulting hybrid, felt the studio, would most definitely attain must-see status among Trekkers everywhere, while serving to establish *The Next Generation* as a viable cinematic franchise all its own. At about the same time, just prior to the start of *The Next Generation*'s 1993–94 TV production, the studio made it official, publicly announcing that the series' seventh season would also be its last. That development was almost immediately bemoaned by most Trekkers as highly illogical.

With *The Next Generation* most often placing first among all syndicated dramatic television programs in the Nielsens, and carrying a built-in, extremely loyal audience of fifteen to twenty million viewers per week, it seemed that Paramount had opted to cook their golden goose. However, upon closer inspection, it becomes clear that Rick Berman's "three reasons" behind the demise of *The Next Generation* were flanked and augmented by at least a half-dozen more.

First and most definitely foremost, as calculator buttons tapped madly in studio cubicles, it was discovered that a successful string of *Next Generation* features, produced with limited overhead and comparatively minuscule shooting schedules, would ultimately prove far more profitable than the TV series ever could. At the same time, having already filmed seven full seasons of hourlong *Next Generation* tales, it was a no-brainer that with or without any additional episodes, the original series' reruns would also continue greasing studio palms for decades to come.

Additionally, by making their well-planned, well-timed and very loud public announcement, very early on, that *Star Trek: The Next Generation* would be leaving the airwaves after the upcoming season and graduating to the silver screen, the studio actually treated themselves to the luxury of almost two years' worth of ravenous and carefully nurtured Trekker hype and speculation. In fact, if you watched closely throughout the media feeding frenzy that surrounded the series' final installment, you undoubtedly noticed that *The Next Generation* cast, creatives and studio personnel made mention of the upcoming movie at even the slightest provocation. "We aren't *really* saying good-bye," they'd almost unanimously tout. "We're just making a movie, which, by the way, is coming this Thanksgiving to a theater near you." Quite wisely, the studio milked the final episode's media spotlight for all it was worth.

Meanwhile, several other factors were further motivating the studio to boot the crew of the *Enterprise* D upstairs. For example, while *The Next Generation*'s first spinoff, *Deep Space Nine*, was rapidly coming into its own both creatively and in the ratings, another, entitled *Star Trek: Voyager*, was hurriedly being readied for air as well. With that, despite *The Next Generation*'s move to the big screen, *Star Trek*'s television universe was undeniably expanding, and the Trekkers who might previously have deluged the studio under a mountain of hate mail, now had a lot to cheer.

Finally, by the time any series reaches the advanced age of seven years, even one with an entire universe to explore, it begins burning out rather quickly. Good, solid, original story ideas begin getting harder and harder to come by, and at the same time, after years of spending fifteen-hour days cooped up on the same soundstages, in the same costumes, playing the same characters, most actors can't help but grow fidgety. The cast of The Next Generation proved no exception, most notably Patrick Stewart, who said, while filming the series' final installment, "For me the timing is perfect. I had been increasingly feeling that I'd already given my best work on the series. The last two years have found me feeling an intense restlessness. I needed to go on to something else. This is the toughest job I've ever done, except maybe when I worked on a building site, unloading cement blocks—that was marginally tougher."

At any rate, all of those things combined to bounce the Enterprise D off the boob tube and onto the big screen, a development that would, very shortly, sentence Captain James T. Kirk to death. Screenwriter Ron Moore, who'd previously written far more than his share of the very best Next Generation TV episodes, explains the early stages of this film's creation:

Rick Berman approached Brannon Braga and me in February 1993, sounding very serious, and saying that we should meet in his office. He was very mysterious about it all, and because we weren't working on anything at the time, and because we'd never really met with Rick unless we had a script for the TV show in progress, we were sure we were gonna be fired. Either that, or the show had been canceled. Either way, we were out of work.

And Rick likes to make people squirm a bit when he can, so there we were, sitting on his couch, while he had this very serious look on his face, and he was sort of pacing up and down, and finally he said, "Well, boys, I've just completed two months of very difficult negotiations with the studio, and I have something to tell you." And I thought, "Oh my God. It's true. It's over. We ARE canceled. I'm out of work."

But then he smiled and said, "I've been asked to produce a *Next Generation* movie and I want you guys to write it." And at that point, we just sat there and stared at him for a long time. It felt weird at first, but by early spring, Rick, Brannon and I were spending a lot of time together, just sort of sitting together in a room, batting ideas around and playing with all kinds of possible stories. It was actually a lot of fun, in that we had a great deal of freedom and didn't really have any formal guidelines or demands from the studio. Their attitude was very supportive. They basically just told us, "You guys know this franchise. You've worked on it a long time. We trust you. Go and make a good movie. Make us a film that's gonna start a whole series of *Next Generation* movies."

From there, we just started throwing ideas around, and right from the beginning, Rick had said that he wanted to develop a script that would have the original cast in it. So we started talking about that, and we said, "Let's have the *whole* original cast in this thing. Let's just put *everybody* in the picture and make it a party." At the same time, we said, "Well, they really can't be in the whole picture, because it's gotta be clear that this is really a *Next Generation* picture, not a 'classic' *Star Trek* film."

And at that point, we decided to start with the original cast, in the twenty-third century, and have a mystery that sorta spans both franchises. But then we moved away from that and started looking for ways to have the two crews meet. I was really in favor, early on, of having the two crews in opposition to one another. Brannon agreed, saying that the best possible poster you could ever hope to have for this picture would show you the two *Enterprises* battling against each other. We all tried our best, but we were never able to come up with any scenario that made both crews look heroic. No matter how we played around with this thing, *somebody* was gonna come off looking like the bad guy.

So then we returned, a little more solidly, to the "mystery that spans two generations" idea, and came up with the idea that would allow Whoopi Goldberg, as Guinan, to act as the tie that binds the two. At about the same time, we began looking for an event: something *really* dramatic, something *really* big, something *really* special that people would talk about, and in the middle of all this, one of us just kinda threw out, "What if we kill Kirk?" And we all kinda looked at each other and said, "Wow. That would be *amazing*. I can't imagine we'll ever be able to actually pull it off, but at the very least, it's an interesting possibility." From that point on, Kirk's death became part of the fabric of our story, and as a big surprise to us all, there was never a moment where it really came into question.

We fully expected that the studio would say, "No, you can't possibly kill the captain," because Kirk really is one of their golden characters, but they didn't have that reaction. Instead, they just asked us, "Are you sure you want to do this?" And when we said, "Yes, we are," they said, "Okay, we're behind you," and we went back to the office and waited for *you* to say "No."

Obviously, I never did that, and in fact, when Rick first called me and told me about wanting to knock off the captain, it really didn't bother me at all. Not one bit. In fact, I got really excited, thinking, "Well if this really is going to be Kirk's last hurrah, what better way to close the book? It's dramatic. It'll be great fun to play, and if it's well written and important to the story, it'll be good for the film as well."

I did waffle just once, for a second or two. But then I spoke with Rick once more, happily agreeing to die should I find myself suitably impressed with the script-in-progress. With that, tucked away just off Melrose Avenue, Ron and Brannon started typing. Ron explains how the script began coming together:

We were amazed at how easily you took to the idea of Kirk's death. Y'know, even as we went into rewrites, we were still waiting for you to drop that other shoe, to call us up and say, "Okay, guys, here's what's bothering me. I don't want Kirk to die." But you never did that, and we had made it *very* clear from the *very* beginning that Kirk was *indeed* going to die. None of this Spock stuff; no gimmicks, no tricks. I said, "Let's not be coy with this. Let's not leave some spirit floating around somewhere, or anything like that. Let's just kill him, bury him, and let that be that. If we're gonna do this, let's really DO it," and we stuck to that throughout.

I really felt that Kirk's death would finally bring

closure to the original *Trek*, and as a writer on *The Next Generation* TV series, I always felt that we *should* close that door, because it was starting to become a cheat to just keep ignoring the question of "Whatever happened to Kirk?" I'd heard Gene say a couple of times that he thought Kirk would most likely be dead by the twenty-fourth century, so we felt that our idea was sort of in that spirit. And it seemed the right thing to do. It's one of the creative decisions I feel really good about in *Generations*. I think it'll be a very poignant moment, and something people will remember for a long time.

As their bare-bones storyline began to take shape, Rick, Brannon and Ron had concocted a tale in which the entire crew of the original *Enterprise*, much to their chagrin, has been reassembled once more to act as the honored guests at a ceremony christening Starfleet's newest starship, the *Enterprise* B. However, amid the pomp, circumstance and condescension of the *Enterprise* B's new, younger crew, there is little joy among our graying heroes. Later, when a mysterious energy field moves in, seriously threatening the very survival of the new ship, the inexperience of the *Enterprise* B's virgin crew rapidly manifests itself all over the bridge, allowing the danger to escalate, and ultimately forcing the entire original crew back into their original positions once more. Moments later, as Kirk rushes about the bowels of the ship in an ultimately successful last-ditch attempt to save her, he is engulfed by a direct hit from the Nexxus and presumed dead. From there, the film flashes forward into the realm of *The Next Generation*. Picard finds Kirk alive, and seemingly better than ever, within that same mysterious energy field. It's a place that provides a highly pleasurable, extremely addictive "reality," wherein time stands still and the inhabitants find themselves invincible, wandering at will throughout all of the most enjoyable moments of their own pasts.

With that basic storyline in place, Ron and Brannon drafted their first script. All three sides of this creative triangle found themselves generally pleased with their progress but disappointed with the film's opening classic cast scenes. It was rapidly becoming clear all around that with seven classic cast member mouths all vying for dialogue, and only about twelve minutes of actual screen time allotted for the cause, this legendary and beloved crew might ultimately come off on-screen as a laughable mob. Ron continues:

Originally, the opening was much more prolonged than it is in the final draft. There was all sorts of stuff about getting this new ship out of space dock, and when it came out of space dock we were gonna have the *Enterprise* do a barrel roll, which I'd always wanted to see. And initially, the original crew's role in this ceremony was to pilot this ship out of space dock on their own while the new crew stood by and watched. Y'know, the old guys were gonna be given one last spin around the block before the new crew took over. Kirk would've been in the captain's chair, Sulu at the helm, the whole bit, just for old times' sake.

Then the Nexxus emergency happens and the new crew has to kick the old guys out of their chairs, and that really rankles them, but one by one, as this emergency escalated, they would've slowly retaken their old roles until the entire classic crew was running the ship once more. And just because it took us so long to get there, we had to start slashing and burning, getting the new guys into the seats right from the get-go.

But no matter what, the original cast members were only gonna be in this thing for *maybe* the first fifteen or twenty pages and at the same time we were gonna be introducing the crew of the new *Enterprise* B and if we hadn't pared that down, those scenes would've been truly awful. We actually got to the point where we were counting lines, saying things like, "Uh-oh, Uhura hasn't said anything in three pages." It was really that bad. Finally, when we realized that there was no way we could make this crowd scene work, we had to bite the bullet, pare down the crowd, rewrite and just go with you, Leonard, and De. Then of course once we had that all first drafted, Leonard and De turned the project down.

Actually, I should take a step backward and explain that not only was Leonard asked to act in this film, he was asked to direct it as well. Berman sent Leonard a copy of Ron and Brannon's most recently revised draft, which he read, several times over, marking up his margins with a long series of creative notes and alternate dramatic suggestions. Leonard then forwarded his ideas to Berman, who sat down with them, studied them and ultimately decided to stay the course, keeping his original script intact and shooting down Leonard's proposed changes, opting instead to place the film, as originally conceived, into the hands of veteran *Next Generation* director David Carson.

I must also explain that Leonard, surprisingly, really wasn't all that upset with this unusual turn of events. As you know, on *Treks III*, *IV* and *VI*, Leonard had been very involved very early on, nursing his projects through the story level and the scripting process, while simultaneously functioning as director and ultimately producer. However, this time around, that simply wouldn't have been his job. This story came from Rick Berman. It was written by his own handpicked writers, and essentially, Leonard was being asked to just shoot their script as written, and he wasn't all that interested. He would much rather have been involved in the overall creation of the film, and ideally, he would have come into this thing six months earlier, when Rick, Ron and Brannon were first hammering out their most rudimentary story points.

At the same time, the role of Spock, as scripted, wasn't very big or very important, and once it became clear that Leonard would not be directing this film, the idea of simply walking through a glorified cameo wasn't all that appealing. He turned down the part shortly thereafter. At that point De Kelley, whose role was similarly skimpy, also declined to appear.

I, having already tentatively agreed to one last tour of duty, made quick phone calls to both men, hoping I might be able to change their minds, but of course changing the mind of either Leonard or De is a Herculean undertaking at best, and despite my best intentions, they ultimately chose to stay out. Both of them felt like they'd already said their good-byes in *The Undiscovered Country*, and told me they'd rather be remembered for their work in our half-dozen outings than to resurrect their characters for the sole purpose of briefly putting their faces into one more film. I couldn't argue. Spock and Bones were exchanged for Chekov and Scotty shortly thereafter. However, we were by no means finished working on Kirk.

During this period of time, I had finally received a script, and when I read it, I immediately came to two conclusions. First, I realized that I had not seen nearly enough of *The Next Generation* to even hazard an opinion as to whether or not those roles were written appropriately. And second, my friend James Tiberius didn't quite seem himself. He had no overall theme, no thrust, nothing that made this part uniquely and absolutely Kirk's. With that in mind, I began meeting with Rick and the writers, suggesting a few changes and rewrites.

Over the course of three separate meetings, we got together and banged around a lot of ideas about what we might do with Kirk in this film. Starting small, we all agreed upon things like rather than having Kirk *talk* about his recent forays into skydiving, we should actually *show* him wafting like a maniac down toward Earth from the wild blue yonder. We also reworked a couple of horseback scenes that Ron and Brannon had obviously added into the script in a shameless (but nonetheless successful) attempt to butter me up, reorganizing the action to make better use of our equine co-stars. Finally, as we all began feeling more comfortable with one another, we began hitting upon some bigger concerns. First and foremost was my fear that Kirk was basically in this film to die, and not much else. Ron Moore continues:

It was an interesting meeting, and it marked the first time that I had met you. It was very weird, because I was a fan of the original series growing up, and you came in playing your cards close to the vest, listening, observing, sort of checking us out more than anything else, and there was one moment where you actually used the Kirk voice.

Brannon was explaining to you why he thought Kirk was integral to our story because of this, that and the other thing, and while he was explaining all of these reasons, you were just sort of watching him, and you suddenly burst out, sounding *exactly* like Kirk, "Well . . . in fact . . . he's NOT . . . in-te-GRAL . . . to . . . the story!" and Brannon's head snapped back, I flinched, and Rick looked startled, but I thought that was really cool.

So we kept doing rewrites, and we'd send 'em back and forth, and you'd say, "I don't like this" or "I don't like that," whatever, but by and large we got the sense as we progressed that you were getting happier, and that you really would do this movie if we could just satisfy some of your problems with the script. We then had another meeting with you, and you said, "I still don't think Kirk's integral to the script. You could do this movie without me." You didn't like the way Picard had to talk Kirk into coming back to help him save the day, because you felt that he looked like a druggie who couldn't figure this thing out on his own. But we added a scene where Kirk jumps his horse over a ravine and realizes for himself that the life in the Nexxus isn't worth living, and little by little we finally came up with a draft you really liked. Once we got you, we knew the movie was really gonna work.

One of the most helpful things that rose out of those meetings was a conversation that began with Rick asking me, "What do *you* think about Kirk? Where is this character in his life? What do you think is going on inside his head?" At that point, the four of us spent the better part of the afternoon psychoanalyzing Kirk, and trying to understand what might be driving him to stay within the Nexxus. Quite obviously, the timelessness of the place would have allowed the captain, who'd now spent the better part of the last three decades cheating death at every turn, to win the battle once and for all, but somehow it seemed that there ought to be something more, something that would've allowed him to blind himself to the worthlessness of an artificial existence within the Nexxus. That's how Antonia was born.

Somewhere in the middle of that meeting, I asked Ron, Rick and Brannon, "What if there's one woman that Kirk really wishes he had married, the love of his life? Maybe the captain's chair somehow caused him to lose her way back when, and maybe she's with him now in the Nexxus." Eyebrows went up all around the room, and as the conversation continued, it began to come out that maybe this sort of domestic life is something that Kirk has always wanted, always missed, and here, within the Nexxus, he'd finally managed to attain it. That's what kept him there.

Over the ensuing weeks, we just kept volleying drafts back and forth across Los Angeles, until finally I had nothing left to find fault with. Within days of closing that draft, I officially signed a contract to whack the good captain. Surprisingly, I still felt very little remorse about the captain's terminal status. In fact, I was a lot more worried about working with Walter Koenig and Jimmy Doohan, two men who have made it clear on any number of occasions that my name is generally near the top of their shit lists.

Toward the beginning of March 1994, I got a call asking me to come on down to the Paramount lot for a first readthrough/rehearsal of my scenes with Walter and Jimmy. When I got there, I found myself hoping for the best while fearing the worst in regard to the unavoidably awkward reintroduction that was about to unfold.

"Well, here's Bill," said Jimmy in a very neutral voice.

"Hi, Jimmy! Hi, Walter! Hi, Rick! Hi, Brannon! Hi, Ron!" I said, smiling as broadly as humanly possible. I then sat down and exchanged pleasantries with everybody for a couple of moments, at which point Jimmy proceeded to hand out "Scotty cards," which had a magnet on the back. "Here," he said to everybody in the cast, "these are some Scotty cards that you can stick up on your refrigerator door." He handed me one, and I was somewhat nonplussed in that I didn't feel I needed a card as an introduction. I mean, I *had* met the man several times before.

Still, we got through our rehearsals just fine, and as the third week of March approached, we prepared to begin shooting all of the film's opening scenes aboard the *Enterprise* B. Everything was ready, except me.

I was driving with my daughter on the Sunday evening before our Monday morning shooting, and she looked over at me and asked, "Dad, where're your Kirk sideburns?" and immediately my gut turned over, as if I'd forgotten to do my homework. I clasped my hands to the sides of my head and I realized that in all the weeks that I'd been preparing to do this film, the script consulting, the wardrobe fittings, nobody had mentioned my sideburns. Everyone just assumed that I *must* know the routine by now, and that I would have the intelligence to grow them myself, which is overestimating any actor, I feel. It's a lesson I want everybody to learn about actors. Never trust us, not for a minute.

The following morning, with my head hanging low in embarrassment, I walked into the makeup room and said to Brian McManus, our makeup man, "What am I going to do? I forgot to grow my sideburns"—at which point he sighed, rolled his eyes and said, "Sit down." He then took out a mustache, cut it in half, pasted the pieces on either side of my head, and proceeded to create instant pointy sideburns. They were a little thick, a little bushy, a little different color at first (don't be surprised if Kirk looks vaguely reminiscent of Edgar Allan Poe throughout this film's opening scenes), but they passed. Luckily, because there were going to be almost eight weeks between the end of my scenes aboard the *Enterprise* B and the beginning of my scenes with Patrick Stewart, I was able to grow my own organic sideburns.

On our first day of shooting, as I was wandering around the interiors of another captain's prefab starship, my first real twinge of melancholy set in. I found myself really missing Leonard, De, Nichelle and George, and for the first time, I found myself feeling as if I were now a guest star in somebody else's show. The bridge was no longer mine, and it seemed almost as if

ALL FOR ONE, AND ONE FOR ALL

someone had broken into my house, redecorated and moved in while I was away. Halfway through my funk, Walter arrived on the set, put a hand on my shoulder and said, "I feel so-o-o strange."

"Me too," I said, thinking I'd found a kindred spirit.

"I really thought I'd put all this *Star Trek* stuff behind me," he continued.

"Oh," I replied, a bit dumbfounded, "I was thinking about how sad I'm beginning to feel about seeing it all end." With that we both retired to the breakfast table, drowning our bipolar sorrows with donuts.

As the days progressed, though the filming went very well and all around me people were trying their best to make me feel at home, I never quite got comfortable, never quite stopped expecting to come into work one morning and find De and Leonard in the adjacent makeup chairs.

Seeking solace, I approached Walter, and over the course of our shooting, we chatted, joked and reminisced through most of our unavoidable shooting delays, and he actually became a bit of a buddy. I then approached Jimmy, cajoling him into telling me his old war stories one more time (as he'll tell you at the drop of a hat, he was a pilot, wounded on D-Day). As always, that request brought a smile to his face, and he was *thrilled* to have found someone interested, someone who'd only heard his stories perhaps two or three times before. And as I listened, his stories really *were* interesting (of course, he's worked on them long enough to make sure of that), and for the first time in a long time, I got the feeling that both of us were trying our best to rebuild some of the bridges we'd previously barbecued. In fact, as shooting progressed, I even managed to talk both Walter *and* Jimmy into posing for a picture of the three of us holding hands, a mind-boggling occurrence in the annals of Trekkerdom. As we sat there smiling, Walter said to me, "Any picture of the three of us holding hands has got to be worth at least five hundred dollars at a convention, signed, fifteen hundred." We all laughed at that, and I spent the better part of our shooting feeling rather pleased that our relationships were making some progress. I was much less pleased with falling off the Enterprise B's "Uhura perch."

You remember how Uhura always sat several feet above the bridge. That's just about where Jimmy, Walter and I were sitting as we began shooting a scene in which the Enterprise B gets hit by the pulsating energy ribbon of the Nexxus, rocking the ship, quite literally, as never before. And throughout our series and six previous films, Paramount has remade, refurbished, upgraded or at the very least redressed the Enterprise bridge with each new go-round. However, despite all that interior decorating, one thing remained a constant. Whenever the Enterprise was about to be hit by a photon torpedo, a meteorite, an energy beam, whatever, one of our AD's would simply stand off in a corner yelling "3 . . . 2 . . . 1— BOOM!!!" At which point we'd all jump out of our chairs while we yelled some variation of "AAAAAAARGH!!!" and proceeded to fall all over the set. Why Scotty never installed seat belts remains a mystery to this day. At any rate, we exploded that way for twenty-five years, but today things were decidedly different.

Here, reclining comfortably aboard the bridge of the *Enterprise* B, we were actually sitting just above a series of very large, very powerful electric motors, each of them possessing a huge acentric flywheel that, when activated, served to shake the entire set with a rather horrifying realism. At the same time, as we prepared to shoot this particular scene, just about two months had passed since one of the worst earthquakes in California history had devastated the entire area. You can understand why the cast and crew of this film decided to keep the rocking and rolling to a minimum by avoiding any full-scale rehearsals of this scene. Instead, we'd just go through our lines, and only when we felt ready to roll cameras would the set begin shaking. If we got really lucky, we might only have to rattle everyone's brains one time. However, that didn't happen, thanks to me.

When we got ready to roll and the AD yelled "Action!" the switch was flipped, the motors rolled, the set shook, I lurched forward, grabbing hold of the banister in front of me, that banister came off in my hand, and I went flying through the air, falling forward about five feet while heading toward the ground face-first. Luckily, as the years of doing my own stunts came into play, I tucked, I rolled, and lo and behold, I was fine.

Everybody came running over to me, asking, "Are you okay? Are you okay?" And then, amid my embarrassment and bruises, the prettiest girl on the set walks over to

ABOVE: A split-second before disaster
BELOW: Kirk drops in on Scotty and Chekov

me, taking my hand and saying, "I hope you're all right." And thrilled with this youthful attention, I glowingly said, "Why, yes, I *am*, my dear," to which she replied "Oh, good, because for a man of your age, a fall like that could've broken your hip." Y'know, she really wasn't all *that* pretty.

Still, I survived, and over the next week and a half we

TRYING MY BEST TO SMILE AMID THE SUN, HEAT AND RUBBER

completed all of Kirk, Scotty and Chekov's scenes aboard the *Enterprise* B. At that point, we were all free to wearily make our way home, where we could relax and recover for the next two months. We would reassemble in late May, at which point Kirk was going to skydive, horseback ride, climb a mountain, have a huge fistfight and die, in that order. With that in mind, I decided to rest up as much as possible.

While I was on hiatus, the *Next Generation* crew went about shooting the bulk of this film, wherein Worf becomes a lieutenant commander, Data struggles with an emotion chip, and Picard gets dragged into battle against the evil Dr. Tolian Soran, a villain willing to wipe out a highly populated planet just to get back inside the addictively pleasurable Nexxus once more. While in pursuit of Soran, Picard would ultimately meet up with "long-dead" space hero Captain James T. Kirk. At that point, I would be reporting back to the set.

By the third week in May, I was back in uniform, only this time it was covered by a strange black rubber suit that passed as the latest in twenty-third-century skydiving wear. We were now shooting the very first scene in the movie, wherein Kirk parachutes to the Earth (encircling the globe three times in the process) and is greeted by Chekov and Scotty, who shepherd the less than excited Kirk to the christening ceremonies aboard the *Enterprise* B.

As I arrived on the set, they were just about to shoot my stunt double performing the actual dive (neither I nor the studio were crazy enough to allow Captain Kirk to achieve *that* level of realism), and as things progressed, I watched, thrilled with the fact that my feet were firmly planted upon Mother Earth. The stuntman, however, wasn't that lucky. Very early on, our art department had decided that by the twenty-third century, parachutes would be smaller, flashier and far more maneuverable than they are today. They outfitted my double with a very unusual, very small parachute, and dressed the poor guy in an identical black wetsuit kinda thing, slapping a black crash helmet onto his head not so much for safety's sake but to ensure that no one could ever notice that William Shatner was indeed *not* the brave soul plummeting toward the Earth from above. Twenty minutes later, this guy jumped.

Looking up into the sky, I watched as this black shiny pinpoint of a dot began hurling toward the planet. Cries of "Wow!" "Look at that!" and "There he is!" sprang up all around me, replaced shortly thereafter by slightly louder cries of "Uh . . . shouldn't his chute be open by now?!" and "Oh my GOD!!!" Plummeting toward us now, this stuntman, whose "Captain Kirk" helmet had limited his field of vision rather severely, was fighting with a parachute that just didn't want to open. At 3,000 feet, he was still freefalling, 2,500 feet, 2,250, and by 2,000 feet with the ground becoming dangerously close, his chute finally deployed. Still, having fallen this far without a chute, he knew a normal landing was going to be impossible. He was going to hit hard, falling at approximately thirty-five miles per hour.

At the same time, with his helmet still in place, this guy couldn't see the ground, so as he approached the ground, he started running in midair, cartoon style, in an attempt to mollify the effects of his fall. It didn't help, and he basically just crashed to the ground with a sickening thud. However, within minutes it was clear that he had defied logic, surviving this thing pretty much unscathed. Now it was my turn in the chute.

I suited up, got zippered into place, and realized for the first time that this rig weighed about twenty pounds, and would almost immediately cause the poor sap inside to begin sweating profusely. The wardrobe sadists then pounded that damn helmet onto my head while covering my hands with black rubber gloves. As a final indignity, the same parachute that had just about murdered our stuntman was then attached, fully deployed, onto my back. Once all of that was in place, I spent the remainder of this late spring day in Southern California, my last with Walter and Jimmy, shooting this scene in which I had to run uphill, fully clad in my rubber regalia, and then wheeze through two pages of dialogue with Scotty and Chekov. By the way, did I mention that the mercury rose to 103 degrees that day? Needless to say, I spent the better part of that afternoon distracted from the death of Kirk, obsessing instead upon the possible death of Shatner.

Still, when it was all over, I had survived, barely. I said my good-byes to Walter and Jimmy and went home, where I collapsed into an exhausted heap for the better part of the evening while preparing myself for the first of my scenes with Patrick Stewart.

Y'know, somebody once summed up the contrasts between these two characters by telling me that when push came to shove, with an enemy brandishing weapons and threatening the very existence of the *Enterprise*, Kirk would say, "I'm going to count to three and then fire. One . . . two . . . fire!" And Picard would say, "I'm going to count to three and then fire: One . . . two . . . three . . . I'm not kidding. Four . . . five . . . six . . . I'm serious about this. Seven . . . eight . . . nine . . . perhaps we should discuss this situation further." With that in mind, I decided to play off the differences between this intergalactic odd couple, highlighting Picard's quiet, dignified strength and reserve by allowing Kirk's humor, his energy and the rest of the bigger, broader aspects of the character to rise to the surface a little more easily than ever before. I had actually discussed that idea with Patrick several weeks earlier, as we got to know one another while roaring through the starry skies over Southern California. I'm not kidding.

JUST AN ORDINARY PAIR OF INTERGALACTIC COWBOYS

At the request of Paramount, the two of us had traveled together to Las Vegas for a convention of movie theater owners called ShoWest. This thing is basically a yearly hype-and-schmoozefest where the studios hawk their upcoming releases, while the stars of those releases press the flesh spreading goodwill and positive public relations, and simultaneously talk up their new film to anyone who'll listen. If all goes well, the studio can expect theater orders for their upcoming wares to increase dramatically. Patrick and I soon found ourselves in Vegas, holding hands at center stage while telling the assembled theater owners all about how great our new film was going to be. Fifteen minutes later, amid a huge ovation and pats on the back all around, we were through.

Backstage now, it was just past 11:00 P.M., and because both of us had early morning appointments, neither Patrick nor I was particularly looking forward to spending the night in Las Vegas. We quickly formulated a plan by which we might take advantage of our combined clout to commandeer Paramount's company jet. Cornering and double-teaming the studio's current chairperson, Sherry Lansing, Patrick and I smiled, tried our best to be incredibly charming, and asked, "Do you think we can use the company plane to get back to L.A. right away?"

Much to our surprise, she smiled right back at us and said, "Sure, it's going back to L.A. at two A.M. and you guys will be the only passengers on board. Enjoy." Mom had officially given us the car keys. So there, in the middle of Las Vegas, in the middle of the night, *Enterprise* captains past and future hopped aboard the large private jet, and over the course of the next hour and fifteen minutes, as we sped back toward the City of Angels, "Kirk" and "Picard" finally got acquainted. To my surprise, I found that we actually had a lot in common, and by the time we'd touched down, I really liked him. We've since become good friends.

By mid-May, as the two of us began ten days of working together on location, I found myself sitting across an aluminum caterer's table from Patrick while both of us picked over our lunches, pondering what the end of this picture would bring. Patrick was glowing, enthusiastically explaining to me that because The Next Generation series no longer existed, he could now return home and spend an extended period of time in London, really for the first time in almost eight years. Additionally, free of the grueling work weeks he'd become accustomed to during the run of the show, Patrick was going to refocus his creative energies toward mounting a revival of Who's Afraid of Virginia Woolf?, a play he had been forced to back away from when a certain Mr. Roddenberry requested his presence in L.A. almost eight years earlier.

Finally, although the rest of the Next Generation cast had now officially wrapped, mothballed their uniforms and hugged their way through an extended series of tearful good-byes just days earlier, Patrick really wasn't all that distraught about their parting. Instead, he felt quite secure in the probability that they'd more than likely spend the next decade or two sporadically reassembling to take yet another spin around the universe amid the spacious deep-pile interiors of the U.S.S. Enterprise D.

Meanwhile, across the lunch table, I wasn't nearly so jolly. The filming of Kirk's death scene was now less than two weeks away, and at the eleventh hour, the finality of that situation was just beginning to hit me . . . hard. I talked about that to Patrick, relating a story I'd heard about a tribe in Africa who live in the desert, with

MCDOWELL AND
I SPENT AN
ENJOYABLE
AFTERNOON
CHEERFULLY
BEATING THE
CRAP OUT OF
EACH OTHER

barely enough food to survive. Their culture prescribes that the elder people, the ones who can no longer pull their own weight or provide their own livelihood, go out in the desert and die. "That's how *I* feel," I told Patrick as his eyes widened. "It's like this elderly captain's been asked to dodder off into the desert, lay down, gasp his last few breaths and die." We both laughed at my melodrama, brushing it aside quickly in favor of less leaden conversation topics, but over the course of those final days of shooting, I couldn't help feeling as if it contained a real kernel of truth.

As the days went by, without any of my former castmates or crew guys to pal around with, I really began feeling like an outsider, like a guest star, like the new kid in school, and at that point I met the school bully. His name is Malcolm McDowell. Hired to play Soran, our villain, Malcolm would be phasering me into oblivion sometime in the fairly near future. At the same time, I'd also been hearing rumors that he'd recently been heard quite gleefully bragging about the fact that after almost thirty years of foiled villainy, *he* was gonna be the man who'd finally knock off Captain Kirk. Basically, he couldn't wait to kill me. When I grilled him about that, he got a bit of a twisted gleam in his eye, laughed, perhaps a little too heartily, and answered:

I've absolutely been bragging about killing you! Because it's something I've wanted to do for a long time. Actually, whenever I'm asked what my character does in this film, I have to say that basically, my function is to shoot Captain Kirk. But of course, having said that, I always have to add, "At least until he renegotiates his next contract."

But I have to say that killing Kirk is frightening.

I mean, these Trekkies are going to be after my hide, aren't they? Half the world's gonna come after me with knives, and the other half's probably gonna applaud, saying, "Thank God they got rid of THAT old bugger at last!"

I should break in to tell you that Malcolm is slightly less crazy than he sounds above, as well as a brilliant actor and an absolute joy to be with on the set. Throughout our days together on location, whenever time allowed, we talked. Here's what he said when I asked him about how he got involved in the film:

When Rick asked me to be in this film, I was thrilled! I said, "I'd LOVE to do it. I want to be THE man to kill Kirk." And when I read the script I thought Soran was an interesting and wonderful character, and obviously he would ultimately be given the honor of pulling the trigger that kills the good Captain Kirk. I'd immediately become a trivia question at *Star Trek* conventions all over the globe.

I had never really been a Trekkie, but I don't care whether you've memorized every single episode, we've *all* seen it, we *all* grew up with it, and I wanted to be a part of the series. I'd also worked with Patrick Stewart, your successor to the crown, back at Stratford-upon-Avon when he was a talented, hardworking actor, making all of four hundred dollars a week.

And I have to admit I've had a tremendous amount of fun making this film. The *Next Generation* people have been fabulous and they've made me feel like a part of the family right away.

They were very, very sweet, and I've just had a ball doing this. Even when I was torturing poor Geordi for three days, I loved every minute of it.

Over the course of the next several days I was tortured, too, both emotionally, as the finality of Kirk's death continued to weigh on me, and physically, as nearly every aspect of my final handful of scenes seemed consciously crafted to cause me as much physical discomfort as humanly possible. Still feeling the effects of Kirk's parachuting nightmare, my next day's scenes found us shooting high atop a mountain at Kirk's cabin in the woods, where the script demanded that I spend the better part of the ensuing fifteen hours splitting logs and running up and down staircases while Kirk does his best to refuse Picard's pleas for help.

The following morning, Patrick Stewart and I traveled to a ranch just about three hours northeast of Los Angeles, where we'd spend the day shooting all of Kirk and Picard's scenes on horseback. It was going to be another tough one. Still, despite the fatigue and the physical abuse I was now enduring on an almost daily basis, I was really looking forward to this particular day of shooting. Not only would I get to spend the better part of the day on horseback, I'd also be riding my own horse, Great Belles of Fire.

Months earlier, upon seeing that Captain Kirk was gonna be spending a lot of time in the saddle throughout the final third of this film, I told the production guys that I had an absolutely wonderful saddlebred that could serve very well as Kirk's horse. Additionally, because she'd be comfortable with me and I'd be comfortable with her, it seemed to me that we might save this production a lot of time that would normally have been spent trying to get the unfamiliar horse and rider in sync. Great Belles of Fire turned out to be a great movie horse, and together we managed to make the horseback scenes between Kirk and Picard pretty special.

For example, as Kirk speaks with Picard, feeling him out and ultimately deciding to leave the Nexxus and join him in his fight against Soran, both men spend almost four pages of dialogue speaking back and forth while astride a pair of horses. Now, in ninety-nine films out of a hundred, due to inexperienced riders or fidgety, uncomfortable horses, that scene would end up having to be shot *extremely* simply. In all likelihood, you'd see one rider on either side of the screen, and there they'd sit, entirely static, until the scene was over. However, on *Generations*, we were able to do a lot more, thanks to Great Belles of Fire.

Watch this scene closely, and you'll find Great Belles physically embodying Kirk's emotions throughout. Galloping away from Captain Picard at first meeting, she then turns, cautiously allowing him to approach, and at that point she slowly, warily sidles up next to his mare and begins a careful walk around him. In effect, Kirk's gradual acceptance of this man, his message and his mission is physically echoed and visually strengthened thanks to his horse. That simply would not have been possible between an unfamiliar horse and rider.

I should also mention that because Patrick is much less experienced on horseback than I, I gave him some advice about how he might protect himself. We talked about how to prevent certain muscles from getting sore after being in the saddle all day, and with at least twelve hours of riding staring us in the groin, I knew that we might very well set a new world's record for chafing. I threw out a suggestion that I had recently picked up at a three-day riding event. It was rather embarrassing, but faced with the ugly alternative, both Patrick and I immediately tried it out. Therefore, unseen on the film, and heretofore known only to Patrick Stewart and myself, we captains of the Enterprise shot all of our scenes on horseback while wearing pantyhose under our uniforms. It really worked well, and of course it makes your legs look fantastic. But that's another book.

Anyway, throughout my final handful of scenes with Patrick, I became aware of two things. First of all, though I'd now begun feeling the emotional effects of Kirk's death and saying good-bye to Star Trek, I was nonetheless surprised at what a hard time I had uttering any of the several Kirk lines that acknowledge that he's no longer the invincible space hero of stardates gone by. Worst by far was the line that signals Kirk's final acceptance of Picard's request for help. "Who am I," he asks, "to argue with the captain of the Enterprise?"

I had read that line in my script dozens of times without ever giving it a second thought, but somehow, here, now, on location, with my impending death looming ever closer and the heir to the Enterprise parked on horseback less than five feet away, I practically choked on my words. The phrase came foreign to my lips every time I tried to say it, and I just couldn't get comfortable admitting my own, now officially subordinate, position. In retrospect, I think that line may have been the one thing that finally broke through the denial, forcing me to fully understand the finality of the situation. Y'know, I liked Captain Kirk, I liked playing the guy, but now, for the first time, and just days away from a fatal phaser blast, I found myself regretting my decision to let Kirk die.

Second, making it even more difficult to walk away

from all of this, was the fact that throughout our scenes together, I found myself feeling really good about the on-screen pairing of captains Kirk and Picard. Here's what Patrick Stewart had to say:

I've been thinking, even from the first day we started rehearsing together, "I really *like* working with this man," and increasingly, as we got through our scenes, I found myself thinking, "What a shame. I really wish this hadn't been so brief." Y'know, there's an undeniable chemistry between us, there's something happening here, and even though I know the death of Kirk is supposed to be terribly final, I can't help but think, "C'mon now Patrick, this is *Star Trek*. Anything can happen, *anything*."

At any rate, with emotional distress now complementing my physical exhaustion rather nicely, it was time for all of us to pack our bags and travel to what would be, far and away, our most difficult and least hospitable location of all. Heading off to Nevada, we were about to start working in a gorgeous but horrendously harsh desert canyon, quite appropriately named the Valley of Fire. About an hour and a half northeast of Las Vegas (which provided the nearest halfway-decent accommodations), this is perhaps the hottest, dustiest, windiest, most uncomfortable place on the face of the planet. It is also staggeringly beautiful.

Here, amid the jagged red rock formations and barren otherworldly beauty, I would spend the next few days completing my remaining scenes, fistfighting with Malcolm McDowell, then performing my death scene with Patrick Stewart. I was looking forward to neither.

The fight scene came first, and it found Malcolm and me running all over a series of scaffolding platforms built upon, around, and on top of a huge desert rock formation. Designed by a black belt, this unusual fight takes place within the very tight quarters of that scaffolding, forcing Kirk and Soran to struggle against one another within an extremely confined space. Basically the fight entails a series of parries, blows and blocks between two very good, equally matched opponents, and I worked really hard with the stunt guys in making sure that Captain Kirk's final fight was also one of his very best. It was also perhaps the most grueling, made far tougher by the tortuous desert conditions. As a matter of fact, I might not have gotten through this thing at all were it not for a horse that decided to fall on me.

In the late spring of 1993, I was riding in a horse show when the stallion I was riding got spooked by an approaching golf cart, reared and fell on top of me, tearing muscles and ligaments in my left leg severely. What followed was an intensive physical therapy program in which I gradually strengthened the leg and ultimately ended up running three to five miles a day, adding push-ups and all sorts of other torture into the mix as soon as I found out that Captain Kirk was gonna be called into duty one last time. As a result, I went into *Star Trek: Generations* in really good shape, feeling far better than I have in many years, and just barely able to survive this film's physical pounding. The only thing I neglected to build up was my eyes.

Quite obviously, when you're running around an earthbound approximation of hell for twelve hours at a pop, you're gonna need sunblock. But as I learned almost immediately, and Malcolm McDowell learned shortly thereafter, our UV protection came along with some really nasty side effects. Once we started running around the desert, beating up on one another while sweating profusely, a lethal mixture of makeup, sweat and sunblock combined to run into our eyes, rendering us nearly sightless. Stinging with unbelievable ferocity, this stuff not only reduced us to teary-eyed, bleary-eyed uselessness, it also managed to create an infection that caused one of my eyes to swell up noticeably. Look closely at the final film and I'm sure you'll see it. At any rate, the production crew rushed an antibiotic to the set, and before long Malcolm and I, both of us squinty-eyed, were uncomfortably beating the hell out of one another once more. When we'd finally finished, having survived yet another day in the furnace, we both slunk back toward our cars like wet dishrags. I congratulated Malcolm on having survived, and he returned the compliment, saying:

Y'know, these scenes have been a pain in the ass, and with the heat, the dust, the fight scenes and just trying to survive in this hellish wasteland, there's a lot of people I'd give a million dollars NOT to do this with. If I were up here muddling through the degrees and the dust with somebody who was out of control in the fight sequences, or just unbearable, I'd have gone nuts.

And now, with the fight scene in the can and nothing else to distract me, I rode through the blackness of the desert night into the neon haze of Las Vegas, back to my hotel, where I spent the night sleeplessly mourning the death of Captain James T. Kirk.

CAPTAIN'S EPILOGUE:
FINAL ENTRY

My little plastic travel alarm is buzzing its annoying wail, but I don't need it. Neither did I need my 4:50 wake-up call, nor my 4:55 *insurance* wake-up call, from the front desk. I've been up pretty much all night, and even at this ungodly hour, I'm wide awake, showered, dressed, shaved and depressed, staring out at the strange alien landscape known as Las Vegas. Here in the waning moments of the night, amid a superabundance of neon, stucco and bad lounge acts, I find myself pondering this gleaming desert monument. Paying homage to every baser instinct known to man—greed, gluttony, lust, take your pick—it's a town where tourists routinely plunk their last handful of quarters into the nearest slot machine, hoping that one lucky pull might make up for a week of constant losing, where billboards advertise "A $3.99 shrimp cocktail as big as your head," where the local cabs hawk "clean, legal, air-conditioned cathouses." It's a town trying hard to be louder, brighter, more excessive and vastly more energized than any other on the planet. Jammed with tourists from all parts of the globe, this "desert paradise" has nonetheless left me feeling entirely isolated. Jim Kirk always predicted that he'd die alone. Turns out he was right.

For years now, Leonard has been telling me about how difficult it was for him to film the death of Spock, and I have to admit, I never really understood what the hell he was talking about. I mean, he'd sit there telling me about how he spent our entire preproduction period on *The Wrath of Khan*, as well as our early days of production, in total denial, blocking the character's death from his mind. Only later, he said, as the actual shooting day approached, did the full depth and consequences of his actions begin setting in. That's when he began having second thoughts, which continued to plague him right up until cameras were ready to roll, at which point he began looking for any excuse to storm off the set and avoid playing the scene at all. Today, for the first time in more than a decade, Leonard's story finally makes sense.

I too had spent months blissfully denying to myself that this simple death scene merited any serious thought, any analysis, any grief, only to later find myself swept under a flood of last-minute anxiety and soul-searching in regard to Kirk, Shatner, and both of their lives.

The Kirk *I* know is not the standard-issue amalgam of fiction, imagination and hype. Instead, the actor's Kirk grew out of memorizing ten pages of dialogue every day and studying scripts in advance, always struggling to come up with the creative ideas that might eventually allow the actor's performance to complement and enhance what already existed on paper. In short, the character was first and foremost a combination of writer's concept and actor's experience.

The Kirk I know was bonded to cast and crew by hours of tedium and occasional moments of creative glow.

What laughs and sorrows had gone into the totality of this fictional character! I thought about a marriage that broke down under the long hours of making a television series, the days that I missed of my children's growing up, the pain of personal tragedy and the single-mindedness—the absolute focus—it took to keep my private life from showing up on Captain Kirk's face. I also remembered the belly laughs that Leonard, De and I shared amid a vast assortment of cheap, rubberized planets of the week. We played practical jokes like kids in a playground, because that's exactly what it was: a playground in which we spent our days telling fanciful tales while pretending to be a troop of futuristic space heroes.

For me, so much has grown from my personal James T. Kirk. He's given me financial security and personal success, as well as the celebrity and accompanying ability to get other works accomplished. He's changed my entire life, and he's fulfilled a lot of my boyhood dreams along the way. I owe him a tremendous debt.

At the same time, I found myself overwhelmed by a sudden awareness of the recent changes in my life, both professionally *and* personally. Y'know, while it is a truism that life *is* change, and that all around us everything changes from instant to instant, the processes are almost always slow enough that only rarely are we forced to stop and be amazed by their effects. Birthdays, weddings, funerals, all of these events add ceremony to the realization, but every once in a while, just when you least expect it, that kind of awareness will sneak up on you from out of nowhere and clobber you over the head. For me, preparing to film Kirk's death marked one of those occasions.

It was clear now that, for me anyway, *Star Trek* was indeed coming to an end. In having Kirk run around basically unfamiliar sets, without most of his former castmates, and calling Patrick Stewart "captain of the *Enterprise*," I couldn't help but realize that things were changing on a large scale, very quickly. At the same time, my personal life had proven equally volatile: I'm in the process of getting a divorce. My life, at my age, has been turned almost entirely upside down. Surprisingly, however, while I am deeply affected by the sorrow of that event, there is a part of me that is intrigued, excited, even fascinated by the prospects, possibilities and chaos that will undoubtedly follow in its wake. For better or worse, this particular change will more than likely bring with it a whole new series of adventures. And so it is with Kirk. At that moment, I decided to extend Kirk's death scene one step further.

Kirk's dying words read, "It was fun," and I quickly determined to make it very clear that Kirk was speaking not only of his escapade with Picard, but of his entire life.

But what about the next step? What would Kirk see as he drew his last breath? In that moment, that unrecordable, heart-stopping moment, what would he see? I wanted to show Kirk looking *into* the abyss, crossing that final threshold, intrigued by the mysteries within. I wanted to speak to the strength of the character, and yet, as he lay dying, I wanted something out there to startle him. I wanted something to emerge from the gathering gloom, something that would frighten and ultimately fascinate the man.

I, on the other hand, am not nearly that brave, and the prospect of my own death has always left me semi-hysterical. Of all the great fearful issues in the world—abandonment, loneliness, helplessness—death, to me, is the most terrifying. I can reason with myself most of the time, but every so often, the fear escapes my control, and I find myself breathless with anxiety.

However, in creating the fictional death of Kirk, I was able to overcome my fears and die the way *Shatner* would like to die. What would the captain see as he crossed the final threshold? I still don't know, but I realized I could sum up his attitude with the words "Oh, my," said with the same mix of emotions that I, at my best, might feel.

And then the phone rang.

At 5:30 A.M., I was summoned to the lobby and tossed into the back seat of a rental car, in which I was being hauled, one last time, out to our Valley of Fire location. Captain Kirk was now officially walking his last mile.

An hour and twenty minutes later, I was at the site, marveling over the fact that our heretofore hellishly hot, dry, dusty and windy location had suddenly gotten . . . a lot worse. Even at this early-morning hour, heat waves were rising all around us, and the weather service was cheerfully assuring us that by lunchtime the mercury in our thermometers would be well on its way to the 112-degree mark. Shortly thereafter, I started fistfighting with Malcolm McDowell once more.

With just a few close-ups left to finish out the filming of our big fight scene, Malcolm and I ascended the hot metal scaffolding once more, and proceeded to spend the morning cursing the heat and pounding on each other's faces. As a final bit of torture, this particular series of shots ended with Kirk falling from the scaffolding and landing, for your ears only, upon a comfortable foam-rubber mattress some ten feet below. Still, though the scene was quite safe and quite good, it was by no means comfortable, pleasant or tolerable. However, after nineteen takes, nineteen falls and nineteen guzzled pints of water, our fight scene was finally complete. Thoroughly exhausted, Malcolm went back to his trailer to lie down. I, however, started climbing a rock.

With the heat continuing to rise and my spirits continuing to fall, I had just one last shot to knock off before doing the same to Captain Kirk. Climbing up a loose sandstone rock formation, I was pleasantly surprised, in fact amazed, by the fact that this shot ultimately came off very smoothly, requiring just minimum takes and maximum sweat. At that point we broke for lunch, and prepared to shoot Kirk's death scene. Needless to say, I wasn't very hungry.

Indulging myself for that hour amid the decadent, ozone-damaging luxury of my air-conditioned trailer, I ran the death scene through my head over and over again. I thought about Kirk's looking into the abyss. I uttered the words "It was fun" at least a hundred times over, and while I was revisiting all of those preconceived ideas, a new idea came into my mind as well. Once again, my thoughts returned to the horse that had fallen upon me several months earlier.

In that moment of extreme pain, just after the horse fell and rolled on me, I quite illogically ignored my pain and tried to get up, refusing to admit to myself, or anyone else, that I was hurt. Several times over, I got up on my feet, fell back down, and repeated the agonizing process. I must have done that a half-dozen times until somebody finally grabbed hold of me and forced me to lie down. Still, even *then* I wouldn't allow myself to accept the injury.

I refused to go to the hospital, and later, when I'd been wisely overruled and an ambulance had arrived, I flatly refused to get in. Somehow, amid the shock and adrenaline, I simply wouldn't allow myself to accept the injury. Back in my trailer, it struck me that Captain Kirk would most likely do the same thing. Y'know, when he gets shot, after a lifetime of near-misses and flesh wounds, it seemed absolutely fitting that he'd put up a futile effort to try and deny the pain, as well as the effects and ultimately the dire consequences, of his injury. With that in place, Kirk was ready to die, and even Shatner found himself feeling a bit more at peace with the idea.

We began shooting shortly thereafter. Soran blasts, Kirk gets phasered in the back, and immediately tries his best not to fall. When he ultimately succumbs, he slowly, painfully rises again, only to collapse once more, this time lying on his back. At that point, the script called for Soran to look up into the sky at the rapidly approaching Nexxus, dropping his gun in his excitement. Picard would then come running up to care for Kirk, conveniently grab Soran's gun, and shoot the villain immediately thereafter. Somehow, that just didn't make sense. I mean, why would our dyed-in-the-wool bad guy, having just emerged victorious from a fight to the death, allow himself to carelessly drop his gun, practically at the feet of Captain Picard?

"Bad storytelling!" I said, and we ultimately decided to expand upon Captain Kirk's resistance to death by having him reach out and trip the "victorious" Soran. The fall would cause Soran to drop his gun, and at that moment, Nexxus would show up in the sky, distracting Soran. Once that was in place, both Soran's fumble and Picard's recovery of the gun became a lot more believable. It also allowed Kirk to chalk up one last victory.

Finally, late in the afternoon, as the heat was just beginning to level off and the dust was just beginning to kick up, we began shooting Kirk's death. Lying on a bridge, straddling a chasm between two sandstone rocks, while we were being rocked by the wind and pelted by flying dust particles, with the lights shaking and the camera hand-held by our director of photography due to lack of space, this difficult scene became nearly impossible.

As the scene unfolds, the mortally wounded Kirk is lying down with Picard kneeling over him. While the various technical crews went about their preparations, Patrick and I rehearsed the scene a couple of times, and also began talking about Kirk's death and that final moment when I had planned to have him see something beyond death itself. Several moments later, with the camera loaded and ready to roll, we began shooting Patrick's close-ups. There, in those takes, as we shot Patrick's dialogue and went through the scene perhaps a half-dozen more times, I was able to begin finding the emotions that I knew I would need in portraying Kirk's death.

By the time Patrick's takes had been completed, I knew I was finally ready to do this. However, with the sun just beginning to go down, the production crew had now decided to play it safe and shoot all of our wide shots prior to my close-up dialogue. That way, even in a worst-case scenario, with the sky rapidly going orange in the distance, they could still hit me with a couple of artificial lights and approximate daylight without its being noticed. However, you know what they say about the best-laid plans of mice and men.

Feeling absolutely ready to play Kirk's death for the first time, I was terrified that I would "lose the moment" during the half-hour to forty-five minutes it would take to shoot our wide shots. With that in mind, I turned to our director, David Carson, and asked, "Could you shoot *me* next?" And David, being an actor's director, immediately understood my request and turned his shooting order upside down. He placed the camera just over Patrick's shoulder, focusing squarely upon Kirk's face, and both of us were quite pleased with the results.

I did it. I killed Kirk and I think I killed him well, using all of the emotions I'd denied for so long in allowing the man to battle, then ultimately accept his impending death, while simultaneously peering into the greatest mystery of all. When we'd finished Kirk's dialogue, I felt absolutely terrific, having performed the scene exactly as I'd hoped. Finally, we went in for one last close-up, this time even closer than before, focusing upon Kirk's dying words. Lying there with the camera now just about a foot and a half from my face and John Alonzo, our director of photography, just behind it, my view of the sky was almost entirely obstructed, save for a small strip of sky and clouds just behind the DP's head.

And as the shot rolled, I was able to effectively summon up those emotions one last time, and as I said my lines, filled with the need of a dying man to see the last of the world around him, I looked up into the sky, and there above the director of photography's head, so high in the sky that there was no sound, was a flying object, obviously some large jet plane, so the last thing I saw as Kirk lay dying was this flying object that for him and all the world could very well have been the *Enterprise*.

With that I was done. One of our AD's then made the official announcement that I was finished on the film, and the crew, by this point only a handful of key personnel, broke into scattered applause. It was a bit ignominious, and certainly there were no trumpets blaring that day; nevertheless, I went back to my trailer feeling a bit sad and more than a bit exhausted. I then paused one last time in front of the mirror to admire the Starfleet uniform that had served me so long and so well, smiled, changed and sped back toward Vegas, smiling through the last orange remnants of a gorgeous desert sunset. It was over. Like it or not, the inevitable had finally happened. After all the near misses, the

Somehow, though the Kleenex flew, test audiences weren't entirely satisfied by Kirk's quick, simple, celluloid demise. Instead, they came away with the feeling that simply blowing the Captain away with one high-voltage phaser blast to the back just wasn't big enough, or important enough, or noble enough, or meaningful enough to be entirely satisfying. Somehow —in perfect 20/20 hindsight, I'm surprised we didn't see this coming—audiences simply refused to accept that Kirk's mortality could be so easily terminated. I mean, here was a guy who'd beaten up a Gorn, who'd won two battles with Khan Noonian Singh, and who'd spent the better part of three decades cheating death at every turn while simultaneously kicking intergalactic supervillain ass all over the cosmos. Never, not in a *million years*, would this guy be dumb enough to turn his back on the likes of a Dr. Tolian Soran. It was really that simple, and when those sentiments proved themselves a running theme throughout Paramount's earliest preview screenings, Rick Berman took action. He ordered a rewrite of "Kirk's death" scenes, and ultimately chaperoned us all back into hell. With visions of sweat, sand, sunburn, and raging eye infections all still fresh in our minds, it would be an understatement to say that none of us was looking forward to the return engagement.

However, I have to admit that once we finally got rolling, this reshoot wasn't nearly as awful as we'd feared. It was great fun to don Kirk's Starfleet uniform one more time. Patrick was gracious and charming as always, and Malcolm was . . . well, insane, but that's Malcolm. The crew was terrific, and best of all, by early October, the Valley of Fire's average daily temperature had dropped from the hundred fifteens of early summer, down into the comparitive nippiness of the mid-eighties. The only down side to the shoot may have been my own nagging perception that Kirk's revised cinematic death might cause Shatner to keel over as well.

You see, in revising their original script based on the comments of those early sneak preview audiences, Ron Moore, Brannon Braga, and Berman saw to it that Kirk would once again assume his status as a running, jumping, fistfighting, villain-vanquishing superguy. No longer did he merely get shot in the back. Now, after a life-and-death, hand-to-hand struggle with Soran, Kirk risks his life one more time, scaling a rapidly deteriorating, steel chasm-crossing in a last ditch heroic attempt to rescue the tiny control device that just might allow the combined Captains to save the entire galaxy from imminent and impending disaster (boy, some things *never* change). Finally, even as the steel couplings around him are beginning to give way, Kirk manages to grab hold of the device, heaving it toward Picard just milliseconds before falling to his doom.

This time around, despite the fact that the end result remains a violent death, Kirk has once again proven himself unbeatable. *This* time around, no mere enemy has gotten the better of the good Captain. Instead, it is Kirk's own heroism, combined with the exigencies of yet another galactically dire situation (and of course some *really* shoddy steelwork) that conspire to do him in. Kirk, in effect, now dies undefeated. Weeks later, this revised ending left a second wave of sneak previewers feeling much more satisfied. It was a very good sign.

Within a month, *Star Trek: Generations* would enjoy the biggest opening weekend in the history of the Trek films, ultimately taking in just about 100 million dollars at the global box office . . . and of course you know what *that* means.

Will there be more Trek films? Absolutely!

Will Kirk be in them? I don't know. This being *Star Trek*, I *do* know that even death is not always an absolute. However, for now, for the forseeable film future, and perhaps forever, Captain James Tiberius Kirk is quite simply dead; buried under six feet of dry red sand on Veridian Three. I, for one, will miss him, but at the same time, I find it very satisfying, even awe inspiring, to realize that the *Star Trek* universe has now grown to the point where Kirk, Spock, Picard, Sisco, Janeway . . . *none* of us are absolutely vital to it's continued existence. It is truly bigger than all of us. As for the *future* of *Star Trek*, your guess is as good as mine. But then again, if *anything* has become clear over the past 450 pages, it's that your guess has *always* been at *least* as good as mine.

Finally, a long time ago, a pointy-eared friend of mine once instructed me to "Live long and prosper," and as I look back over nearly three decades' worth of friendships, accomplishments and memories, I have to think I've taken him up on that advice pretty well. Turning my thoughts to the future, with my kids and *their* kids effectively guaranteeing that I'll never really be alone, and a whole world full of brand-new adventures to explore, I find myself rather exhilarated about the rest of my life, my thoughts traveling once more to the wisdom of that same green-blooded colleague. According to him, the only thing that is ever certain in life is this: "There are always possibilities."

I couldn't agree more.

Star Trek Enterprise: The First Adventure

Vonda N McIntyre

From the moment James T. Kirk steps aboard the *Enterprise* – the youngest captain in Starfleet's history – things begin to go wrong. His Vulcan officer, Mr Spock, considers Kirk impetuous; the ship's chief engineer thinks him an inexperienced young hotshot; his chief medical officer hasn't bothered to show up yet; and the new helmsman would rather be somewhere else entirely. To cap it all, Starfleet has assigned the *Enterprise* a disappointingly tame task: to ferry a troupe of vaudeville performers on a morale-raising mission to Federation starbases – in short, a USO tour.

Then the largest spacecraft anyone has ever seen suddenly appears in the ship's flight path . . . and on their first mission together, Kirk and the entire *Enterprise* crew are facing what could truly be man's *final* frontier . . .

ISBN 0 586 07321 3

Space:
Above and Beyond

The novelization of the TV Movie

Peter Telep

The book of the most ambitious science fiction production in television history tells a story of high adventure and suspense as a courageous band of heroes wage an unprecedented fight for human survival.

From the executive producers of *The X-Files*, *SPACE: ABOVE AND BEYOND* is set 100 years in the future and features a group of rookie military cadets hurled unexpectedly into all-out war with an unknown alien race. Riveting adventure with the added advantage of Peter Telep's fine writing and concern for atmospheric detail.

ISBN 0 00 648245 7